FLIGHT OF FANCY

Flight of Fancy

The Banishment and Return of Ornament

Brent C. Brolin

ST. MARTIN'S PRESS NEW YORK

All photographs courtesy of the author unless otherwise noted.

Design by Manuela Paul

Library of Congress Cataloging in Publication Data
Brolin, Brent C.
Flight of fancy.

1. Decoration and ornament, Architectural—History.
I. Title.

| NA3310.B76 | 1985 | 729′.09′04 | 85-10057 |

ISBN 0-312-29613-4

First Edition
10 9 8 7 6 5 4 3 2 1

To Tally

Contents

Numerals in brackets in the text refer to the illustrations.

Acknowledgments

I WOULD LIKE TO acknowledge the advice and support generously offered in the course of the past three years by Hans Zeisel and Eva Zeisel. I would also like to thank Samuel Y. Edgerton, Jr., Sarah Bodine, David Levy, for giving their professional opinions on all or parts of the manuscript, and my friend Phil Ehrenkrantz for suggesting the title. Finally, I must extend my deepest appreciation and admiration to Jean Richards, whose love and attention provided me with the peace of mind needed to write this book.

Foreword

Fashions in design rarely develop along a simple course, like the ballistic curve of a projectile, and, therefore, their evolution cannot be realistically illustrated by a direct line from point A to point B. If I have been fortunate enough to present events in what appears to be an orderly sequence, it is not intended to imply a simple one-to-one relationship between complex historical events.

When speaking of "modernism" or "modernist principles" in this book, I frequently use the present tense. This is not an oversight. Various claims have been made about the death of modernism over the past two decades, but it seems to have evaded the grim reaper thus far. For sheer volume, the majority of new buildings are still designed in styles whose modernist parentage is rarely in doubt. In listening to acknowledged leaders in the profession, men and women allegedly at the "leading edge" of "new" movements, we are all too frequently left with a sense of déjà vu—that the old ideas are justifying yet another "style for our times." Even the most respected reference books, scholarly works, and architecture journals use the same words without a hint of irony, implying—or stating outright—that buildings designed in the "modern" styles of the 1920s and after are, for example, more "functional" than those of a generation before. If this book does nothing more, I hope it dispels forever the notion that design ideologies have something to do with the way things look.

Introduction

A few years ago, excavators uncovered a grave in an Iraqi cave. They found the remains of many flowers under the bones, including bachelor buttons, hollyhocks, and grape hyacinth, all of which had been gathered from surrounding hillsides and lovingly woven into a funerary litter of pine boughs. The grave is sixty thousand years old, one of the earliest and most touching expressions of humankind's desire to embellish.

From the beginning, it would seem, ornament has been an integral part of virtually all cultures, gracing buildings, clothing, bodies, utensils, weapons, vehicles—almost every appurtenance of daily life. [1, 2, 3] Ornament has beautified the most utilitarian and the most luxurious of objects, from the screws securing the knight's armor to the jars holding his lady's unguents. [4] Perhaps ornament has been such a consistent part of human history because it has satisfied a need for beauty that all people share. With rare exceptions, when ornament could be used, it was; and, in most cases, in proportion to wealth. If there has been one constant in the history of the arts, it has been the lack of debate about the use of ornament—until our time. The nearly ornament-less, modern design of our century is an aberration, barring the occasional sumptuary law. For perhaps the first time in the history of mankind, the surroundings of the most sophisticated and elegant classes of society have been characterized by a consciously celebrated poverty of ornament.

1

2

Figs. 1, 2, and 3.   The desire to ornament influences virtually every aspect of daily life: clothing, eating utensils, lighting fixtures, cars, electric appliances, and, of course, architecture. (1) Sign for umbrella shop, Venice. (2) Misericord, St. George Slaying the Dragon, Wells Cathedral, England 14th century. (3) Roof of St. Stephen's Cathedral, Vienna (14th–15th centuries, restored completely to original state after being destroyed in World War II).

4

Fig. 4.   Few things have escaped ornamentation in the past, regardless of their functional value. This decorative screw fastens a tilting shield *(manteau d'armes)* to a 16th-century suit of jousting armor. German, ca. 1550. Attributed to Anton Peffenhauser of Augsburg. *(Photograph by Brent C. Brolin. Courtesy of The Metropolitan Museum of Art, New York, gift of William H. Riggs)*

This book is written in an effort to understand why ornament, which had been an integral part of life for millennia, should have virtually disappeared at the beginning of this century. (It would be more precise to ask why traditional ornament has been suppressed, for we shall see that modernists, too, found ways to slake the thirst for embellishment.) Understanding how this came about will take us a long way toward learning how to make "serious" architecture and design a meaningful part of the lives of more people.

A decade and a half ago, I spent four postgraduate years studying architecture. I never once heard the words "ornament" or "decoration" uttered in the context of contemporary architecture. Nor, for that matter, can I recall having heard any building, traditional or modernist, described as "beautiful" during that time.

The fact is that both "ornament" and "beauty" have been out of favor for a long time. The aversion to these terms did not begin with the "modernism" of the 1920s—as many might think—but much earlier. From the middle of the nineteenth century, designers made it increasingly difficult to talk about the beauty of a design, or the attractiveness of its decoration, *in purely aesthetic terms.* Buildings were not beautiful, cozy, foreboding, gracious, stiff, or comfortable. Instead, through the so-called principles of design, they appealed to our intellect and sense of morality: we were to appreciate their *honest expression* of structure, function, material, and so on. Succinctly stated, ideology replaced taste as the basis of discussion about the nature of beauty.

I hope to make the reasons for this clear in the following chapters, but, in sum, designers found it difficult to impose what they felt was "good taste" on a growing middle class whose "bad taste" was epitomized by an unrestrained love of ornament. The "principles of design" appealed because they put designers on a wholly different, intellectual plane. They no longer needed to speak in terms of taste or mere fashion. That was for decorators. Designers were concerned with *morality.*

The sincere desire to believe in this kind of morality in art encouraged designers to ignore popular taste, and shoulder the tiresome but necessary burden of "educating the public in its own best interests," to paraphrase a modern critic.

The ideology created in the nineteenth century served our own as well. The ability to ignore popular taste in good conscience ultimately made it possible, among other things, to banish traditional ornament— and to view that banishment as a public service. But the reader should not let such a remarkable feat obscure the fact that the principles of design never determined appearance; they only rationalized it. Even today, when ornament has again become acceptable, we are told that it has returned because it is "suited to our times."[1]

Over the decades, the purpose of these principles has remained consistent: to influence the "uninitiated" to accept styles that they could not be convinced to accept solely on aesthetic merit. Once that is understood, laypeople and professionals alike should find it easier to ignore such self-serving ideologies. If that can be done, it will be possible to be less coy and self-conscious in using ornament, and perhaps to recapture the uninhibited pleasure in embellishment that marks the architecture and design of the past.

Without the lens of ideology distorting our vision, we may also find it easier to address ourselves to certain critical design questions that have been ignored for the past half century. The most important of these is ensuring a humane, livable townscape by the addition of sensitively designed buildings, which respect their surroundings through the free use of ornament.

---

1. Robert Venturi, Denise Scott Brown, and Steven Izenour, *Learning from Las Vegas: The Forgotten Symbolism of Architectural Form* (Rev. ed., Cambridge: MIT Press, 1977), p. 161.

CHAPTER I

Ornament in History

Modern designers have continually claimed that their work represents the "spirit of the times" while, from a popular perspective, they have remained on the fringes of cultural relevance. There are surely several interwoven causes for this phenomenon, but one thing is clear: their rejection of the warmth, familiarity, and inspiration of traditional ornament guaranteed their failure to make contact with the great majority of those whom they proposed to enlighten. The modern designers' reasons for forsaking ornament have most often been couched in moral terms—the need for the honest expression of structure, and functionalism, the earnest desire to express the "spirit of the times," and so on. These homilies mask the real reason behind the death of traditional ornament in our century, which is found in the inability of a new artistic elite to tolerate the taste of an equally new middle class, which, by virtue of its wealth, is imposing its preferences on the art marketplace. The taste of the middle classes has been unacceptable to this elite, and ornament (along with the historical styles which it defined) is the most apparent, insistent, and easily graspable artistic manifestation of their "bad taste."

The Exile of Ornament

The ease with which design shed its traditional, ornamental skin in our century is some indication of the length of the molting period. The new status that artists (and later architects and designers) had attained was an important factor in the eventual suppression of ornament. Since antiquity, artists and artisans had been lumped together, relegated to lower rungs of the social ladder. In large part, artists' low rank was due to the fact that theirs were manual rather than intellectual arts. A sequence of events originated in fifteenth-century Italy, which began to raise the status of some of these manual arts by establishing an intellectual basis for them.[1] By the late 1700s, an important shift in values had taken place in virtually all of Europe: The "artist" had been isolated from the "artisan." The visual arts of painting and sculpture were designated "fine," by virtue of their exclusive concern with beauty as opposed to utility (hence the *beaux arts*). The others, by implication, were less fine.[2] This institutionalized a hierarchy among the arts of design where none had been recognized formally before, making ornament a concern of second-class artistic citizens.

Some decades after the abbé Batteux's definitions postulated this difference between artist and artisan, the coup de grâce was delivered. For all the glories of Western art that have come down to us from antiquity and Byzantium, from Europe of the Middle Ages and the Renaissance, it was not until 1790 that the first systematic philosophy of art was written in the West: Immanuel Kant's *Critique of Judgment.* Its densely argued thesis succeeded in placing the fine art artist above all others, elevated because he, and he alone, possessed "genius," the essence of which was "originality."[3] This had the obvious and inevitable effect of stigmatizing the decorative arts as the province of the less gifted.[4]

Kant's *Critique* forms one of the most important bases for modern aesthetic theory. One particular aspect, however, is germane to our discussion here: the notion that, because of genius and its demand for

5

Fig. 5. The first philosophy of art was put forth by
Immanuel Kant, in *Critique of Judgment* (1790).
According to Kant, genius was the defining
characteristic of the artist, and originality the most
important property of genius. Hence the artist-genius
was obliged to ignore conventional rules governing
popular taste. (*Photograph by Brent C. Brolin. Courtesy of
The New York Public Library*)

originality, artists are expected to ignore conventional taste. Indeed, to
be "conventional" is tantamount to admitting that you lack genius.

In theory, at least, Kant freed artists from the chains of the
marketplace, for they no longer had to cater to the taste that still fettered
the artisan, a lesser soul who lacked genius. [5] Within a few years, this

view had permeated the philosophy, literature, criticism, and cultural myths of the West.

This exponential gain in prestige for fine art artists was to have a novel, if unexpected, impact on the development of the decorative arts. By mid-nineteenth century, leading figures in the English arts confronted what they considered a disastrous decline in the quality of that country's decorative arts. In seeking ways to remedy this—first by improving the quality of design, and later by teaching "good taste" to the entire English buying public—the reformers adopted an approach similar to that which had enabled "fine art" artists to think of themselves as above the demands of conventional taste.[5] The English reformers provided artisans with their own *intellectual* justification for their worth, an approach intended to raise them above the demands of popular taste.

This intellectual foundation took the form of design principles. Couched in moral rather than visual terms, these appeared to transcend mere "taste." With such an all-important intellectual platform, designers no longer needed to concern themselves with vulgar discussions of taste; with the best of intentions, and in good conscience, they set out to impose their own tastes on an obdurate, often disinterested, public.

The foremost English artists, designers, and critics ultimately lost the battle to set standards of "good taste" in the marketplace. It was a slow-motion defeat, lasting for decades, and comprised of small skirmishes in which designers fired bolts of rhetoric and volleys of "good design" at the impregnable fortress of middle-class aesthetic values. The failure to breech the battlements and subdue the excesses of the nouveau riche was perhaps the single most important, and least acknowledged, component in the decision to abandon traditional ornament. By the beginning of this century, traditional ornament had come to symbolize the enemy, the dreaded philistine. Artists' and designers' frustration at having failed to assert their own values played the key role in a unique reversal of the definition of beauty: what had been beautiful became ugly, and vice versa. But the objection was not yet to ornament, per se; it was to the taste of the middle class. By the turn of the century, therefore,

6

Fig. 6.   Once designers were deprived of the traditional means of developing new kinds of ornament—borrowing from nature and/or from other styles—they were forced to rely upon other means to satisfy the urge to embellish. The most common approach has been to push and pull the form into an "interesting shape," making the building itself into an ornament. Bertrand Museum/DeSoto Visitors' Center, Missouri Valley, Iowa; Astle/Ericson & Associates, Architects. (*Photograph courtesy of Astle/Ericson & Associates*) "progressive" designers had rejected the popular "historical" ornamental styles, but were creating new decorative styles of their own.

By the 1920s, the campaign to rally the middle class behind the banner of "good design" had brought the avant garde to the point of renouncing all ornament as part of a program that rejected virtually all middle-class values. In doing so, the modernists took over the same principles that the English reformers had used to justify their still-ornamented styles, and used them in turn to rationalize the banishment of all traditional ornament.

Ironically, modernists proved no more resistant to the infectious urge to embellish than preceding generations. Fervent protests aside, modernists created their own ornament—based on the natural colors and textures of materials, on structural exhibitionism, and on the vague notion of "expressing" a function. Modernists moved away from the "fussy," small-scale details of the traditional styles, and toward buildings whose forms became so fussy that they themselves became ornamental, as rich in their own kind of convolutions as any Baroque extravagance. And these new forms were justified with the same principles that had been used to explain the Gothic Revival and Art Nouveau. [6]

Now all is well, we are told, for modernism is dead and ornament recalled from exile. This is only half-true. It is impossible to be completely at ease when breaking a taboo, and the self-conscious awkwardness of much of today's ornament attests to the intimidating power of modernism. Furthermore, the principles—that shield of ideology which the modernists used so well—remain largely in place, protecting designers from the annoying task of having to concern themselves with the taste of others.

To understand how principles of such profound ambiguity have exerted so great an influence through so many changes in styles, we must recognize that the modern view of the power of art and the role of the artist is unique in the history of Western art. To understand why our era abandoned traditional ornament, and to welcome it back to a useful role in the arts of design, we should look briefly at how artists and the arts fared in earlier times—for our attitude toward ornament has been defined by our attitude toward the artist and the fine arts.

NOTES: CHAPTER I

1. See Leon Battista Alberti, *On Painting,* trans. John R. Spencer (2nd rev. ed., New Haven: Yale University Press, 1966), and Leonardo da Vinci, *Paragone,* trans. I. A. Richter (Oxford: Oxford University Press, 1949).

2. See abbé Charles Batteux, *Les Beaux Arts réduits à une même principe* (1747). The "ornamental arts" included all other arts based upon "design," from the Italian *disegno* (drawing).

3. Kant, *Critique of Judgment,* Div. 1, bk. 2, para. 46, trans. J. H. Bernard (New York: Hafner Publishing Company, 1951), p. 150.

4. According to one scholar, Aristotle's mention of music as an appropriate leisuretime occupation for free citizens *(Politics)* is "perhaps the only explicit recognition in Greek literature of aesthetic enjoyment (apart from aesthetic appreciation of the physical beauty of the human body) as an end in itself"—Harold Osborne, *Aesthetics and Art Theory: An Historical Introduction* (New York: E. P. Dutton, 1970), p. 37, note 3.

5. I speak here of men who were involved in the massive experiment to "improve" the English public through art education, including William Dyce, Henry Cole, Owen Jones, and Sir Charles Eastlake, rather than John Ruskin and William Morris. The latter two are better known in this century because of their influence on the most important Continental art reform movements, including the Viennese Secession, the German Werkbund, and the Bauhaus. The Werkbund presents an interesting sidelight. Several art historians, including Nikolaus Pevsner, indicate that Gottfried Semper played a major, if not seminal, role in the development of the English Arts and Crafts movement. From recent research, however, it would seem that Semper's role was exaggerated during the hostilities of World War I—for blatantly political reasons—and German art historical education would likely have reflected this bias: "[Before World War I], the Werkbund had freely acknowledged the English Arts and Crafts movement as its progenitor. Now, however, it claimed priority for Germany by stressing the seminal role of the German architect Gottfried Semper, who had lived in England for some years around 1850. . . . While it is true that Semper was in close contact with the Arts and Crafts reformers of his day, to conclude that they would have done nothing without him is obviously an exaggeration"—Joan Campbell, *The German Werkbund: The Politics of Reform in the Applied Arts* (Princeton: Princeton University Press, 1978, p. 93).

CHAPTER II

The Artist in Antiquity

For thousands of years, artifacts of extraordinary beauty and refinement were created without the aid of an articulated philosophy of art, or an elite group of artists deemed qualitatively superior by virtue of their genius and originality, or the intercession of nonvisual, moralistic principles to guide the visual arts. Why should such notions have come to the fore in the late eighteenth and early nineteenth centuries?

It is only in the past two hundred years that educated society has come to accept the idea that artists (and even architects) are invested with a near-mystical power, enabling them to provide insight into the deeper meaning of life through their Art. They did not always enjoy such an exalted position. Who but the scholar can name the architect of the Parthenon, keystone of Western architecture? And Phidias, whose sculpture graced that glorious monument, belonged to a trade that Plato found less vital to his *Republic* than shoemaking. [7]

One fact leaps out when we consider the attitudes toward arts in antiquity. The arts of design were grouped with other "manual" trades, all of which had a relatively low status. No specifically art historical literature was developed in the ancient world, and there was certainly nothing remotely resembling a philosophy of art. Neither "artists," "artisans," nor their works were of more than passing interest to classical poets, philosophers, and chroniclers. And seminal figures in the development of

7

Fig. 7.   Ancient attitudes toward art and the artist were quite
different from our own. The most famous building of antiquity
is not associated with its architects, Ictinus and Calicrates, but
with Pericles, the politician whose clever financing made the
Parthenon possible. And Phidias, its master sculptor, practiced a
trade that no self-respecting Greek gentleman would consider
taking up.

Western culture—Plato and Aristotle, to mention the most obvious—
not only neglected to develop theories of art; the former *specifically
excluded the visual arts from his theory of the Beautiful.* [1] In fact, the most
influential philosophical themes of antiquity tend to denigrate the senses
relative to the intellect, and therefore the arts of design. [8, 9]

Fig. 9.   The ancients never thought of art as a self-justifying pursuit—"Art for Art's sake" as the saying goes. Art was a tool, propaganda for the ruling class, a votive offering of a leader for his people, or vice versa. It was never a vehicle for expressing a personal point of view. This bas-relief, from an altar known as the Ara Pacis, was a politic offering of the Roman Senate to Augustus, their first emperor, given upon his successful completion of military campaigns in Gaul and Spain.

Fig. 8.   (*Facing page*) While today's patrons of the arts may increase their prestige through an association with a famous artist—a Picasso for the plaza, for instance—the flow of prestige was reversed in antiquity. Art was but one manifestation of the power and beneficence of the state, political figures and events being immensely more influential in forming the arts than any "individual creativity" the artist might bring to his work.

The Artisan/Artist

In trying to understand the way cultures other than our own have viewed the arts, our vision is distorted because we are forced to judge by our standards. Often, even our words do not match the meanings of other times. For example, our differentiation between "artist" and "artisan" did not exist in antiquity, and even as late as the beginning of the twentieth century the word "designer" did not have its current meaning. The most striking evidence is that there was no ancient Greek or Roman equivalent for our word "art," as in "fine art." The closest Greek approximation, *tekne* (or *tekhne*), has the same meaning as a variety of modern terms, including art (as in artfulness), skill, craft, trade, the regular method of making a thing, or a work of art. *Teknites* (or *tekhnites*) can refer to an artificer, artist, craftsman, workman, or anyone who works by the rules of an art. We find similar ambiguities in the Greek word for architect: *architekton* can mean chief artificer, director of works, architect (of buildings), engineer, or master-smith, as in shipwright (not mason)—all of which are, however, distinguished from the very lowest of manual laborers.[2] The appropriate Latin words have similarly broad meanings. *Opifex*, for example, can mean artisan, worker, mechanic, artist, producer, maker, or fabricator.[3]

If we were to jump ahead in time to try to discover what painters and sculptors were doing in seventeenth-century England, it would seem reasonable to study the "artists" of that time. But the seventeenth-century English artist was anyone who pursued a "practical science."[4] The magnitude of our difficulty in understanding earlier views of art and ornament is suggested by the metamorphosis of the word "artist" over the past four centuries:

1667: One who pursues some practical science.
1686: A chemist [then a new science].
1761: A medical practitioner and astrologer or chemist.
1783: A learned man, a Master of [Liberal] Arts.

1793: A follower of a pursuit in which skill comes by study or practice; hence a proficient; a practical man, as opposed to a theorist.

1815: A follower of a manual art, a mechanic, etc.

1832: *Artiste* (Fr.), re-introduced in consequence of the limited sense now given to the word.

1849: One who makes his craft a "fine art." Cf. French *artiste.*

It should be apparent from this progression of meanings that there was no formal distinction in the English language between "artist" and "artisan" until quite recently. And the expression "fine art" became common usage as late as circa 1767,[5] soon acquiring the special connotations we now attach to the word "artist," namely, one with the inspired quality of "genius," who raises his work beyond mere craft.

The Arts of the Elite

The unified conception of art and ornament in antiquity—and hence of artist and artisan—is more difficult to grasp because of yet another difference between our view of art and that of even the recent past. As late as the eighteenth century, the educated elite of Western society still assumed that a class difference existed between those who practiced the manual arts and those who pursued the liberal arts. The differentiation between tasks requiring physical labor and those requiring only contemplation was based upon an aristocratic bias, "liberal" coming from the Latin *liberalis,* pertaining to freeborn men. Occupations that were unsuitable for freemen included our "fine" arts of design (painting, sculpture, and architecture) as well as our "decorative" arts (wood carving, ceramics, clay and plaster modeling, metal smithing, stone carving, weaving, embroidery, and the like). Although the list of liberal arts has varied from time to time,[6] the most familiar grouping comes from the fifth-century-A.D. Latin writer Martianus Capella, and includes grammar, rhetoric, dialectic, geometry, arithmetic, astronomy, and music.[7]

A few artists were well known in antiquity, among them Apelles, court painter to Alexander the Great, and Phidias, whose sculpture commissions for the Acropolis came about, at least in part, because of his friendship with Pericles.[8] But these were the exceptions. Although the results of an artist's work may have been appreciated, this was rarely if ever reason enough for a person of high birth to take up such a trade. The great majority of those whom we would now call fine art artists came from humble beginnings, and would have been lumped together at the lower end of the social scale, in the same class as other manual laborers.

The disdain for manual labor influenced the extent to which a man of gentle birth should pursue those of the liberal arts that demanded some degree of manual dexterity. According to Aristotle, it was fine to go beyond the theory of music and learn to play an instrument, but only to refine one's appreciation.[9] To develop a facility that challenged the professional musician's was both unwise and improper, for it reduced the freeman to the level of those who used music to make a living rather than for the loftier goal of intellectual betterment.[10] [10]

Another indication of the relatively low status of the visual arts came from the Muses themselves, in testimony by omission. The daughters of Zeus and Mnemosyne gave inspiration to mortals, but there were no Muses for the visual arts, as they were too menial to merit divine attention. When the Muses were assigned specific subjects, in late Roman times, only the following arts were considered worthy of divine inspiration:[11]

Epic poetry (Calliope)	Erotic poetry (Erato)
Sacred hymns (Polyhymnia)	History (Clio)
Lyric poetry (Euterpe)	Tragedy (Melpomene)
Astronomy (Urania)	Comedy (Thalia)
Choral song and dance (Terpsichore)	

Fig. 10.   (*Facing page*) The "liberal" arts were those suitable for study by freemen. The mechanical arts, including our "fine" arts of painting, sculpture, and architecture, were stigmatized because they were manual arts. Aristotle even restricted the freeman's study of music—a liberal art—because its performance required a degree of manual dexterity. (*Photograph by Brent C. Brolin. Courtesy of The Metropolitan Museum of Art, New York*)

Mind versus Body

The lack of differentiation among the ancient arts of design was reinforced by still another attitude that differs from our own, and which may help to explain why the antique view of art seems strange to us. The equation of spiritual truth with physical beauty, which was fixed in a systematic philosophy of art only at the end of the eighteenth century, was virtually unknown in antiquity: when the ancients spoke of "Truth and Beauty," they referred not to physical but to spiritual beauty.

The relationship of physical to spiritual beauty was similar to that of the manual to the liberal arts. Plato never doubted that knowledge gathered through the senses was inferior to that gleaned by the mind. "Absolute" beauty referred to the constant and invariable truths of wisdom—of philosophy—which were impossible to apprehend "except by thinking; they are invisible to our sight."[12] "If someone tells me that the reason why a given object is beautiful is that it has a gorgeous colour or shape or any other such attribute," said Socrates, in Plato's *Phaedo,* "I disregard all these other explanations—I find them all confusing—and I cling simply and straightforwardly and no doubt foolishly to the explanation that the one thing that makes that object beautiful is the presence in it or association with it of absolute Beauty."[13] If sight was the foremost sense, it was only first among lesser faculties, which, singly or in combination, were unable to discover Truth.[14]

The physical world was a constant source of deception for those interested in the higher truth and beauty of philosophy:

> Don't you think that the person who is likely to succeed in this attempt most perfectly [apprehending the true nature of anything] is the one who approaches each object, as far as possible, with the unaided intellect, *without taking account of any sense of sight in his thinking,* or dragging in another sense into his reckoning—the man who pursues the truth by applying his pure and unadulterated thought to the pure and unadulterated object, cutting himself off as much as possible from his eyes and ears and virtually all the rest of his body, as an impediment

which by its presence prevents the soul from attaining to truth and clear thinking? (my emphasis)[15]

Perhaps the most famous example of Plato's opinion of the arts is found in Book Ten of the *Republic,* in which he spoke of them as occupations of no real value as they produced mere representations of the physical world, itself only a faint reflection of the essence of things.[16]

The Wages of Art

Financial records of ancient building projects give an interesting insight into the status of our categories of artists, artisans, and architects in ancient times. As the accounts were public affairs in many cases, they were often tallied on stone slabs. Portions of the Erechtheum accounts indicate that the standard day wage for any kind of building-related work was 1 drachma, whether lowly laborer or architect.[17] Parthenon accounts show that the carvers of the pediment sculptures, who presumably translated the clay models of Phidias into marble, were earning little more than the masons and carpenters who worked on the Erechtheum.[18]

The workshop system that produced the sculptural frieze of the Erechtheum is equally disconcerting, given our emphasis on originality of concept as the difference between artist and artisan. The frieze consisted of relief figures in white marble, fixed to a dark, limestone background, and was not the product of one sculptor, but was contracted out, figure by figure, to a number of carvers. The general layout of the figures was presumably decided upon first, by a person or persons whose identities have not come down to us, and individual figures were then assigned to different individuals: five are mentioned on one stone fragment.[19] Payment to the ancient sculptors was apparently not based upon the quality of the work, but was made per adult figure. Each sculptor received 60 drachmas for one adult figure, with two exceptions: Lasos of Kollytos received 80 drachmas for carving a woman and child (presumably 60 for the adult and 20 for the child); Mynnion of Melite carved a stele and a man striking a horse, and was paid 127 drachmas (presumably 60 each for the man and the horse, plus 7 for the stele).[20]

While this may seem an appropriately rational apportionment of funds for the homeland of Socrates, Plato, and Aristotle, it confounds our evaluation of the aesthetic experience to pay for "beauty" by the figure, rather than to judge it on the basis of aesthetic merit. Furthermore, this kind of virtually anonymous joint effort flies in the face of our notion that creative freedom is essential to the arts. It is almost beyond our comprehension—and certainly beyond our experience—to imagine a situation in which artisans of uniformly superb skill were so easily at hand that what we must assume was a sculpture of impeccably consistent style and exquisite beauty could be produced by commissioning different pieces from different stonecutters. It strains credulity to imagine five modern artists in the same medium reining in their artistic wills long enough to work on the same project, let alone produce a work of artistic merit and coherence.

The Uninvolved Eye

The lack of any significant treatment of painting, sculpture, and architecture in ancient literature reinforces the notion that those who practiced the design arts at that time did not have a high status. The most famous encyclopedic writer of Rome, Pliny the Elder, included no history of art in his multivolume *Natural History,* and painting and sculpture are only mentioned as subentries, under Mineralogy.

A few artists did sign their work as early as the sixth century B.C., and some scholars have interpreted this as an indication that they "regarded a work of art as being distinct from other crafts."[21] Books *by artists* on their art also began appearing toward the beginning of the fifth century B.C.[22] Although none has survived,[23] it has been suggested that at least some of these might have dealt with theoretical as well as technical matters.[24] Given the difference in status between intellectual endeavors and manual labor, we can assume that any link with theory (as opposed to technique) would have lent prestige to a craft, and helped raise its status relative to other crafts. But it is unlikely that the artisans' estimation of their own worth would have been reflected in the opinions of their social betters. We might get a more accurate idea of that opinion by looking at the notice taken of these arts in the other literature of the time, where we find that

> neither the artists of the classical period nor their works are mentioned in contemporary literature. Herodotus and Thucydides describe precious materials but not the works they enrich. Pindar praises victorious athletes but not the monuments erected to perpetuate their fame. Aristophanes mentions citizens of all walks of life—musicians, poets, wrestlers, politicians—but never artists. And none of the great Attic orators down to Demosthenes (384–322 B.C.) and Aeschines (389–314 B.C.) reveal the slightest interest in art and artists.[25]

Although the status of the manual arts remained low, "an interest in art and criticism became a status symbol of the educated" in Hellenistic times; "Aristotle himself agreed to the teaching of art in the schools, and drawing and even modeling were regarded as a suitable pastime for dilettanti," all of which was accompanied by the growth of a busy art market that serviced private collectors.[26]

This new attitude, which permitted the appreciation of sensual beauty for its own sake, seems to have brought with it a new relationship to nature.[27] Socrates had perfunctorily dismissed the glories of natural beauty, saying: "people in the city have something to teach me, but the fields and trees won't teach me anything."[28] Writing four centuries later, in the first century A.D., the younger Pliny overflowed with enthusiasm for the site of his Tuscan villa:

... the countryside is very beautiful. Picture to yourself a vast amphitheater such as could only be a work of nature; the great spreading plain is ringed round by mountains, their summits crowned by ancient woods of tall trees, where there is a good deal of mixed hunting to be had."[29]

The sensibility that enabled sophisticated Romans to appreciate natural beauty was coupled to an ability to appreciate the art of man in a way that had hardly been expressed before or after, until the Renaissance. The younger Pliny sounds like a sophisticated connoisseur of today in this letter to a friend:

Out of a sum of money I have inherited I have just bought a Corinthian bronze statue, only a small one, but an attractive and finished piece of work as far as I can judge. . . . The bronze appears to have the true colour of a genuine antique; in fact every detail is such as to hold the attention of an artist as well as delight the amateur, and that is what persuaded me to buy it, novice though I am.[30]

But did the Roman sculptor or painter (our "artist") profit from this interest in the aesthetic quality of his work—in terms of an enhanced status relative to his fellow craftsmen, or in comparison to the more prestigious occupations of the liberal arts? [11] The paradoxical answer seems to be No, at least in a general sense.[31] And, in a devastating observation on the status of the artist in the first century A.D. that goes a long way toward reconciling the interest in aesthetics with the traditional disdain for the manual arts, Plutarch stated unequivocally that

it is quite possible for us to take pleasure in the work and at the same time look down on the workman . . . who occupies himself with servile tasks proves by the very pains which he devotes to them that he is indifferent to higher things. *No young man of good breeding and high ideals feels that he must be a Pheidias or a Polycleitus after seeing the statue of Zeus at Olympia or Hera at Argos.* (my emphasis)[32]

Fig. 11. (*Facing page*) The design of the Roman Pantheon is attributed to one of the most renowned practitioners of the architect's trade, but one whose design skills were not his claim to fame, the emperor Hadrian. Those responsible for laying it out and supervising its construction—the "engineers" or "architects" of ancient Rome—are little known to us. As workers in a manual art, they were grouped with other freeborn and slave tradesmen such as weavers and shoemakers.

Furthermore, even with this identifiably "aesthetic" appreciation, the interest in qualities that we find essential to art appears to have been nonexistent, and "there does not seem to have been much awareness of its intellectual values, let alone spiritual [values]."[33]

Pliny's lively account of his small bronze statue is the exception, rather than the rule, in ancient literature. The accounts of works of art that have come down to us are disturbingly matter-of-fact, given the value we now place on art. Pausanias, a Greek writer of the second century A.D., compiled a guide to Greece that was notable for its almost casual treatment of the arts: "It was Pheidias who made the statue, as an inscription written below Zeus's feet bears witness: 'Pheidias the son of Charmides from Athens has made me.' "[34] So said the description on the famous Olympian statue, according to Pausanias. This passage continues for several hundred words, but the following excerpt gives the flavor:

> The god is sitting on a throne; he is made of gold and ivory. There is a wreath on his head like twigs and leaves of olive; in his right hand he is holding a Victory of gold and ivory with a ribbon and a wreath on her head; in the god's left hand is a staff in blossom with every kind of precious metal, and the bird perching on this staff is Zeus's eagle.[35]

The remainder offers a detailed account of the size, materials, and symbolism of what Pliny the Elder allegedly referred to, in the previous century, as the "unrivalled Zeus of Olympia."[36] Not a phrase of Pausanias' recitation of fact was devoted to the now familiar *visual* analysis, nor does it make reference to aesthetic effect. At no point in this account do we find any recognizable aesthetic connotation, no sense of a "delight" in "every detail." This is a startling omission considering the sculptor's reputation and the importance of the shrine.[37] Occasionally, these descriptions seem more familiar because they refer to the qualities of an object rather than to its quantities. Pliny described an Apollo of the sculptor Myron as being "more rhythmical" than the work of Polyclitus, his "proportions more carefully studied."[38] But in describing the work of

Phidias, Pliny emphasized its "believe-it-or-not" characteristics, rather than what we would think of as its aesthetic attributes:

> . . . to this end I shall employ, not the beauty of Olympian Zeus, nor the grandeur of the Athena which he made at Athens, though she is 26 cubits in height, all of ivory and gold—but the fact that on her shield he wrought in relief the battle of the Amazons on the convex surface, and the combat of gods and giants on the concave side, while on her sandals he represented those of the Lapithai and Centaurs; so true was it that every spot furnished a field for his art to fill.[39]

If we sensed a kindred spirit when we read Pliny's account of his new bronze, it only serves to increase the contrast, for as sensitive and thorough an observer as Pausanias, who wrote a century later, did not seem to have noticed—or care enough to have characterized—the simple, visual qualities that made Phidias' statue of Zeus at Olympia so impressive. How could he have failed to mention the satiny sheen of its gold, the warmth and power that emanated from it as it glistened under the oil lamps, or the metallic curls beneath the olive branch, rendered so realistically that they seemed to move with the mountain breezes? Was he blind to the cunning way Phidias positioned the fierce visage, to transfix the viewer at first sight; or to the subtle proportioning of the base, which made that noble form still more imposing? And, finally, did he not notice the terrifyingly regal bird, poised on the staff, straining to do his master's bidding?

Of course this glorious image of Zeus was lost long ago, but the format of my "viewing" is familiar to all of us; it articulates the most rudimentary aspects of our aesthetic experience of a work of art. Was Pausanias unable to isolate these elements from the mythological, religious, and cultural? Or did he not care that facets of this experience could be separated out and appreciated in their own right?

Pausanias came closest to describing something we would recognize as an "aesthetic" quality when he acknowledged that his careful measurements of the statue of Zeus at Olympia "fall a long way short of the impression this statue has created in those who see it."[40] Given the overwhelming impact that statue must have had when it was revealed to the Greek pilgrim, we can only marvel at the incomprehensible inadequacy of this descriptive gesture. [12]

The fact that such meticulous observers hardly isolated the aesthetic ingredient, and that visual arts were the subject of no analysis comparable to that of modern times, indicates that they did not assign high priority to what is, for us, the artist's very stock in trade: the *physical beauty* of the form. If the aesthetic element was not isolated and studied in the literature of the classical world, it is unlikely that it was isolated in the life of those times. This further supports the importance of the ancients' apparent failure to separate artist from artisan. If the aesthetic element was not isolated for special consideration, they could hardly have shared our aesthetic distinction between fine and decorative art.

This is not to say that Greek and Roman sculptors, painters, and architects were oblivious to the aesthetic qualities we encompass with the term "beauty." Nor, obviously, were their contemporaries who practiced the other design arts. It would be silly to argue that ancient stone carvers did not delight in a beautiful line, form, or texture, or that painters did not thrill to the glow of their colors in the splendid Mediterranean light. But whatever it was that "impressed" the ancient temple-goer, as Pausanias put it, was a combination of ingredients, thoroughly dissolved in the total experience of ancient life, which combined to accomplish the broad social function of art. That elusive potion can no longer be concocted, largely because the self-consciousness of the eighteenth century brought a division of the arts that differs vastly from the unity of artist and artisan and the unified perception of the place of art in society that characterized antiquity.

Fig. 12. (*Facing page*) The experience of the Greek citizen who visited the shrine of Zeus at Olympia was probably much like that of the fourteenth-century Christian who confronted this *Madonna and Child,* by Duccio (shown here in Orcagna's Tabernacle in the Orsanmichele, Florence). It is unlikely that pilgrims of either period would have been able to isolate and analyze the "aesthetic" ingredient of their experience.

The Postclassical View

The senses continued to be viewed as inferior to the intellect long after
the Greek and Roman pantheons were replaced by the Christian God. St.
Augustine's attitude toward the arts was not dissimilar to that of the
ancients, whom he studied, and the senses remained a secondary source
of information for him: "In this world the soul looks for permanence,
constantia, and eternity, but never finds them, because only the lowest
kind of beauty can be achieved by such transience."[41] The great drawback
of sensual knowledge was the same for Augustine as it had been for Plato
and Aristotle: it lacked discernment compared to the intellect. [13] One
could be delighted with the form of a sculpture, for instance, while being
completely misinformed by it. A sculpture showing a winged Venus and
a cloaked Cupid (reversing the attributes of those two mythological
figures) could be pleasing to the eye even though, as Augustine said,
"through the eyes [the forms and their confused meanings] would offend
the mind."[42] The message was clear. The senses were sometimes useful—
the soul did perceive objects of delight through them, for example—but
placing one's faith in them alone could lead to serious misunderstandings,
because it meant relying on the frail world of the physical senses rather
than on the eternal kingdom of God.

For Augustine, as for his classical forebears, beauty of a superior
nature was only attainable through the intellect, which he pointed up in
this explanation of the origin of geometry:

> [Reason] realized that nothing pleased it but beauty; and in beauty,
> design; and in design, dimensions; and in dimension, number. And it
> asked itself whether any line or curve or any other form or shape in
> that realm was of such kind as intelligence comprehended. It found that
> they were far inferior, and that nothing which the eyes beheld, could
> in any way be compared with what the mind discerned.[43]

While it simplifies a complex matter, one might say that the
pagan art of antiquity served the state by instilling appropriate civic

13

Fig. 13. The early Christians borrowed freely from the classical world. Fourth-century bas-relief. (*Photograph by Brent C. Brolin. Courtesy of The Vatican Museum*)

virtues in its citizens, and the art of the early Christians was to provide one of several tools through which the individual was instructed in Church doctrine and prepared for the next life. The emphasis on purpose in Christian art was partly due to the persistence of the antique notion that art was there to perform a social function; but it was also connected to a long-standing controversy over the worship of icons, which some churchmen considered an undesirable carryover from pagan practice. The Church's attitude toward the uses of art was codified during the reign of

Pope Gregory the Great (590–604). In a letter to the bishop of Marseilles, who wanted to destroy all the religious images in his diocese, the pope wrote:

> It is one thing to worship a picture and another to learn from the language of a picture what that is which ought to be worshipped. What those who can read learn by means of writing, that do the uneducated learn by looking at a picture . . . that, therefore, ought not to have been destroyed which had been placed in the churches, not for worship, but solely for instructing the minds of the ignorant.[44]

Thomas Aquinas also spoke of superior beauty in metaphysical terms similar to those of Plato and Aristotle, as a spiritual beauty unconnected to the sensual world of art.[45] He did acknowledge that all the arts (using that word in its comprehensive, antique sense) possessed some good, and that some were more valuable than others. But, as we would expect by now, the more intellectual the art, the greater its value, the more useful it was in instructing the faithful in the higher conduct of life, and the higher its status: "the theoretical arts are good and honorable, the practical arts are only praiseworthy."[46]

Like Aristotle, Aquinas considered statesmen to be the most valued citizens, more so than generals, as matters of war were part of the overall good of the commonwealth for which the statesman was responsible. This line of reasoning invariably placed the visual arts at a disadvantage, for they were much less useful than shoemaking, cooking, or any number of other activities which Aquinas encompassed by the term "art."

Once we are aware of the continuing low assessment of the design arts relative to intellectual pursuits, we will not be confused by titles such as *doctus, expertus,* and others, which were frequently used in the Middle Ages to describe artisans. These "should not . . . be too highly valued as individual characterizations," says Rudolf Wittkower, "but should, rather, be regarded as referring to the expert handling of execution." Indeed, one twelfth-century bishop felt that artists should never be con-

sidered for higher positions, but were to be kept away "like the plague
. . . from more honorable and liberal studies."[47]

NOTES: CHAPTER II

1. Rudolf Wittkower and Margot Wittkower, *Born Under Saturn: The Character and Conduct of Artists. A Documented History from Antiquity to the French Revolution* (New York: W. W. Norton, 1963), pp. 3, 5.
2. *Liddell and Scott's Greek-English Lexicon.*
3. *Follett Latin Dictionary.*
4. *The Shorter Oxford English Dictionary on Historical Principles,* s.v. "artist."
5. The definitions and dates of first written occurrence are taken from *The Shorter Oxford English Dictionary on Historical Principles.*
6. Cicero, and his contemporary Marcus Terentius Varro, both listed medicine and architecture along with the more familiar liberal arts. These were acceptable to Cicero because they required "greater knowledge," or resulted in "more than ordinary usefulness." *Oxford Classical Dictionary,* s.v. "Encyclopaedic Learning"; Cicero, *De Officiis/On Duties,* trans. Harry G. Edinger (Indianapolis: Bobbs-Merrill, 1974), I.150.

   In his *Natural History,* Pliny (A.D. 23–79) spoke of a fourth-century Greek named Pamphilus, who claimed that painters could not "maintain perfection" without a thorough knowledge of all branches of learning, particularly the liberal arts of arithmetic and geometry. And so, according to Pliny, painting was raised to the front rank of liberal studies. But just as one of our fine arts seems to have risen to what we feel to be its rightful place, we find Pliny saying that painting fell from favor again in the middle of the second century B.C., and was no longer "esteemed as handiwork for persons of station" (9.35.36; 9.35.7)—Pliny the Elder, *Natural History,* trans. H. Rackham (10 vols., Cambridge: Harvard University Press, 1938–63).

   About the time Pliny compiled his *Natural History,* Seneca (54 B.C.?–A.D. 39) wrote a series of *Epistles* (see above) on ethical behavior, in which he flatly refused to consider painting a gentlemanly undertaking; yet the circumstances of the rejection are ambiguous. From his argument, Seneca appears to have been bucking a trend: "In this discussion you must bear with me if I do not follow the regular course. For I do not consent to admit painting into the list of liberal arts, any more than sculpture, marble-working, and other helps towards luxury." But before we take his remark as a sign of the high value accorded "fine" art by some of his contemporaries, we should mention that he also felt obliged to specify his disapproval of wrestlers, perfume makers, cooks, and all those involved with knowledge "compounded of oil and mud," who had apparently also been nominated to the ranks of the liberal arts at one time or another—Seneca, *Epistles,* trans. Richard M. Gummere (3 vols.; London: W. Heinemann, 1917–1925), 88.18. See also Harold Osborne, *Aesthetics and Art Theory: An Historical Introduction* (New York: E. P. Dutton, 1970), p. 40, note 4.

   Vitruvius (first century B.C.) mentioned that architects should know the liberal arts —an indication that he felt they had, or should have, some standing in the intellectual community. (See Vitruvius, *The Ten Books on Architecture,* trans. Morris Hicky Morgan [1914; reprint, New York: Dover Publications, 1960], bk. 1, ch. 1.) But it is not certain that the writers of his time, who were far more esteemed by their contemporaries, would have shared this view.

7. *Oxford Classical Dictionary,* s.v. "Martianus Capella."
8. Plutarch, *Lives,* "Pericles," 13.
9. Aristotle, *The Politics,* ed. Betty Radice, trans. T. A. Sinclair (Baltimore: Penguin Books, 1962), 8.3.
10. In the view of one scholar, Aristotle's mention of music as an appropriate leisuretime activity for free citizens was "perhaps the only explicit recognition in Greek literature of aesthetic enjoyment (apart from the aesthetic appreciation of the physical beauty of the human body) as an end in itself"—Osborne, *Aesthetics,* p. 37, note 3.
11. Hesiod, *Theogony,* 25ff.; *Anthologia Palatina,* 9.504, 505. Martin Shaw Briggs has argued that because we frequently know the names of ancient architects, they enjoyed a high status in those societies. But the cataloguing of names accompanied by honorific formulas cannot obscure the fact that, as Plutarch pointed out, while the object might be revered, the elite of those cultures looked with disdain upon those who were obliged to pursue such activities —*The Architect in History* (1927; reprint, New York: Da Capo Press, 1974).
12. Plato, *Phaedo,* trans. Hugh Tredennick (Baltimore: Penguin Books, 1959), 77c–80a.
13. Ibid., 99d–101a.
14. Ibid., 64b–65c.
15. Ibid., 65c–66e.
16. Plato, *The Republic,* ed. Betty Radice and Robert Baldick, trans. H. D. P. Lee (Baltimore: Penguin Books, 1951), bk. 10.1.602; see also bk. 10.1.597, 2.603.
17. Robert Scranton, "Greek Building," in *The Muses at Work: Arts, Crafts, and Professions in Ancient Greece and Rome,* ed. Carl Roebuck (Cambridge: MIT Press, 1969), p. 26.
18. Alison Burford, "The Builders of the Parthenon," *Parthenos and Parthenon Supplement to Greece and Rome,* 10 (1963):23–4.
19. Scranton, "Greek Building," *The Muses,* p. 33.
20. Ibid. If the method of payment can be taken as an indication of the status of the artist, as a number of historians seem to feel (from Arnold Hauser to Rudolf and Margot Wittkower), then it should be mentioned that the payment-by-piece method of ancient Greece was still being practiced as late as the fifteenth century, when Filippo Lippi "received six times as much money for the Crowning of the Virgin (1441–47) than [sic] for his Barbadori altarpiece in S. Spirito . . . no doubt because the later picture, although not much larger, contains about five times as many figures"—Wittkower and Wittkower, *Born Under Saturn,* p. 22.

21. Ibid., p. 2.
22. Ibid.
23. The only ancient treatise on the arts that has come down is *On Architecture,* by Vitruvius, the Roman engineer and architect of the first century B.C., which was a "how-to" book.
24. Wittkower and Wittkower, *Born Under Saturn,* p. 2.
25. Ibid., p. 3.
26. Ibid., p. 5. Aristotle took a crucial step toward the appreciation of beauty for its own sake when he separated goodness from beauty, making it possible to have a purely aesthetic experience of art or nature. (See *Metaphysics,* trans. Richard Hope [Ann Arbor: University of Michigan Press, 1960], 13.1078a.)
27. Frank P. Chambers, "The Aesthetic of the Ancients," *RIBA Journal,* 32 (Feb. 1925):241–52.
28. Plato, *Phaedrus,* 230. The first interest in the female nude came in what is usually referred to as the decline of Greek art, in the fourth century B.C. See Chambers, "The Aesthetic of the Ancients."
29. Pliny, *Letters,* 5.6. He also gloried in the relaxed atmosphere offered by country living, where "I need never wear a formal toga and there are not neighbors to disturb me." Pliny's enthusiasm for nature—not to mention his success as a lawyer—led him to acquire at least two villas. His Laurentum home, the Roman version of a bedroom suburb, was "seventeen miles from Rome, so that it is possible to spend the night there after necessary business is done, without having cut short or hurried the day's work." His directions to a friend read like an automobile club brochure: the villa "can be approached by more than one route," he advises, "the roads to Laurentum and Ostia both lead in that direction, but you must leave the one at the fourteenth milestone and the other at the eleventh"—Pliny, *Letters,* 2.17.
30. Pliny, *Letters,* 3.6.
31. While we find objects being appreciated for their beauty alone in Hellenistic and early Roman times, apart from their useful qualities, the Puritanical strain that rejected the senses as deceiving persisted. Seneca, for example, found the visual arts incapable of offering the means to achieve anything truly virtuous, specifically because of their connection to manual labor —*Epistles,* 20.
32. Plutarch, "Pericles," *The Rise and Fall of Athens: Nine Greek Lives by Plutarch,* ed. Betty Radice, trans. Ian Scott-Kilvert (Baltimore: Penguin Books, 1960), 1–2.
33. Jacques Barzun, *The Use and Abuse of Art,* Bollingen Series XXXV·22 (Princeton: Princeton University Press, 1974), p. 32.
34. Pausanias, *Guide to Greece,* ed. Betty Radice, trans. Peter Livi (2nd rev. ed., 2 vols., Baltimore: Penguin Books, 1979), 2:5.10.1.
35. Ibid., 5.11.1.
36. Pliny, *Natural History,* xxxiv.54.
37. The famous temple at Olympia fared no better under Pausanias' curiously uninvolved eye: "The style of workmanship of the temple is Doric, with a pillared portico around it; it is made of local stone. . . . Its height up to the pediment is sixty-eight feet, its width is ninety-five, and its length is two hundred and thirty. . . ."—Pausanias, *Guide to Greece,* 5.10.1.

In a similar, inventory approach, Herodotus described a Babylonian temple in which there was "a sitting figure of Zeus, all of gold. Before the figure stands a large golden table, and the throne whereon it sits and the base on which the throne is placed are likewise of gold.

The Chaldaeans told me that all the gold together was eight-hundred talents in weight"—Herodotus, *The Histories,* ed. E. V. Rieu, trans. Aubrey de Selincourt (2nd rev. ed. Baltimore: Penguin Books, 1972), 1.183.

38. Pliny, *Natural History,* xxxiv.57.

39. Ibid., xxxvi. 18.

40. Pausanias, *Guide to Greece,* 5.17–5.19.10; 5.11.10.

41. Augustine, *De Musica,* xiv.44, in Albert Hofstadter and Richard Kuhns, eds., *Philosophies of Art & Beauty: Selected Readings in Aesthetics from Plato to Heidegger,* various trans. (Chicago: University of Chicago Press, 1976), p. 195.

42. Augustine, *De Ordine,* 11.34, in Hofstadter and Kuhns, eds., ibid., p. 176.

43. Augustine, *De Musica,* xiv.48, in Hofstadter and Kuhns, eds., ibid., p. 197.

44. *Encyclopaedia Britannica,* 11th ed., s.v. "Iconoclasts."

45. Paul Oskar Kristeller, "The Modern System of the Arts," *Journal of the History of Ideas,* 12, 13 (1951, 1952):496ff., 17ff.

46. Ibid., 13, pp. 48, 43.

47. *Dictionary of the History of Ideas,* s.v. "Genius: Individualism in Art and Artists." V.2, pp. 297–312.

CHAPTER III

Art, Craft, and Ornament

"Artisan" . . . on the Way to "Artist"

Only in the Renaissance do we begin to sense an attitude toward art and the artist that seems familiar. It is in the early fifteenth century, too, that we find the first indications of a new way of looking at art, one which argues that painting (and possibly even sculpture) should be valued more highly than other mechanical arts. This was the beginning of a metamorphosis that would eventually undermine the traditional unity of the design arts, and have a quite unexpected effect on ornamental art in the nineteenth and twentieth centuries.

At the heart of this change, and crucial to the evolution of modern attitudes toward ornament, was the hint of a division among the visual arts, which would eventually separate "artist" from "artisan." The reason for this new way of looking at art was straightforward. It was, in the words of Erwin Panofsky, to "wrest a place for [their art] among the *artes liberales* by enumerating its dignity and merits," and thereby improve their own status.[1] It is impossible to pinpoint the beginning of this trend, but Boccaccio's *Decamerone* (1353) was one of the earlier signs. [14–19] There Boccaccio lauded Giotto as a painter who "had brought back to light that art that had been buried for centuries under the errors of those *who painted rather to delight the eyes of the ignorant than to please the intellect of the wise*" (author's emphasis).[2]

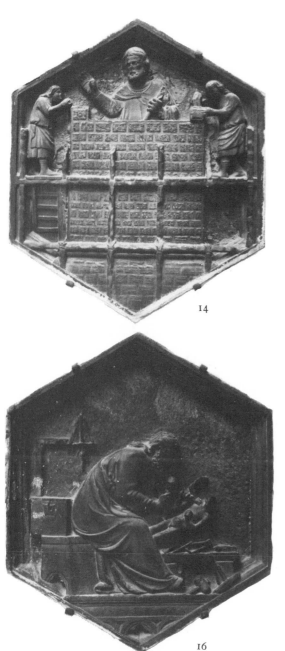

14

15

16

Figs. 14–19.   Giotto's relief sculptures for the Florentine Campanile were perhaps the first art works to link the three arts of painting, sculpture, and architecture, which were shown between the seven liberal and the three mechanical arts. (14) Art of Building, (15) Architecture, (16) Sculpture, (17) Art of Blacksmithing, (18) Painting, (19) Weaving.

17

18

19

Early champions of the painters' cause went about improving their lot in a predictable way, given the traditional importance assigned to the senses versus the intellect. They invested painting with the same intellectual qualities that had given stature to the liberal arts for the preceding two thousand years. This activity was portrayed less as the result of refined manual dexterity (what would eventually come to be described as "craft"), and more as the product of intellect, requiring knowledge that heretofore had been necessary only when studying the liberal arts.

Leon Battista Alberti's treatise *On Painting* (1435) may appear to have little to do with the plight of ornament in the twentieth century, but it was the first indication of the trend toward elitism within the design arts that would make mere ornament a matter for craftsmen rather than "creative artists," and eventually set artists above any concern for the taste of others. Alberti made claims for painters that Vitruvius had once made on behalf of architects: that a knowledge of the more intellectually demanding liberal arts was essential to the proper practice of their craft.

But while Vitruvius' admonition had little or no effect on the status of the architects of antiquity, Alberti's marked the beginning of a new way of viewing art and the artist.

Painters had to observe nature systematically, said Alberti, in imitation of the approach to the observation of the natural world that was coming to be adopted by those interested in the sciences. They should be aware, for instance, that elements of the same size appeared smaller when farther away, and that atmospheric haze diluted colors that were nearer the horizon.[3] *On Painting* also contained the first written exposition of the science of linear perspective. This alone made a strong case in favor of a much-improved status for painters, for to execute a proper perspective painting demanded a specialized knowledge of geometry, a discipline that had once been the guarded province of liberal art.[4]

Leonardo da Vinci made even bolder suggestions in a posthumously published portion of his notebooks known as *Paragone,* arguing for the superiority of painters over poets and even philosophers. Painting served sight, Leonardo maintained, and sight was acknowledged by both Plato and Aristotle as the noblest of the senses. Furthermore, painting was the most useful "science," as Leonardo called it, since it communicated the most information. And, while philosophers only understood the inner qualities of the human being, painters revealed both inner and outer truths.[5]

Like Alberti's, Leonardo's line of reasoning hinged on the link between painting and the liberal arts, particularly the painter's need to know geometry, which formed the basis of his argument that painters should be ranked above sculptors. In a series of detailed, direct comparisons between these two arts, Leonardo explained his reasons. Like astronomy, painting originated in the intellect and demanded the same kind of scientific observation of nature. Painters were also required to call upon the powers of the intellect to invent their own color, light, shade, and perspective. Sculptors, on the other hand, had no need for painters' sophisticated intellectual equipment; they simply made literal, three-dimensional copies of what was before their eyes.

Finally, with what may seem a tongue-in-cheek remark, Leonardo went to the core of the differences between the mechanical and the intellectual arts when he disdainfully observed that painters could dress comfortably and remain clean while they worked—they could even work to the accompaniment of music, one of the sister liberal arts—while everything in a sculptor's house was filthy with marble dust, including the sculptor himself!

While the artist's interest lay in raising his trade from a mechanical to an intellectual, or liberal art, his intellectual contemporaries—the literary humanists—were often unwilling to admit that one who worked with his hands could ever share their elevated status. When Leonardo Bruni was asked to make a list of Old Testament topics that might serve as sculptural motifs, he carefully pointed out that he "would like to be close to the designer to make him grasp every point of significance that the episode carries," as he did not feel an artist would be able to under-

20

Fig. 20. Like their medieval predecessors, Renaissance artists received little or no formal education. One consequence was that the intellectuals of the day frequently assumed that the interpretation of biblical events was beyond their abilities. Baptismal font showing the legend of St. Nicholas of Myra, in Winchester Cathedral, England (black Tournai marble, Belgian workmanship, 12th century).

stand the subtleties of each biblical event.[6][20] Like other professional humanists, Bruni was skeptical about the wisdom of trafficking with manual workers who had pretensions to a higher station in life, and left the unmistakable impression that these artisans should not try to better themselves by basking in the reflected glory of the liberal arts:

An artist who has acquired a certain perfection and standing in his art, such as Apelles in painting or Praxiteles in sculpture, does not need to understand military science or the government of the state or to have a knowledge of the nature of things. Indeed as Socrates says in the Apology it is a common vice in artists that one who excels in his own art deceives himself into thinking that he has other faculties which he has not. An art therefore should be distinguished from other intellectual virtues.[7]

The attitude was not so patronizing as it first sounds. Painters and sculptors rarely received liberal arts educations at the time, although those who sought to improve the artist's status felt it was essential. Artists were generally apprenticed to their trade as children, leaving no time for esoteric and irrelevant studies.

The differentiation between manual and intellectual tasks had held the design arts down for centuries. Petrarch was only reiterating the Aristotelian view when, in the fourteenth century, he wrote: "To noble minds money is no fit reward for intellectual pursuits. Manufacturers [literally, those who made things with their hands] are quite right to look for cash: the liberal arts have a finer end in view."[8] Needless to say, painters and sculptors always did things very much by hand, and "For many patrons [of the arts], even from the upper clergy, the artist still remained no more than another manual employee with whom one did not need to concern himself much." Again, "For the vast majority, even of the cultured middle class, artistic creation counted then as earlier only as a branch, at best somewhat elevated and especially esteemed, of the artisan trades."[9]

Florence was the most liberal in terms of its treatment of artists, and there are indications that Florentine patrons had begun a slow change of attitude toward artists by the middle of the fifteenth century. But even in the most artistically forward-looking of European cities, the "better" families rarely permitted their sons to become artists, for it was a trade that placed its practitioners no higher than the lower ranks of the petty bourgeoisie.[10] The fathers of Uccello, Botticelli, and Andrea del Sarto were a barber, a tanner, and a tailor, respectively. Michelangelo's father, who was serving as *podestà,* or chief official, of two small towns in Tuscany when his son was born, wanted him to take up the respectable study of letters, and sent him to school for this purpose when he came of age. As soon as Michelangelo's real interests became known, he left school, an act for which "he was resented and quite often beaten unreasonably by his father and his father's brothers who," as his biographer says, were "impervious to the excellence and nobility of art, detested it and felt that its appearance in their family was a disgrace."[11] The notion that the artist's self-image was not necessarily shared by his "betters" in the community—the intellectuals and literati—is supported by analyses of the literary output of the time: fewer than 5 percent of the biographies written in the fifteenth and first half of the sixteenth century were of artists, the other 95 percent being devoted primarily to writers, followed by civic and military figures, churchmen, and physicians.[12]

The Renaissance writers who, like Vasari, wanted to raise painters above their fellow "mechanics," preferred their compatriots to be more exclusive in the type of work they took on. Vasari, for example, felt that applied art tasks were not suited to his elevated vision of the artist's worth, and frequently said that artists should no longer concern themselves with this kind of work. But like the generations of artisanartists who had preceded them, most Renaissance artists did not confine their activities within the narrow boundaries that now circumscribe the fine arts.[13] Documentary evidence indicates that even well-known artists in Vasari's time, not to mention lesser lights, did not take his advice, and unself-consciously pursued the "decorative" as well as the "fine" arts. In his study of *The World of the Florentine Renaissance Artist,* Martin Wackernagel writes that the "inclusion of the most varied and sometimes even humblest tasks of everyday applied arts [were] within the scope of the work of famous, highly qualified ateliers."[14] He notes that Botticelli designed processional banners,[15] and painted carts for similar festivities came from the hands of Andrea del Sarto and Pontormo.[16]

Brunelleschi rigged up an "ingenious mechanism in San Felice that made possible a representation of the vault of heaven with live child angels revolving in it and the angel of the Annunciation hovering suspended from it."[17] Donatello and the della Robbias were said to have fashioned coats of arms,[18] and there were small bronze statuettes, some by Donatello, "which were first used as church or household utensils."[19] Well-known artists and their studios also designed portrait medals, coinage, and seals,[20] and painted wainscot paneling, including, again, Botticelli or his workshop.[21] Vasari spoke of a small Botticelli, probably part of the paneling of the Vespucci house.[22] A number of paintings also exist in a wide and rather narrow format—often the reclining lovers, Mars and Venus—which probably decorated the headboards of beds.[23] "Finally there was the aristocratic, sporadically distributed higher level of chest paintings for which, as for many *spalliera* pictures and *cornicioni,* wealthy customers frequently employed well-known artists. The authors of these, according to documentary evidence or convincing attributions, include Uccello, Domenico Veneziano, Pesellino, and Sellaio."[24]

The list of craft occupations of Renaissance artists goes on: small, portable pictures were painted for well-to-do bourgeoisie; special occasions required platters ornamented with "painstaking decoration of high artistic quality," for which established masters were hired. The inventory of the Palazzo Medici mentions decorated platters by Masaccio.[25] There were also small devotional paintings for the house, overdoor panels, and bed canopies; one, "painted or embroidered" by Botticelli, is mentioned in the Medici inventory.[26]

Indeed, when Florence was besieged by Pope Clement and the Spaniards, artists even became engineers. Michelangelo designed catapults, battering rams, mantlets, tortoises, ironclad towers and bridges, and the "shape and proportion" of forts, bastions, moats, and other fineries of battle, right down to the "cunning designs" of arms and emblems of banners, standards, and the devices for shields and helmets.[27]

It is impossible to assign one status to all artists of a given period. A minority had great prestige and wealth in the Renaissance—among them Brunelleschi, Michelangelo, and Raphael—and were not reticent about expressing their sense of worth. "O to punish as they deserve those foolish critics who presume to speak about painting!" Michelangelo reportedly said, "O to teach them to be more courteous and to speak properly of what they do not understand, however noble or illustrious they may be."[28]

Strong words, to be sure, but Michelangelo was a rare case. The majority of artists led a far more humble existence, burdened by restraints on the practice of their trade that modern-day painters would find hard to imagine. Martin Kemp tells us that most fifteenth-century art patrons continued to feel that choosing subject matter was far too delicate a task to be left to the discretion of the painter or sculptor; although by the end of that century, artists were challenging this custom as they strove to have their own creative powers acknowledged.[29] Nevertheless, as late as the early sixteenth century, only a few painters enjoyed the luxury of liberal-minded patrons who permitted them to pursue their own innovative ideas.[30] Even the contract for Michelangelo's famous *David* had what seem, by hindsight, remarkable stipulations: "When the said work and the said male figure of marble shall be finished, then the Consuls and Overseers who shall at that time be in authority shall judge whether it merits a higher reward, being guided therein by the dictates of their own consciences."[31]

Indeed, even Michelangelo was plagued by problems that would hardly befall a lesser artistic light today. Early in his career, Pope Julius II entrusted Michelangelo with the preparation of his tomb, in the Medici church of San Lorenzo, in Florence. Sculpture was Michelangelo's greatest love, and it was a coveted commission. However, through the connivings of his rivals, according to Vasari, the pope took him away from that commission, and ordered him to decorate the ceiling of his private chapel, the Sistine.[32] Following Julius's death, Pope Leo X directed the sculptor to complete the facade of San Lorenzo instead of continuing the tomb sculpture, [21] and although Michelangelo objected he could do nothing.[33] When Clement VII asked him to paint a Last Judgment on the altar wall of the Sistine, he was once again forced to comply against his wishes.

It is difficult to conceive of a similar scenario today, even assuming one could find an artist of comparable stature. It would have been hard to imagine Albers painting ellipses instead of squares in order to comply with a client's preference. Today's artist is not so easily coerced. More to the point, our reverence for the artist, and his need for a free artistic hand, is so deeply ingrained that no "sensitive" art lover would think of designating the subject matter, size, and medium for a work of

Fig. 21. (*Above*) In some ways, even minor artists of today are treated with greater respect than the most celebrated artists of the Renaissance. According to Vasari, the most famous biographer of artists, Michelangelo was obliged to execute one of his greatest triumphs virtually against his will. (*Photograph by Brent C. Brolin. Courtesy of The Vatican Museum*)

art—though he may be well aware that most of the great works of the past were created under precisely those conditions.

Recounting Michelangelo's plight, Vasari made a revealing comment about the nature of the patronage system, which gives an insight into one of the differences between our modern view of art, and that which held sway long past the Renaissance. Clement was not interested in paying homage to the artist, according to Vasari (though he would naturally have chosen the best to execute his commissions). In fact, the pope would probably be astounded to discover that the Sistine Chapel is known today for its painter, and not for the pope who commissioned it. Clement chose his artist solely in the interest of self-glorification, the ruler's motivation in commissioning works of art since time immemorial. Clement, as Vasari put it, was "no less anxious than Leo and his other predecessors to leave a name glorified by the arts of architecture, sculpture and painting."[34] Michelangelo's work was not yet the self-justifying creation which would characterize eighteenth-century art. It was not yet "Art for Art's sake," at least as far as the patron was concerned. Art was still primarily a tool of propaganda, as it had been since ancient times.

The Academies

Alberti and Leonardo laid the groundwork for the formation of an elite among the arts of design. Leonardo's pointed remarks about sculptors are particularly telling in this respect. The academies of art were a more organized manifestation of that trend, "the thin end of the wedge driven officially between arts and crafts," and the first real step toward freeing artists from the protective, and restrictive, guild system.[35]

Through Giorgio Vasari's initiative, the Accademia del Disegno was begun in Florence in 1563, jointly sponsored by Cosimo de'Medici and Michelangelo. The Roman Accademia di San Luca followed later in the century, and, within two hundred years, art academies were flourishing in most European capitals.[36]

Scholars seem to agree on the motivation behind the formation of these academies: artists wanted to increase their prestige and social standing. "To become a member of an academy was everybody's ambition, not only for reasons of professional prestige, but also because the glamour of an academic title was considered a passport to the higher spheres of society."[37] While their very existence enhanced the position of those associated with them, it cannot be said that the academies came into being solely to give prestige to certain arts and artists over others. For example, one proposal suggested the creation of an Academy of Spectacles, which would have included circus performers and other public shows; another recommended grouping all the arts (not just the ones we now call fine) under a single academic roof.[38] In France, governmental ministers were instrumental in creating the academies in their country, in part to consolidate political and economic power under the monarchy. Cardinal Richelieu established the French Academy of Literature in 1635, and Cardinal Mazarin founded the royal academies of painting and sculpture (1648). Colbert, who became chief minister to Louis XIV upon the death of Mazarin in 1661, extended the king's control, forming a number of provincial academies of painting and sculpture. He also began a major fiscal reform program under which the royal tapestry works at Gobelin and the porcelain factory at Sèvres both developed drawing schools in an attempt to raise the quality of their designs, and increase the value of their production.[39] [22]

From the fifteenth century on, the status of artists slowly but steadily improved. One measure of this was the degree of freedom they wrested from traditional regulatory bodies, the guilds. In Florence in 1434, Filippo Brunelleschi was jailed as a result of a guild complaint. In one of the earliest instances of an artist successfully resisting his guild's power (albeit with outside help), the Church fathers secured his release in less than two weeks, as his services were essential to construct his dome for the Cathedral of Santa Maria del Fiore.

There is no question that artists' enhanced status offered them new opportunities. Already in the late fifteenth century some Italian cities were permitting them to hold public office. But in spite of these strides, the improvement in the artists' position was not as rapid as either they or the theoreticians had hoped. If Brunelleschi's case marked a hairline crack in the prison of the guilds, the final breaching of those walls was a long time coming. Nearly two hundred years after Brunelleschi's release, as prestigious an artist as Rubens could still have difficulties with his guild.[40] One of Rubens's letters offers personal testimony to the continuing prejudice facing even the most successful artists in his time. At the peak of his career—recognized as a man of great learning, recipient of commissions from the royal houses of Europe, and trusted executor of diplomatic missions—Rubens took his second wife, a merchant's daughter named Hélène Fourment. He would have made a "Court marriage," he wrote, had it not been for "pride, that inherent vice of the nobility," which would have made him seem an upstart intruder in their ranks. Therefore, he continued, "I chose one who would not blush to see me take my brushes in hand."[41]

One hundred years later, and three centuries after Alberti's literary and artistic milestone, a Spanish artist named Antonio Palomino wrote a treatise in which he felt obliged to reiterate Alberti's argument that painting should be considered a liberal art, a clear sign that this standing had not yet been assured, by any means. Palomino's reasons for pleading the artists' case were practical: "If it could be proven that painters practiced a liberal, not a mechanical art, they would be free from the *alcabala,* the sales tax."[42]

There are, of course, many anecdotes of haughty artists who ridiculed patrons with impunity, but we should bear in mind that this was a small portion of the total number. In England, for example, " 'face

Fig. 22. (*Facing page*) The commercial purposes of art academies created in 17th-century France have often been overlooked. In addition to the better-known academies of painting and sculpture (1748), schools were established at the Gobelin tapestry works and the Sèvres porcelain factory in order to raise the quality of French design, and thereby improve the balance of trade. (*Photograph by Brent C. Brolin. Courtesy of The Metropolitan Museum of Art, New York*) painters,' coach-painters, and house-painters were, on an equal footing, members of the Painter-Stainers' Company throughout the seventeenth century, and painters remained low-class tradesmen even longer than in France." Well into the eighteenth century, "the majority of artists had by no means climbed as high on the social ladder as optimistic theorists of the fifteenth century had expected they would. It was owing to the discrepancy between the actual and the hoped-for conditions that large numbers of the public continued to hold the profession in low esteem."[43]

NOTES: CHAPTER III

1. Erwin Panofsky, *Idea: A Concept in Art Theory,* trans. Joseph J. S. Peake (Columbia, S.C.: University of South Carolina Press, 1968), p. 51.
2. G. Boccaccio, *Decamerone,* "Giornatta" VI, "Novella" 5, as cited in E. H. Gombrich, "Visual Metaphors for Art," *Meditations on a Hobby Horse: And Other Essays on the Theory of Art* (3rd ed., New York: Phaidon Press, 1978), p. 17. See also Dante's reference, in the *Divine Comedy,* to Giotto having usurped Cimabue's position as the most famous painter (*Purgatorio,* xi, 94–6).
3. Leon Battista Alberti, *On Painting,* trans. John R. Spencer (2nd rev. ed., New Haven: Yale University Press, 1966), p. 48.
4. Brunelleschi is generally acknowledged to have invented perspective (having painted the first, true perspective picture around 1425), and painters such as Mantegna and Masaccio practiced it before the publication of Alberti's treatise. See Samuel Y. Edgerton, Jr., *The Renaissance Rediscovery of Linear Perspective* (New York: Harper & Row, 1976), for a detailed discussion of perspective in Renaissance painting and its larger implications. See also Edgerton, "Linear Perspective and the Western Mind: The Origins of Objective Representation in Art and Science," *Cultures,* no. 3 (1976):77–105.
5. Leonardo da Vinci, *Paragone,* from the Codex Urbinas 1270, in the library of the Dukes of Urbino, trans. I. A. Richter (London: Oxford University Press, 1949), pp. 27, 29, 30, and 72.
6. Leonardo Bruni, letter written in 1424, quoted in George Holmes, *The Florentine Enlightenment: 1400–1450* (New York: Pegasus, 1969), p. 234. See also Martin Kemp, "From Mimesis to Fantasia: The Quattrocento Vocabulary of Creation, Inspiration and Genius in the Visual

Arts," *Viator,* 8 (1977) 8:359, on the status of the artist at this time.

7. Bruni, quoted in Holmes, *Florentine Enlightenment,* p. 235. See, in general, Kemp, "From Mimesis to Fantasia," pp. 347–98.

8. Petrarch, letter on "Scholarly Method," in *Renaissance and Reformation: 1300–1648,* ed. A. R. Elton (New York: The Macmillan Company, 1963), pp. 50–51.

9. Martin Wackernagel, *The World of the Florentine Renaissance Artist,* trans. Alison Luchs (Princeton: Princeton University Press, 1981), pp. 290, 295.

10. Rudolf Wittkower and Margot Wittkower, *Born Under Saturn, The Character and Conduct of Artists: A Documented History from Antiquity to the French Revolution* (New York: W. W. Norton, 1963), p. 253.

11. Ascanio Condivi, *The Life of Michelangelo,* ed. Hellmut Wohl, trans. Alice Sedgwick Wohl (Baton Rouge, La.: Louisiana State University Press, 1976), p. 9.

12. Wittkower and Wittkower, *Born Under Saturn,* p. 13.

13. Wackernagel, *Florentine Renaissance Artist,* p. 335, note 62.

14. Ibid., p. 335.

15. Ibid., p. 140.

16. Ibid., p. 195.

17. Ibid., p. 202.

18. Ibid., p. 106.

19. Ibid., p. 107.

20. Ibid., pp. 107, 109.

21. Ibid., pp. 156ff.

22. Ibid., pp. 157–58.

23. Ibid., p. 158. One, by Botticelli, in London, another, by Piero di Cosimo, in Berlin.

24. Ibid., p. 160, note 125.

25. Ibid., p. 168.

26. Ibid., pp. 172ff., 178, note 172.

27. Francisco de Hollanda, *Four Dialogues on Painting,* trans. Aubrey F. G. Bell (London: Oxford University Press, 1928), p. 50.

28. Ibid., p. 82.

29. Kemp, "From Mimesis to Fantasia," pp. 384ff. According to Kemp, the concept of "genius" in the Renaissance did not carry exactly the same connotations as it does now. The visual arts of the Renaissance were governed by rational procedures of discovery and making, and could be given "almost infinite extension by imaginative invention, rather than by capricious creativity of an anarchically modern kind," p. 397. See also pp. 347, 348–9.

30. Ibid., pp. 290, 295.

31. Contract for *David,* quoted in Elizabeth Holt, *Documentary History of Art* (2 vols., Garden City, N.Y.: Doubleday Anchor Books, 1958), 2:5.

32. Vasari, *Lives of the Artists,* trans. George Bull (2nd ed., Baltimore: Penguin Books, 1965), p. 349.

33. Ibid., pp. 362ff.

34. Ibid., p. 365.

35. Wittkower and Wittkower, *Born Under Saturn,* p. 233. See also *Dictionary of the History of Ideas,* s.v. "Genius." V.2, pp. 297–312.

36. Wittkower and Wittkower, *Born Under Saturn,* p. 233.

37. Ibid., p. 229; see also *The Oxford Companion to Art,* s.v. "Academies."

38. Paul Oskar Kristeller, "The Modern System of the Arts," *Journal of the History of Ideas,* 12 (1951):522–3.

39. *The Oxford Companion to Art,* s.v. "Academies," "Art Education." In view of what was to happen in the nineteenth century, it is interesting to note that, while the French ministers had aims similar to those of the English decorative art reformers, they did not invent any new, nonvisual "principles." Perhaps the difference, or the key difference, was the growth of the middle classes in the intervening two centuries.

40. Wittkower and Wittkower, *Born Under Saturn,* p. 11.

41. Ruth Saunders Magurn, ed., *The Letters of Peter Paul Rubens* (Cambridge: Harvard University Press, 1955), p. 393, quoted in Wittkower and Wittkower, *Born Under Saturn,* pp. 96–7.

42. Antonio Palomino, *Theory of Painting* (1715), quoted in Holt, *A Documentary History of Art,* 2:225, note 2.

43. Wittkower and Wittkower, *Born Under Saturn,* pp. 11, 22.

CHAPTER IV

Fine Art and the Art Marketplace

Introduction

The eighteenth century marked a milestone in the evolution of attitudes toward art, and hence toward ornament. In 1747, a new category called "fine art" was defined and generally accepted, which placed painting and sculpture above the decorative arts. In 1790, the creation of a philosophy of fine art reinforced that separation by providing an intellectual basis for these "fine" arts, and, in the process, transformed the artist into a *Wunderkind*. The fine arts of design—painting and sculpture—gained enormous prestige from this intellectual underpinning, while the decorative arts remained mired in the age-old prejudice against manual labor. In spite of earnest attempts by reformers in the next century, the prestige of the decorative arts could not be raised, and the "lesser" arts remained, by and large, the pursuit of "lesser" artists.[1]

One ingredient stands out as having been most important in bringing these new attitudes toward fine and decorative art into being: the taste of the newly emerging middle class. Several factors point to this, the most obvious being that beautiful art had been created for thousands of years without either a category called "fine art," or a philosophy of art; these were only needed once an economically powerful, culturally influential, and relatively uneducated class had begun to exert its influence.[2] Another indication of the importance of this new group is that "taste" had rarely if ever been a subject for prolonged intellectual debate before the emergence of this class, for artist and patron generally agreed on the definition of beauty. Yet in the late seventeenth and early eighteenth centuries, lengthy treatises on taste were as easy to come by as stock in new trading companies. Aesthetic judgment became a focus of interest because the taste of a growing body of new art consumers differed noticeably from that of the cultured elite and the refined art supplier. As early as 1750, these newcomers had irrevocably changed the artist's life, creating a "culture market"[3] for the arts, which eventually supplanted the traditional patronage system. Unable to escape the influence of this new class, serious artists and art lovers were sustained by the unquestioned belief that taste could be improved through reason.[4] Unfortunately, faith in the ultimate triumph of reason was little consolation to the artist trapped by the marketplace, and obliged by custom to satisfy a client whose ideas of "good taste" were often painfully different from his own. This dilemma was ultimately "resolved" by the philosophy of art. It established that "true" artists ignored conventional taste, and, to that end, provided the wedge of *genius* and the hammer of *originality* to shatter the chains of convention which bound artists in the service of popular taste. But the artisan—the creator of ornament—remained at the mercy of the marketplace.

A half century later the upstart middle class, deep in a passionate love affair with ornament, dominated a mass market of unprecedented size. The decorative art reformers of that time knew that they, too, needed weapons of the intellect that would enable decorative artists to ignore popular taste. As we shall see, they eventually found them in the "principles" of design. But now let us look more closely at the apotheosis of the fine arts, for the decorative art crusade was modeled on the events that took place in this arena during the eighteenth century.

A Matter of Taste

"The great business in this (as in our lives, or in the whole of life) is 'to correct our taste,' " wrote Anthony Ashley Cooper, third earl of Shaftesbury (1671–1713).[5] Before the end of the seventeenth century, relatively little interest appears to have been shown in the faculty that judges beauty, so it seems reasonable to assume that some new circumstance or circumstances brought it on. There are several possibilities.

The intense interest in taste might have been a simple by-product of the reassessment of all knowledge—known as the "battle of ancients and moderns"—then under way. This grand examination of the cumulative wisdom of mankind was a response to fundamental questions about the validity of ancient wisdom, which had been raised by the revolutionary approaches to science of Descartes and Bacon. It was a time when "enlarged experience and more precise speculation made necessary a sharper division of the sciences,"[6] and to that end, the warriors in this "battle" analyzed all areas of knowledge in an effort to determine whose was better. (It was finally decided that the ancients were superior in the arts, the moderns in science.)

A second factor contributed more directly to a preoccupation with the topic: the growing importance of subjectivity in the experience of beauty. The aesthetic doctrine of classicism, which dominated the seventeenth century, held that the test of beauty was to measure a work of art against the tried and true rules laid down by antique authorities. But the hegemony of the ancients was under attack in art and literature just as it was in science, and new appraisals tended toward the view that beauty was not a property of the object itself (and therefore not the result of following a given formula for composition or proportion), but a subjective response to that object.[7] This placed the determination of beauty within the realm of personal taste—"I mean by the word Taste no more than the faculty or faculties of the mind which are affected with, or which form a judgment of the works of imagination and the elegant arts."[8]

The exponential growth of international trade offers another plausible explanation for the surprising interest in taste. Merchants welcomed frequent changes in fashion, which would surely have stimulated discussions of taste. " 'Fashion or the alteration of Dress . . . is the spirit of life of Trade,' " wrote a seventeenth-century French observer: "thanks to fashion, 'the great body of trade remains in movement' and man lives in perpetual springtime, 'without ever seeing the autumn of his clothes.' "9

The fourth and most convincing explanation for the focus on taste is linked to the growth of trade: the emergence of a new and wealthy class, particularly in England. Artists, whose kind had been trying to improve their lot for centuries, now found yet another obstacle blocking the path toward autonomy. Although no special notice was needed to point it out, it was heralded by the introduction of completely new terms to describe social standing. The word "class," connoting a difference in social status, entered European languages in the latter half of the eighteenth century. "The terms 'higher classes,' 'middle classes,' and 'middling classes' appear in the 1790s, and 'upper classes' in the 1820s. . . . Slightly later than in England, but roughly in the same period, the French terminology shifts from *état* to *classe,* and the German from *Stand* to *Klasse.*"10

The social changes came first in England, partly because it was the leader in trade, and partly because its social structure accommodated movement up from the lower classes more readily than did the Continental countries.11 By 1750, a substantial "middling" class was on the social scene, having grown wealthy and powerful from trade with both the East and West Indies. In his encyclopedic volume on the state of "the Several Kingdoms of the World," William Guthrie wrote in 1771 about the "vast fortunes" made during the late seventeenth and early eighteenth centuries, which

> introduced a species of people among the English, who have become rich without industry . . . *and an emulation among merchants and traders of all kinds, to equal, or surpass the nobility and the courtiers.* The plain

and frugal manners of men of business which prevailed so lately as the accession of the present family to the crown are now disregarded for *tasteless extravagance in dress and equipage,* and the most expensive amusements and diversions, not only in the capital, but all over the trading towns of the kingdom. (my emphasis)[12]

Voltaire commented on the importance of this merchant class to English society when he questioned the French failure to acknowledge the tradesman's importance:

In *France* the title of Marquis is given *gratis* to any one who will accept of it; and whosoever arrives at *Paris* from the midst of the most remote Provinces with Money in his Purse, and a Name terminating in *ac* or *ille,* may strut about, and cry, such a Man as I! A Man of my Rank and Figure! And may look down upon a Trader with sovereign Contempt; whilst the Trader on the other Side, by thus often hearing his Profession treated so disdainfully, is Fool enough to blush at it. However, I cannot say which is most useful to a Nation; a Lord, powder'd in the tip of the Mode, who knows exactly at what a Clock the King rises and goest to bed; and who gives himself Airs of Grandeur and State . . . or a[n English] Merchant, who enriches his Country, dispatches orders from his Compting-House to *Surat* [the Indian headquarters of the British East India Company] and *Grand Cairo,* and contributes to the Felicity of the World.[13]

The deference shown to this new breed of consumer had a simple explanation: "There is among the English of all ranks, a most unpardonable preference given to wealth, over all other considerations. Riches, both in public and private, compensate for the absence of every good quality"[14]—including taste. No matter how loudly sophisticated lovers of the arts deplored the values of this new, consumer class, their sheer economic power guaranteed them the ability to impose their artistic values on the marketplace they had created. They constituted an overriding fact of artistic life, irrevocably undermining the traditional authority of enlightened patron and artisan/artist as arbiters in matters of taste. De

Tocqueville's later chronicle of the new American democracy provides an astute analysis of one way in which this transformation affected the arts: "The handicraftsmen of democratic ages . . . strive to give to all their commodities attractive qualities which they do not in reality possess. In the confusion of all ranks every one hopes to appear what he is not, and makes great exertions to succeed in this object."[15]

Taking the earl of Shaftesbury's earlier-quoted remark at face value, it is apparent that the imperfect taste of the merchant class had been an irritation to lovers of the arts as early as the beginning of the eighteenth century. According to Samuel Taylor Coleridge (1772–1834), the poet and philosopher, its impact was apparent even earlier. In the mid-seventeenth century, wrote Coleridge,

> the spirit of the nation became much more commercial, than it had been before; a learned body, or clerisy, as such, gradually disappeared, and literature in general began to be addressed to the common miscellaneous public. That public had become accustomed to, and required, a strong stimulus; and to meet the requisitions of public taste, a style was produced which by combining triteness of thought with singularity and excess of manner of expression, was calculated at once to soothe ignorance and to flatter vanity. The thought was carefully kept down to the immediate apprehension of the commonest understanding, and the dress was as anxiously arranged for the purpose of making the thought appear something very profound.[16]

By the 1750s, English writers depended almost entirely upon public approval for their livelihoods. A combination of inexpensive paper production, increased literacy, and new ways of distributing books and periodicals (including lending libraries) made it possible for writers to live from the public sale of their work.[17] The "possibility" of living from public sales of one's work was more like a necessity, for the shift from private patronage to public marketplace was very nearly complete by that time. The potential for misunderstanding—even hostility—between artist and client was profound, and quite clearly lay in artists' increasing contact with those whose values they did not respect: "It is not from the textbooks of political theory that the artist learns to decry the vices of the bourgeoisie; it is from contact with the stolid playgoer, the greedy middleman, the wayward patron. These are the living obstacles barring the way to fame."[18]

Coleridge frequently commented on the trials to which the popular marketplace subjected literary artists, curtailing their freedom and, therefore, threatening the quality of the artistic creation:

> In former times a *popular* work meant one that adapted the *results* of studious meditation or scientific research to the capacity of the people, presenting in the concrete, by instances and examples, what had been ascertained in the abstract and by discovery of the Law. *Now,* on the other hand, that is a popular work which gives back to the people their own errors and prejudices, and flatters the many by creating them, under the title of THE PUBLIC, into a supreme and inappellable Tribunal of intellectual Excellence.[19]

Changes of this sort stimulated not only general discussions on taste but, inevitably, debates about whose taste was better. Eighteenth-century thinkers generally agreed that, in theory at least, there was a universal standard for judging beauty.[20] Furthermore, virtually everyone was assumed to possess at least the rudiments of taste. If the groundwork of this faculty was "common to all mankind,"[21] as Edmund Burke put it, that foundation had clearly been doled out in unequal amounts. "Thus, though the principles of taste be universal," said Hume, "and nearly, if not entirely, the same in all men; yet few are qualified to give judgment on any work of art, or establish their own sentiment as the standard of beauty."[22]

As "popular" taste in the arts rarely if ever pleased the sophisticated artist and critic, on no account did they feel the taste of the public could be relied upon to determine standards of artistic excellence.[23] The very thought that members of this uneducated class might consider themselves sufficiently cultivated to render judgments of taste sat poorly with the select circle who knew they knew better:

> Without assigning causes for this universal presumption [of taste], we shall proceed to observe, that . . . this folly is productive of manifold evils to the community. . . . Hence, the youth of both sexes are Debauched to diversion, and seduced from much more profitable occupations into idle endeavours after literary fame; and a superficial, false taste, founded on ignorance and conceit, takes possession of the public.[24]

The elite, therefore, among whom there was "almost perfect uniformity of judgment," was obliged to set the standard, and their concurrence determined "the merit and rank of every work," wrote the Scottish philosopher Alexander Gerard.[25] If that judgment was ignored, the fault lay not with the tastemakers: "whoever dissents ought to impute it solely to his own want of taste."[26]

Nevertheless, it was the "dissenters" who had the upper hand in coloring the artistic spectrum, as we can see from the events at Thomas Coram's Foundling Hospital in London. Coram was a member of this new class, a self-made man who had retired from a career in shipbuilding around the age of fifty in order to devote his life to public service.[27] [23] William Hogarth was a founding member of the hospital's board of governors, and recognized the institution's potential for advancing an artist's career. He therefore encouraged his artist-friends to donate works so they could be seen by the patrons of the hospital, who were also potential clients.[28] The usefulness of this tactic was quickly appreciated, and it was not long before public exhibitions became the accepted way for artists to contact prospective customers. [24]

In 1758, Foundling Hospital held a benefit show of paintings under the auspices of the recently founded Royal Society for the Encouragement of Arts, Commerce, and Manufactures. It was one of the first

Fig. 23. (*Right*) William Hogarth's portrait of Thomas Coram has been described as a turning point in the cultural evolution of England, marking a "significant moment in British social life, when the genius of the rising middle class asserts itself with confidence and power, and permits an image to be produced unlike anything that had gone before" —Benedict Nicholson, *The Treasures of the Foundling Hospital,* p. 36. Coram established a home for foundling children in London, which eventually became one of the first public exhibition places for painters. The value of public displays for the painter's reputation and pocketbook was soon noted, and swiftly became the most important way of establishing and maintaining a career for English artists. (*Courtesy of the Thomas Coram Foundation for Children, London*)

Fig. 24. (*Below*) Canaletto's view shows an exhibition of paintings for the festival of S. Roch in Venice. Such shows, connected to feast days, occurred as early as the beginning of the 18th century, but were intended primarily for the glory of the saint rather than the enhancement of the artist. (*Reproduced by courtesy of the Trustees, The National Gallery, London*)

23

—if not the first—exhibitions of paintings in England to which the general public was invited. According to John Gwynn, a contemporary observer, this public showing of paintings was intended as "a polite, entertaining and rational amusement" for the public.[29] Instead, it turned into a near-riot. What Gwynn called the "prostitution of the polite arts" caused considerable embarrassment to the more eminent painters of the day, who were appalled to find their work criticized by vulgar crowds, including "kitchen maids and stable boys" who wandered in off the street.[30] But another occurrence at the same show proved cause for even greater consternation on the part of artists.

The society had decided to give prize ribbons to the best historical and landscape paintings at the show. The judging was to take place beforehand, so that winners' ribbons would be in place when the exhibition opened. To their eventual chagrin, the more eminent painters boycotted this pre-show judging, refusing to submit their work for "so trifling a premium" as a prize ribbon. They did not withdraw their works from the exhibit, apparently relying on the reasoned good taste in which that century believed so passionately. Their faith was misplaced, however, for the painters who had not participated in the competition found that even some of the more cultivated visitors failed to notice that the "better" paintings were not the ones with ribbons on them, and the new, uncultured class of consumer who came to view the show was naturally drawn to those paintings with ribbons—the sign that some authority had approved them. The offended artists declined to show their work at future Foundling Hospital shows[31] and, over the next few years, held their own exhibitions. Eventually they formed the Society of Artists of Great Britain in 1765, and received a charter from George III to found the Royal Academy of Arts in 1768.

The influence of this new public on the arts was acknowledged in more subtle ways as well; the most common subject matter in these early exhibitions gives some indication of the pressure exerted by the growing marketplace. History painting, the depiction of noble events from the past, had long been the most prestigious undertaking for a painter. Yet few history paintings graced the walls of early public art exhibitions in England. The catalogue, *The Society of the Artists of Great Britain* (May 9, 1761), listed 5 history paintings out of a total of 141 works. Sir Joshua Reynolds, who would later become the first president of the Royal Academy, contributed one such painting *(Hercules),* and twelve portraits of noblemen, ladies "of quality," gentlemen, and children. The absence of the more highly esteemed genre is puzzling until we take market forces into account—the greater demand for portraiture because it appealed to a public uncomfortable with obscure references of history painting: "If this Exhibition can boast of few Historical subjects, compared with the number of exquisite landscapes and incomparable Portraits, it may partly be attributed to the contempt with which the best modern productions of this kind have of late been treated."[32] In other words, the uneducated public who thronged to these exhibitions was interested in social events, not ancient history, and found the exhibitions a source of amusement and delight because they could view "the Portraits of known and living persons of eminence."[33]

Hogarth himself commented on the English preoccupation with portraiture, and in doing so pointed up the relative ease with which class boundaries were crossed in his country, and what that social migration meant for artists. The demand for portraits in England was bound to be constant, he said, because there were always "new faces" coming up in English society.[34]

The English preference for portraiture was noted well into the next century. Edward Edwards in *The Administrative Economy of the Fine Arts in England* (1840) commented on the surprise of foreign artists at the "great proportion" of portraits shown at Royal Academy exhibitions. The author explained the phenomenon by way of a comment which pictured a society increasingly dominated by those coming up from the lower classes, and a class of artists who depended upon them for their livelihood. "The number of portraits may be referred to the great wealth of the country, and the want of acquaintance with the arts generally among our population; another reason is—the Royal Academy existing by the profits of exhibitions, there is no class of art that brings more money to the doors than the portraits."[35]

The importance of the public as "both Judge and Jury" in the new culture market was candidly admitted.[36] Its opinion, rendered at these exhibitions, could make or break the season of a well-known artist—or snuff out the hopes of an aspiring unknown. The annual exhibition of the Royal Academy was the most important of all these showings. That hallowed body exercised extraordinary power, as no artist could show at the Academy if he had once had the temerity to exhibit with a rival organization.[37]

Although frankly admitting that "the favour of the public was openly solicited," artists' opinions of the public jury to which they were obliged to submit their work was often unflattering.[38] Tradesmen were accused by one critic of treating artists with a "rigor and contempt more unreasonable than that exercised by the Algerines over their slaves."[39] The introduction to an early catalogue characterized the crowds who attended such showings as "ignorant," and generally made up of envious and disappointed artists who had failed to get their works in the show. Certain visitors found a particularly ungracious reception, such as the "connoisseur" who prefaced his remarks with "'I am no great judge of Painting, but I know what pleases me.' The judgment of such men is like that of a butcher who, on his first tasting of ice-cream, declared it was the best ice-cream he ever eat [sic] in all his life."[40]

The crux of the artist's displeasure lay, of course, in the loss of control over who established the criteria of Beauty: "The decline of the court reduced [artists'] prestige, their source of support, and their privileges. The rise of a huge market for the popular arts meant for them not only a severe reduction of cultural standards but also a loss of control over the setting of standards for publics of lower status and education."[41]

At least as early as the end of the eighteenth century, the majority of those making their living as painters did so at what we would classify, derogatorily, as "popular" art—paintings or engravings to be hung on the parlor walls of middle-class homes.[42] In 1790, the American painter John Trumbull proposed to create a series of canvases recounting thirteen important events of the recent American Revolution. The series was not to be "patronized," in the traditional sense of having a patron, but was to be financed by first selling engravings of the paintings-to-be at three guineas a print. The completion of this series hinged upon public response to advertisements such as one that appeared in the *Gazette of the United States,* on January 23, 1790, in which Trumbull stated his hope to "meet with such [public] Patronage . . . as will justify him in involving himself in such considerable expenses of Time and Money."[43]

In the collection of clippings from which the Trumbull example was taken, the overwhelming preponderance of artists who placed ads were trying to earn their living by painting miniature portraits—"likeness guaranteed."

With the invention of Arkwright's spinning frame, and the perfection of steam power for factories during the last quarter of the eighteenth century, there was a phenomenal increase in wealth, paralleled by an increased demand for all goods, including the arts. The "dissenters" in taste, as Alexander Gerard branded them, had seized power. The naive notion that the "ignorant" should meekly follow the "educated" was swept away by the overwhelming tide of supply and demand. By the end of the eighteenth century, those who had acknowledged the prestigious status of the new fine arts were already looking upon the artist as an unapproachable seer of cosmic truth. Yet at the same time these "seers of truth" had to peddle their artistic wares in the art marketplace like any other merchant. It was near the end of the century before a means by which they could seem to free themselves from the demands of the marketplace presented itself.

The Apotheosis of the Artist

Attempts at separating artist from artisan (and hence fine from decorative art) had already been in the making for nearly 350 years by the beginning of the eighteenth century, yet relatively little progress had been made toward that end.[44] The elusive goal of autonomy remained the same for eighteenth-century artists as it had been for their fifteenth-century counterparts; but the stakes were higher now, for the standard taste of the marketplace in which they found themselves was set by the middle class.

Several unsuccessful attempts had been made to establish a common ground linking the design arts around the middle of the sixteenth century. It was variously suggested that the shared characteristic might be their nobility or ingenuity, or that they were all commemorative, metaphorical, or figurative.[45] But only two hundred years later, in 1747, did painting and sculpture finally shed the ancient stigma of manual labor, when a generally accepted set of criteria was put forth by a French abbé and critic, Charles Batteux, which institutionalized a hierarchy in the arts:[46] [25]

> *Fine Art*—painting, sculpture, poetry and music—was concerned with beauty alone (*les beaux arts,* in French).[47]
>
> *Art combining pleasure and utility* was a mixture of high and low, and included architecture and eloquence.
>
> *Mechanical art* served a purely practical purpose, and included all the arts not previously mentioned.

It should come as no surprise that our modern vocabulary of art also came into being around this same time. The English word "taste"

Fig. 25.   (*Facing page*) With the invention of *les beaux arts,* it became possible to conceive of art as something without a practical purpose. The fine arts were concerned only with beauty. What remained were the decorative arts, which embellished the practical objects of daily life. This new view of the purposes of the arts placed architects in artistic limbo: their trade was concerned with both beauty and utility, and was therefore a mixture of fine and un-fine art. St. Martin's-in-the-Fields, London; architect James Gibbs, 1722–6.

—meaning "the faculty of perceiving and enjoying what is excellent in art, literature, and the like"—first appeared in print in 1671. "Artist," or "one who practises the arts of design; or, popular and more usually, one who cultivates painting as a profession," had its first literary usage in 1747. And "genius," or "Native power of an exalted type . . . often contrasted with talent," appeared in 1749.[48]

The earliest recorded use of "fine art" in the modern sense of an art concerned only with beauty was in 1767, and this definition was in common use in Europe by the beginning of the nineteenth century. Théophile Gautier used the now-familiar *l'Art pour l'Art* formulation in the preface to his novel *Mademoiselle de Maupin* (1835): "Nothing is really beautiful unless it is useless; everything useful is ugly, for it expresses a need, and the needs of man are ignoble and disgusting, like his poor weak nature."[49] By 1849, the modern distinction between artist and artisan (and therefore between art for beauty, and craft for use) was fixed in the English language.

Although the fine arts of design (painting and sculpture) had been isolated from the decorative arts by mid-eighteenth century, forty years passed before they acquired a full-fledged philosophical underpinning. Immanuel Kant's *Critique of Judgment* (1790) was the first intellectual system in the history of Western art to incorporate the aesthetic feeling, and marks the beginning of the philosophy of art as we know it.[50] Coming after the critiques of *Pure Reason* and *Practical Reason* (1781 and 1788, respectively), Kant considered it "the coping stone of his critical edifice."[51] For all its obscurity and novel terminology, his philosophy was quickly embraced by the European intellectual community, and was being taught in leading German universities soon after the publication of the first *Critique*. By the time the last appeared, Kant had turned the university at Königsberg into a shrine of modern philosophy.[52]

The new concept of genius, put forth in the *Critique of Judgment*, would have a profound effect on later attitudes toward ornament. Although genius had been an attribute of the artist for centuries, Kant's appraisal of that characteristic was different in several respects, the most

Fig. 26. As late as the end of the 18th century, one still did not have to be born with "genius" in order to become a great artist. One could learn to make great art through sheer diligence, as did the Renaissance artist Verrocchio, according to Vasari. Artists learned their craft in the same way bakers learned baking, and potters potting. Bas-relief of a stone carver's studio, from Orsanmichele, Florence, 15th century.

important being that, *for the first time in the history of Western art, genius had become the quintessential characteristic of the artist.*[53] [26] Like others before him, Kant saw genius as an inborn quality, a faculty "no science can teach and no industry can learn."[54] Unlike his predecessors, however, Kant found genius neither refinable through hard work nor accessible to reason. It was a force of nature, beyond even the artist's own comprehension:

> [Genius] cannot describe or indicate scientifically how it brings about its products, but it gives rule just as nature does. Hence the author of a product for which he is indebted to his genius does not know himself how he has come by his ideas.[55]

And "originality" (and hence unconventionality) was its most important characteristic:

> We thus see (1) that genius is a *talent* for producing that for which no definite rule can be given; it is not a mere aptitude for what can be learned by a rule. Hence *originality* must be its first property.[56]

I am not suggesting that *Critique of Judgment* was constructed with an eye toward plucking the artist from the clutches of the marketplace; but that is precisely what it did. As genius could not be subordinated to reason—which earlier critics and philosophers had thought proper—one could hardly expect it to submit to the whims of popular taste. In fact, to qualify as an artist in Kant's terms, one was *obliged to disregard conventional taste.* The practical effect of this definition was that a worker who once would have been considered the finest of artisans—having reached the pinnacle of his craft through a combination of talent, genius, and skills acquired in a laborious apprenticeship—was suddenly transformed into a self-made, self-justifying creature, operating in a vaguely uncontrolled and uncontrollable way, on a plane far removed from that inhabited by mortals. In theory at least this conception freed artists from all worldly constraints, catapulting them into the sacred realm of pure intellect, from which they were to instruct—rather than pander to—conventional taste.

Communication within the European intellectual community was rapid, even in the eighteenth century. Within a decade of the publication of *Critique of Judgment,* educated English ladies and gentlemen were fully acquainted with its lessons as far as the place of the artist was concerned. These first came through the writings of Coleridge,[57] who traveled to Germany in 1798–9, and attended lectures for several months at the University of Göttingen, then a center of German thought. The influence is apparent in his definition of beauty, to take the most obvious example, which derives directly from Kant: "The BEAUTIFUL is thus at once distinguished both from the AGREEABLE, which is beneath it, and from the GOOD, which is above it: for both these have an interest necessarily attached to them."[58] The poet's disdain for the marketplace and revulsion at its effect on artists also betrayed the mark of the German philosopher. Artists should not cater to vulgar taste, said Coleridge, but should follow their own path in search of truth. Unfortunately for the writer, he remarked, progress along that path was perpetually hindered by the taste of the

> Reading Public—as strange a phrase, methinks, as ever forced a splenetic smile on the staid countenance of meditation; and yet not fiction. For our readers have, in good truth, multiplied exceedingly, and have waxed proud. . . . But what is the result? Does the inward man thrive on this regime [of circulating libraries and the popular press]? Alas! if the average health of the consumers may be judged by the articles of largest consumption; if the secretions may be conjectured from the ingredients of the dishes that are found best suited to their palates; from all that I have seen either of the banquet or the guests, I shall utter my *profaccia* with a desponding sigh. From a popular philosophy and a philosophic populace, Good Sense deliver us![59]

If, after the revelation of their genius, artists still ran up against practical problems while trying to make a living in the arts, the popular perception of their revised status did afford them unique prestige and an undeniable cachet, providing the keenest of edges to wield in defense of their aesthetic province. And, as it turned out, the new view of art proved as beneficial to their pocketbooks as to their psyches. In *The Book of Trades, or Library of the Useful Arts,* published in the first decade of the nineteenth century, we already see the effects of the prestige that had accrued to the fine art artist. On the one hand, the trunkmaker, wheelwright, iron-founder, copperplate printer, painter, and sculptor are listed side by side, without any distinction between art and craft. The difference comes in the way they earn their living: while the journeyman wheelwright can earn "from a guinea to thirty shillings a week," the artist's earnings "cannot be defined; *he is paid according to his talents, and to the celebrity which he has acquired*" (my emphasis).[60]

Freedom from the traditional wage structure of manual laborers was but one happy result of the artist's stunning ascent. [27] Only a handful of celebrated Renaissance artists had ever felt the equal of the

27

Fig. 27.   The separation between "artist" and "artisan" was nowhere more apparent than in the details of their employment: "August Lepère [an artisan-illustrator of great talent] . . . entered . . . a studio in 1862 at the age of thirteen. The deed of apprenticeship he signed shows the strict conditions imposed on the young wood-engraver: five years' apprenticeship without receiving any wages: ten hours' work a day; the only rest days Sundays and occasional public holidays. . . . A young adolescent subjected to this system could hardly do otherwise than envy his comrades preparing for entry to the Ecole des Beaux-Arts in comparative freedom to dispose of their time and their talent as they would. But success for them was uncertain whereas the engraver was sure of a living, and had he become an artist he might perhaps have failed to shine"—Jacques Letheve, *The Daily Life of French Artists*, p. 164.

intellectual elite of their time, and had received little or no encourage-ment in their belief.[61] Now the artist was on a par with the philosopher. Indeed, for some, art even replaced religion as the spiritual balm of mankind. Fifty years later, decorative artists would find themselves in a similarly elevated position, as the art reformers of mid-century England fitted them out with intellectual and philosophical tools intended to raise them, too, above the crass taste which governed their artistic lives.

A breathtaking power now resided in the artist, which was not to go unnoticed by the later, decorative art reformers. Its sublime scope was apparent from the artists' mission, put forth most eloquently in a series of letters entitled *On the Aesthetic Education of Man* by Friedrich Schiller. The traditional, unself-conscious wholeness of the individual (Rousseau's "natural" man) had been shattered by the forces shaping modern society: *"Utility* is the great idol of the age, to which all powers must do service and all talents swear allegiance."[62] . . . "State and Church, law and customs, were now torn asunder; enjoyment was separated from labour, means from ends, effort from reward."[63]

And the greatest tragedy of this disruption lay in the rending of the human spirit:

> We see not merely individual persons but whole classes of human beings developing only a part of their capacities, while the rest of them, like a stunted plant, shew only a feeble vestige of their nature. . . . What individual modern [man] will emerge to contend in single combat with the individual Athenian for the prize of humanity? . . . [The] essential bond of human nature was torn apart, and a ruinous conflict set its harmonious powers at variance.[64]

Such a terrible schism could only be healed by the balm of art.[65] Through it, according to Schiller, man could progress to a logical and moral state—"from Beauty to truth and duty."[66] This synthesis, induced by Beauty, was capable of healing the "division of the inner Man" and creating a "freedom" or state of equilibrium between "reality" (the Sensual world) and "form" (the Rational world).[67] Beauty brought those ruled by sensuality back to reason, and those ruled by reason back to the sensual world.

As the giver of this healing beauty, the artist-genius was the vehicle for a miraculous reunification of the spirit and of society. Like the protagonist of Kant's *Critique,* the savior of Schiller's heady *Letters* was safely beyond the reach of convention, responsible only to himself: "Let [the artist] look upwards to his own dignity and to Law, not downwards to fortune and to everyday needs," and "Live with your century, but do not be its creature; render to your contemporaries what they need, not what they praise."[68]

The fully evolved philosophy of art heralded the apotheosis of the artist. From the humblest of beginnings as manual laborers, artists had scaled the intellectual heights. Not even poetry, revered as it was in antiquity, had been deemed capable of touching metaphysical truth. Yet by the end of the eighteenth century, painting and sculpture had gained the power to reveal the most arcane and abstract principles of life, the "holy of holies."[69]

The philosophy of art also offered the means through which artists could at least appear to make a dignified withdrawal from the marketplace. Those who were knowledgeable about new developments in art came to think of artists as figures who should be free from interference, particularly the irksome task of pandering to the taste of others.[70] As a unique creative species, artists became part of a brotherhood whose rites of initiation would ultimately come to demand the rejection of all popularly accepted fashions.[71]

The events that bore fine art artists to unheard-of reaches in the pantheon of Art had a predictably opposite effect on decorative artists, who were permanently relegated to the backwaters of artistic importance. It is not surprising that the term "decorator" (1755) was coined around the same time "fine art" entered the English language; among "serious" artists, that term continues to mark the lowest-echelon design professional.[72]

Before "fine" art came into being, all manual, or "mechanical" arts were decorative; even painting and sculpture were seen as embellishment. Ornament was not thought of as something separate. Along with stairs, lids, windows, handles, walls, spouts, and so on, it was an indivisible part of buildings and objects.[73] The creation of "fine" art institutionalized an elitism among the design arts that necessarily dictated a new way of "seeing" decoration. This vision did not strike like a bolt from the Olympian heights of Art. Its effects were not even immediately apparent. But while ornament continued to be used after the creation of fine art, it was never again used in the same unself-conscious way. Knowledge of "fine" art made artists aware of decoration just as the knowledge brought by the apple had made Adam sense his nakedness. When ornament ceased to be an integral part of a work, it was possible to think of it as separable from the arts, and—more importantly—as something of lesser consequence. The implication for later decades was profound, for once it had been made "visible" in this way—once it had been isolated intellectually—ornament became vulnerable.

With this in mind, we should take special note of one particular quality that Schiller demanded of his artist-genius, for it offers a key to understanding the progressive rejection of all conventional styles of ornament: *Artists should be modest and intelligent,* said Schiller, *but need not be "decent,"* by which he meant they need not have a traditional, bourgeois morality.[74] Here is the core of the sanctioned hostility that grew up between the fine art artist and the rest of society; the rationalization for the contempt which most artists felt, or were beginning to feel, toward those on whom their livelihoods now depended.[75]

When the decorative art reformers opened the second front in the war against "bad taste," raising the status of the decorative arts and giving them an intellectual foundation, they took to heart Schiller's admonition that the bourgeois mentality should not be condoned. In spite of very real differences in the details of their approaches to educating the public, virtually all those who wished to improve the quality of decorative design urged designers to reject the reigning premise of commerce—that *popular demand* should be satisfied. The values against which these men rebelled were quickly identified with the rules governing the familiar, historical styles, beloved by the middle classes for the grand associations they brought to modest parlors. Instead of gratifying these desires, the reformers extended the fine-art litany, which had proclaimed that artists need not, indeed must not follow the dictates of popular taste, and decreed that the decorative artist too should educate through example.[76] The assumption that popular styles had no validity made the twentieth-century elitists' rejection of traditional decorative design inescapable.

NOTES: CHAPTER IV

1. Today, an artist can be involved in the decorative arts—Robert Venturi or Michael Graves, for instance—but the prestige of the product derives from the status of its maker. "Artisans," who have been making these beautiful objects all their lives, seldom get the same attention.
2. The seventeenth-century Dutch experience would seem to be the only exception to this in more modern times, and deserves study.
3. Herbert Gans, *Popular Culture and High Culture* (New York: Basic Books, 1974), p. 53.
4. Part of the reason for this optimism came from the mechanistic view of the world that was prevalent in the eighteenth century. "The least hindrance to such small springs," wrote David Hume, describing the bodily mechanism that determined taste, "or the least internal disorder, disturbs their motion, and confounds the operation of the whole machine"—David Hume, *Of the Standard of Taste and Other Essays* (reprint, Indianapolis: Bobbs-Merrill, 1965), p. 8. If the mechanical flaw in the human machine could be discovered, went the assumption, it could be repaired. The physical analogy operated on many levels, and Burke was not alone in feeling that human passions were controlled by mechanisms similar to those that regulated events in the physical world, and, therefore, should be as accessible to reason as the mechanical principles governing the movement of the planets. "Thus," said Alexander Gerard, "as in natural philosophy [the rational world of science] it is not the collection of experiments and observation, but the general conclusions legitimately deduced from them, that amounts to an explication of the course of nature; so in the fine arts it is not the several sentiments of individuals, but just conclusions deduced from them, concerning the qualities in objects which justify taste, and the simple mental principles from whose operations the gratification is derived, that serve immediately for estimating excellence or faultiness"—Gerard, *An Essay on Taste,* intro. Walter J. Hipple, Jr. (3rd ed., 1780; Gainesville, Fla.: Scholars' Facsimiles & Reprints, 1963), p. 266.

5. Shaftesbury, *Second Characters,* treatise IV. 5, in Albert Hofstadter and Richard Kuhns, eds., *Philosophies of Art & Beauty: Selected Readings in Aesthetics from Plato to Heidegger,* various trans. (Chicago: University of Chicago Press, 1976), p. 272.

6. Friedrich Schiller, *On the Aesthetic Education of Man, in a Series of Letters* (1793), trans. Reginald Snell (New York: Frederick Ungar, 1965), 6th Letter, p. 39.

7. *Dictionary of the History of Ideas,* s.v. "Theories of Beauty."

8. Edmund Burke, *A Philosophical Enquiry into the Origin of Our Ideas of the Sublime and Beautiful,* ed., intro., and notes by J. T. Boulton (New York: Columbia University Press, 1958), p. 13.

9. Nicholas Barbon (1690), quoted in Fernand Braudel, *The Structures of Everyday Life,* trans. Siân Reynolds (New York: Harper & Row, 1981), p. 324.

10. *Dictionary of the History of Ideas,* s.v. "Class." V.1, pp. 441–49.

11. See Hester Lynch Piozzi, *Observations and Reflections Made in the Course of a Journey Through France, Italy and Germany,* ed. Herbert Barrows (1798; reprint, Ann Arbor: University of Michigan Press, 1967), pp. 36, 51.

12. William Gutherie, *A New Geographical, Historical, and Commercial Grammar: and Present State of the Several Kingdoms of the World* (London, 1771), p. 184.

13. Voltaire, "On Trade," *Letters Concerning the English Nation,* trans. John Lockman (London: P. Davies, 1926), p. 56.

14. Gutherie, *Geographical Grammar,* p. 184. See also Chamberlayn, *Angliae Notitia: or the Present State of England* (London, 1707), p. 296, pt. 1, chap. 5, "Of its Inhabitants, their Number, Language, Character," pp. 47ff.; pt. 1, chap. 7, "Of Trade," pp. 62ff.; pt. 2, chap. 9, pp. 285ff. The contrast between "vulgar" (of the common people) and "respectable" became a commonplace comparison, "vulgar" always being used when referring to "bad" taste. Although it had been used to describe "the common people" since the late sixteenth century, it only acquired a social stigma, describing a person "not reckoned as belonging to good society," in 1763 *(OED).*

15. Alexis de Tocqueville, *Democracy in America,* trans. John Stuart Mill (2 vols., New York: Schocken Books, 1961), 2:59.

16. Samuel Taylor Coleridge, *Select Poetry, Prose, Letters: Miscellaneous Literary Criticism,* ed. Stephen Potter (London: Nonesuch Press, 1971), pp. 319–20.

17. Leo Lowenthal and Marjorie Fiske, "The Debate Over Art and Popular Culture in Eighteenth Century England," in *Common Frontiers of the Social Sciences,* ed. Mirra Komarovsky (Glencoe, Ill.: The Free Press, 1957), p. 33.

18. Jacques Barzun, *The Use and Abuse of Art,* Bollingen Series XXXV•22 (Princeton: Princeton University Press, 1974), p. 63.

19. Coleridge, "Aids to Reflection," in *Select Poetry, Prose, Letters: Miscellaneous Literary Criticism,* p. 460. It is important to note that when Coleridge used the term "artist," he was referring to the man of literature, not painters or sculptors, whom the writer would quite likely have still considered his inferiors.

20. Burke, for example, based his assumption of the existence of a general level of taste on the fact that certain stimuli (vinegar, sweets, etc.) evoked the same general response in large groups of people. Therefore, he argued, the same objects should elicit the same response in all men; to postulate otherwise would be logically absurd—*Sublime and Beautiful,* p. 23.

21. Burke, ibid., p. 11. See also Voltaire, Shaftesbury, Hume, Young, and Gerard, among others.

Theory aside, there were woefully evident differences in taste between the sophisticated observer and the general public, and time did not seem to lessen them. These differences were generally attributed to distortions in the perception of this universal standard, arising from individual imperfections and national prejudices. What was more, argued Burke, taste had not yet been subjected to the same intellectual scrutiny as had reason—*Sublime and Beautiful*, p. 11.

22. Hume, *Standard of Taste*, p. 17.

23. Gerard, *Essay on Taste*, p. 225.

24. Goldsmith, "Taste," in *Miscellaneous Works*, p. 313, quoted in Lowenthal and Fiske, "The Debate Over Art and Popular Culture," p. 96.

25. Gerard, *Essay on Taste*, p. 227.

26. Ibid., p. 240.

27. The Foundling Hospital received a royal charter in 1739, and a grant of £10,000 from Parliament in 1756—*Encyclopaedia Britannica*, 11th ed., s.v. "Thomas Coram."

28. Benedict Nicolson, *The Treasures of the Foundling Hospital* (Oxford: The Clarendon Press, 1972), p. 24.

29. The *Encyclopaedia Britannica*, 11th ed., puts the date of the show at 1758. Gwynn placed it in 1760.

30. John Gwynn, *London and Westminster Improved* (1776; facsimile ed., Westmead, U. K.: Gregg International, 1969), pp. 23–5. Gwynn was well known enough to have had Dr. Samuel Johnson edit an essay of his on the coronation of King George III (1761).

31. Gwynn, *London and Westminster Improved*, p. 25.

32. *The Bee: or The Exhibition Exhibited in a new light: being a complete catalogue-raisonné of all the pictures with comments, illustrations, and remarks: in which also will be found the Names of the Principle Portraits* (London, 1788), preface.

33. *The Bee*, p. 3.

34. William Hogarth, quoted by Sandby, *The History of the Royal Academy of Arts* (London, 1862), 1:27.

35. Edward Edwards, *The Administrative Economy of the Fine Arts in England* (London: Saunders & Otley, 1840), p. 170.

36. *The Bee*, p. 1.

37. Quentin Bell, *The Schools of Design* (London: Routledge & Kegan Paul, 1963), p. 23.

38. *Society of the Artists of Great Britain: A Catalogue of the Pictures, Sculptures, Models, Drawings, Prints, etc. Exhibited by the Society of the Artists of Great Britain at the Great Room in Spring Garden, Charing Cross, May 9, 1761*, p. iii.

39. Gwynn, *London and Westminster Improved*, p. 54.

40. *The Bee*, pp. 1–2.

41. Gans, *Popular Culture*, p. 53.

42. The term "popular writer," used in a derogatory sense, is found for the first time in the eighteenth century—Lowenthal and Fiske, "The Debate Over Art and Popular Culture," p. 71.

43. Rita Susswein Gottesman, comp., *The Arts and Crafts in New York, 1777–1799: Advertisements and News Items from New York City Newspapers* (New York: The New-York Historical Society, 1954), pp. 20–21. (The response was not forthcoming, for only eight of the thirteen were completed. They are now in the Yale Art Gallery.)

44. There was no general term or idea for sculpture before 1500, for example. Instead, five different terms were used to describe carvers who worked in different materials. Only at the beginning of the sixteenth century did the term "sculptor" come to be used for all five activities—*Dictionary of the History of Ideas,* s.v. "Classification of the Arts."

45. Ibid. Little thought had been given to the creation of a hierarchy within the arts of design (the mechanical arts) before the sixteenth century, although the conceptual groundwork had been laid by the earlier writings of Alberti and Leonardo. It was only in the fifteenth century, for example, that painting, sculpture, and architecture came to be thought of as "arts of design," that is, arts that had a common starting point in drawing (It. *disegno*).

46. Charles Batteux, *Les Beaux Arts réduits à une même principe* (1746).

47. Architecture was a latecomer to this select group, in limbo between fine art (because of its reliance on sculpture and painting) and ordinary art (because of its dependence on utility).

48. Along with the term "fine art," which was eventually broadened to include architecture, we are indebted to the eighteenth century for our modern definitions of "sentiment," "originality," and "creative imagination," none of which had taken on their current meanings before that time.

49. Théophile Gautier, *Mademoiselle de Maupin,* trans. Joanna Richardson (Baltimore: Penguin Books, 1981), p. 39.

50. Introduction to Kant, *Critique of Judgment,* trans. J. L. Bernard (New York: Hafner Publishing Company, 1951), p. xiv.

51. *Encyclopaedia Britannica,* 11th ed., s.v. "Immanuel Kant."

52. Ibid.

53. Harold Osborne, *Aesthetics and Art Theory: An Historical Introduction* (New York: E. P. Dutton, 1970), p. 195.

54. Kant, *Critique of Judgment,* Div. 1, bk. 2, para. 49. Verrocchio had become a great artist by improving his lesser skills through diligence and hard work, according to Vasari—Giorgio Vasari, *The Lives of the Artists,* trans. George Bull (2nd ed. Baltimore: Penguin Books, 1965), p. 232.

55. Kant, *Critique of Judgment,* Div. 1, bk. 2, para. 46.

56. Ibid. The advent of this kind of artistic genius deprived the Muses of their ancient role of inspiration. Artists no longer had the luxury of being "interpreters of the Gods by whom they are severally possessed," as Plato had once said of poets, for external inspiration contradicted the idea of a self-sufficient creative genius (see *Phaedrus,* 245, *Ion,* 533–5). The weighty burden of creativity, therefore, now rested squarely on the artist's shoulders. While much has been made of Plato's speaking of the poet's divine madness, of the four kinds of "divine madness" he identified—those of poets, mystics, prophets, and lovers—Plato found that of the lover to be the best (*Phaedrus,* 265). At the time Kant was writing, as influential a figure as Sir Joshua Reynolds, first president of the Royal Academy, still thought that the genius of an artist was best subjected to reason—*A Discourse Delivered to the Students of the Royal Academy, on the Distribution of the Prizes, December 11, 1769* (London: Thomas Davies, 1769), particularly pp. 22–3.

57. ". . . even his many borrowings from the German were assimilated with a rare power of development, which bore fruit not only in a widening of the field of English Philosophy but in the larger scientific thought of a later generation"—*Encyclopaedia Britannica,* 11th ed., s.v. "Samuel Taylor Coleridge."

58. Coleridge, *Miscellaneous Literary Criticism,* p. 313. See also p. 311.

59. Ibid., p. 435.

60. *The Book of Trades, or Library of the Useful Arts* (3 vols., 3rd ed., London: Tabart & Co., 1806), 2:102, 118.

61. See Appendix for a discussion of earlier attitudes toward genius.

62. Friedrich Schiller, *On the Aesthetic Education of Man, in a Series of Letters,* trans. Reginald Snell (New York: Frederick Ungar, 1965), Letter 2, p. 26.

63. Ibid., Let. 6, pp. 39–40.

64. Ibid., pp. 38–9.

65. Ibid., Let. 7, p. 46; Let. 9, p. 51.

66. Ibid., Let. 23, p. 109.

67. Ibid., Let. 6, pp. 42–3.

68. Ibid., Let. 9, pp. 52, 54.

69. Schelling, *System of Transcendental Idealism,* Sect. IV.3, in Hofstadter and Kuhns, eds., *Philosophies of Art & Beauty,* p. 373.

70. The academies had provided additional status, but those who exhibited in them still found themselves at the mercy of an "uninformed" public whose taste they generally disapproved of.

71. Unless, as with Pop Art or some postmodern architecture, the intention is to "comment."

72. The demeaning nature of that kind of work was pointed out as early as Vasari, and the proliferation of art academies in the seventeenth and eighteenth centuries was another sign that artists wanted to distance themselves from more menial design tasks. But the philosophy of art provided the first systematic rationale that encouraged talented and ambitious artists to shun the decorative arts.

73. Mass production has often been accused of bringing on the decline of the decorative arts because the "division of labor," which it created, gave rise to the notion of "applied art"— decoration that was added on to the "essential" form. But ornament was applied, as a separate part of the production process, long before the factory system was introduced. Pottery has probably been produced that way for as long as clay has been molded by hands. It was the demands of fashion which caused what the reformers called "bad design," by depriving designers of the slow evolution of styles.

74. Schiller, "On Naive and Sentimental Poetry," quoted in Barzun, *Uses and Abuses of Art,* p. 29.

75. Hegel, *Philosophy of Fine Art,* in Hofstadter and Kuhns, eds., *Philosophies of Art & Beauty,* p. 397. The artists' only difficulty with this noble aim was in convincing the public to accept their new role as purveyors of their own values, rather than as interpreters of those of society. Such changes are slow in taking place, however, and in practical terms, most artists continued to pay unquestioning homage to the omnipotent marketplace: "The object of an exhibition [of fine art] is to afford every candidate for the favour of the public an opportunity of obtaining it . . . it is at once the means of judging the propriety of such distinctions . . . and the court of final appeal . . . the very means of subsistence of the rising artist . . . [the] artist's only remaining means of attaining success in his profession"—Edwards, *Administrative Economy of the Fine Arts,* pp. 168, 169.

76. Reformers with views as widely divergent as John Ruskin and Henry Cole both rejected the notion that popular taste should guide the designer.

CHAPTER V

Educating the Market

"Improving" the Masses

By the mid-nineteenth century, many influential English artists and critics felt that the decorative arts were in a predicament that bore similarities to that of the fine arts some decades before. The most critical of these was that both were subject to the demands of a marketplace in which the standard of beauty was no longer set by the artisan-artist and patron, but by an unsophisticated class whose only qualifications for assuming that privilege were their social ambition and newly acquired wealth. The impact of this group was even more noticeable in the decorative than the fine arts, as the former lacked any forbidding philosophical rampart to provide a defense against the encroachment of the middle class. The effects of the market had already been noted for a century when Edward Bulwer-Lytton, in his *England and the English* (1833), commented that popular fashions changed so quickly, manufacturers could not possibly afford to waste time having things designed, finding "a meretricious and overloaded display cheaper than exquisite execution."[1]

This overloading of manufactured goods did not seem to offend Bulwer too much, for as a sophisticated observer of these trends, he stated with some authority that his countrymen had successfully domesticated and popularized the recently established fine arts through their (ornamental) application to manufactured goods, already an important part of English commerce in 1833.[2]

A number of Bulwer's contemporaries had a far harsher assessment of the marketplace's impact upon the "progress" of the ornamental arts in England. Although the criticism of the decorative arts would come to a dramatic head with the first great commercial exhibition, it had begun decades before the Crystal Palace opened its doors in 1851. In the 1830s, reformers were already criticizing the taste of the marketplace—and for notably less esoteric ideals than those of the Art-for-Art elite. Many of the most influential reformers of the nineteenth century based their criticism on hard-nosed, practical considerations with which the most devout laissez-faire capitalist felt quite at home: They were dedicated to the improvement of public taste in order to sell more English goods.

The idea of "Art for Art's sake," signaling the pursuit of art for other than pecuniary motives, was familiar early in the last century. Those who held this view derived their considerable authority from the new philosophies of art, as set forth by Kant and elaborated by Schiller, Schelling, Hegel, and others. But the state of the decorative arts was a matter of national interest. Most of those who pursued these reforms were artists of stature themselves, and, unlike the Art-for-Art elite, fervently believed that progress in art could no longer be the private concern of the artist. The very health of the nation's economy depended on improving the design quality of its manufactured goods. In the words of one reformer, the "true interest of the workman, the man of science, and the artist, whether as producer, as inventor, or designer, is the true interest of the manufacturer and the capitalist."[3]

The decorative goods about which we speak—textiles, ribbons, paper hangings, ornamental metalwork, furniture, pottery, and other "fancy goods"—constituted the largest part of English manufacture at that time, and were therefore of considerable economic importance.[4] Parliament first took an interest in the state of public taste with regard to these and other goods after the passage of the Great Reform Bill of

1832, which redistributed the seats in the House of Commons, transferring substantial political power from the landed aristocracy to the centers of industry and to members of the wealthy, manufacturing middle class, who stood to lose their fortunes if English goods could not compete with those of other countries.[5] In 1835–6, a few years after the Reform Bill had passed, a Select Committee of the House of Commons on Arts and Manufactures conducted hearings in which concern was expressed over the advantage enjoyed by foreign "manufacturing artists" over their English counterparts. The latter were assumed to be at a disadvantage because the foreign public, and particularly the French, benefited from a greater knowledge of the arts. "Art [was] comparatively dear in England," as opposed to France, where "it [was] cheap, because it was generally diffused."[6]

The committee expressed a viewpoint that was to have a decisive impact on the way the reformers construed their task in the coming decades. The focus of the problem was the public's lack of acquaintance with art. (In the eighteenth-century terms in which we have just been speaking, their taste had not been refined through the rational process of education.) The reformers were prepared to shoulder this artistic "white man's burden," and to undertake the education of the manufacturer and public for the betterment of the balance of trade. The work of these reformers would help to change attitudes toward design and the designer in their own and the next century. Among the better known were: William Dyce, a Scottish painter, involved in the early administration of the Schools of Design; Henry Cole, educator, artist, and administrator of the Schools of Art[7] from 1852 to 1873; Owen Jones, an architect, superintendent of the Crystal Palace Exhibition of 1851, and author of the comprehensive *Grammar of Ornament;* and Charles Eastlake, painter, director of the National Gallery, and author of a popular guide to proper artistic behavior, *Hints on Household Taste* (1868). And, of course, the reformers who are most familiar to us: John Ruskin, William Morris, and Walter Crane. But these did not share the enthusiasm of the others for the commercialization of art. Ultimately, out of a conviction that the subjugation of art to commerce had degraded both art and the artist, Ruskin and Morris turned on the very economic system which the others strove to accommodate. For them, improvement in the arts could only come with the end of the economic system dominated by the new middle classes.

Teaching "Good Taste"

Within a few years of Bulwer's remark on the happy integration of art and daily life, William Dyce was sent to study the Continental design schools with an eye toward establishing similar institutions in England. The decision to create such schools was generally applauded, although some manufacturers feared they would interfere with the free and natural course of commerce.[8] The idea also met with some resistance from a less well organized quarter: the traditional drawing masters correctly guessed that the new design schools would siphon off their pupils and so put them out of business.

Notwithstanding these reservations, a Normal School of Design was established in 1837.[9] In an article supporting the Schools, a contemporary critic stated:

> The essential and characteristic business of the School of Design, by which it is distinguished from other schools of Art, is to offer instruction of the highest description to all who desire to obtain a knowledge of ornamental Art, and to supply a complete and systematic course of education in relation to every kind of decorative work; more especially to such persons as are, or intend to be, engaged in the preparation of designs for the various manufacturers of this country.[10]

Because this was the primary aim (although there were suggestions of broader goals), the hope for improving decorative design lay not in cultivating genius or encouraging artistic novelty, but rather in guarding against the false hope of becoming a great artist—the dream that had been fostered by the cult of genius, and which threatened to lure all talented designers away from the ornamental arts.[11] The differences between fine and decorative arts which we have noted earlier were clearly acknowledged, at least at first.

In spite of the impressive statistical progress of the Schools—twenty-one branches were created between 1837 and 1851[12]—they did not achieve the hoped-for results. Imported goods, and imported taste, continued to dominate the marketplace. The precise reasons for this were the subjects of heated debate.[13] To Dyce, whose influence was waning by the time of the Great Exhibition, the Schools' failure to have a substantial influence on the quality of decorative art manufacturing was clearly due to the "jealousy and apathy of manufacturers, the intractability of artists, and anything but the management [of the Schools]"—for which he had been partly responsible.[14]

According to others, the Schools' lack of success could be laid to very specific causes, not the least of them being that they educated relatively few designers, and fewer still were able to find jobs in the industries they had been trained to serve. Matters were not helped by the manufacturers, who assumed that if their goods sold, they were "satisfying" the demands of the market and their duty to society had been discharged. What need did they have for the allegedly advanced skills of school-trained designers? Furthermore, the Schools offered public subsidies to private individuals, which was a heretical perversion of the "natural" state of the free-market economy.[15]

On top of that, the "mania of becoming artists, so prevalent among young men who have had opportunities of studying the art of design," threatened to undermine the very purpose of the Schools. Some critics claimed that as many as half of the students came to the Schools not to apprentice for industry, but to get a general art training before applying to the Royal Academy.[16]

Given the strong competition of a more glamorous fine arts career, the emphasis of the training offered by the Schools also became a point of contention. Should it lean toward fine art instruction and let the student learn the technical side when he was in industry? Or should the Schools try to instruct students solely in the more practical side of their profession? Neither reformers nor manufacturers seemed satisfied with the way the Schools were operating. In testimony before the Select Committee of 1849, one owner of a furniture factory said he had never found a pupil "who was at all perfect in his art, able to assist me in his profession, or to be of essential service in raising the character of taste in manufactures."[17] The matter was not helped by the manufacturers' preference for training their own workers, thereby ensuring that what they learned was practical rather than theoretical, and directly connected to the manufacturer's method of production.

Learning from the Great Exhibition of 1851

Although the efforts to improve English decorative design began long before 1851, the Great Exhibition was a milestone, for it offered the first chance to judge the success of those early efforts against the products of other countries. To many influential English artists and critics, the capitulation of the decorative arts to the whims of the marketplace (and by implication the Schools' failure to accomplish their appointed task) was evident in every field of manufactured goods, and nowhere more strikingly than at the Great Exhibition of 1851. [28, 29, 30]

Figs. 28, 29, and 30.   There are many definitions of "bad taste," but only one ingredient is common to all: The other person has it. Important critics felt that the Crystal Palace Exhibition of 1851 showed a deplorable lack of "good taste" on the part of English manufacturers, but their reasoning is hard to fathom. This tea and coffee set, for example, was applauded simply for the "novelty" of its ornament. The recently created principles of design were already exerting a strong influence at the 1851 Exhibition. One of them—that ornament should be an honest *expression of function*—implied that decoration should be able to do what it appeared to be doing. This pitcher of "leaves" (29) was criticized for the "inappropriateness" of its ornament: How could a vessel of leaves hold liquid? Yet the strongest part of the plant, the stem, could theoretically serve as a handle, as in this ewer and basin (30).

28

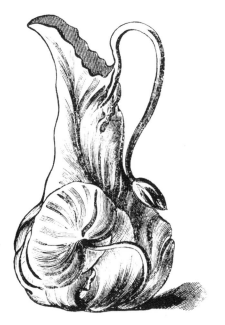

29

30

London had been the site of the first commercial exhibition of modern times, held under the auspices of the Society of Arts in 1756. At that event, the sponsors had offered prizes for improvements in tapestry, carpet, and porcelain manufacturing. In 1797, the French held a display of goods from all domestic art factories, including Sèvres and Gobelin. Other exhibitions, of varying sizes, were held throughout the first half of the nineteenth century, including one with 4,500 exhibitors organized in Paris after the political upheavals of 1848. All of these early exhibitions had one thing in common: They were limited to the products of the countries in which they were held.[18]

The Exhibition of the Industry of All Nations in 1851 was the first to draw exhibitors from around the world. Like the first modern commercial exhibition, it was sponsored by the Society of Arts. The idea for the unprecedentedly wide-ranging exhibit was suggested by the Prince Consort, then president of that organization.[19] Prince Albert was "specially interested in endeavours to secure the more perfect application of science and art to manufacturing industry," and the success of the Great Exhibition was said to have come largely from his intense interest in its development.[20]

Prince Albert's idea was not entirely unopposed. In the House of Commons, a Colonel Sibthorp "prophesied that England would be overrun with foreign rogues and revolutionists, who would subvert the morals of the people, filch their trade secrets from them, and destroy their faith and loyalty towards their religion and their sovereign." Being a foreigner himself, Prince Albert too was accused of "being intent upon the corruption of England."[21]

In spite of such opposition, the Great Exhibition opened, and during five months and fifteen days, 6,039,000 visitors passed through glass and iron galleries housing nearly 14,000 exhibits, almost half of which were from British manufacturers. When the doors finally closed, the exhibition had realized a profit of £186,000, which became the endowment of the South Kensington Museum of Decorative Art, now the renowned Victoria and Albert.[22]

Critical observers at the Great Exhibition were aware that a "sense of the artistic" was lacking in the British people, and that, in the words of the *Art-Journal,* the inferiority of English products was "in great measure attributable to the absence of good designs, and to the superior taste and delicacy of the finish in the foreign workmen."[23] Prince Albert hoped, through exposure to the variety of foreign goods, to awaken a new sensitivity among English manufacturers.

As a commercial venture on a hitherto unimagined scale, the Great Exhibition proved to be precisely what the Prince had hoped: an excellent means of testing British products against their competitors around the world. In that sense, it was pronounced a "colossal success."

As part of this aim, the exhibition was "calculated to advance our National Taste," wrote Ralph Wornum in his prize-winning essay, "The Exhibition as a Lesson in Taste."[24] Yet in reality, he continued, the display of English goods demonstrated "the most debased taste in design ever tolerated."[25]

Wornum's sharp criticism of the English contributions to the exhibition did not mean that he felt there had been no improvement in the country's design efforts during the years immediately preceding the exhibition. On the contrary, "[it] has been universally admitted that England, ten years ago, would not have made so good a display as she did make in the Great Exhibition last year. We claim this immense improvement in taste and manufacture generally as the result of a direct and indirect influence of the Schools of Design."[26]

But there was still some distance to go, and Wornum's analysis of the English entries is revealing on this point. His countrymen's work had not come off badly in terms of general design; the products were by and large well suited to their tasks.[31] Nor were they deficient in quality —nothing was comparable to British hardware or gratings, for instance. There was, however, a "decided inferiority" in national taste when it came to ornamental design: the way in which these useful, well-crafted objects were made "beautiful" through decoration.[27][32]

Of the few English manufacturers and designers whom he

31

Fig. 31. With the growth of the "middling" classes, ornament came to symbolize the culture and social position to which they aspired. Heavily ornamented objects were frankly characterized as "magnificent and costly," and certain objects were admittedly intended to demonstrate one's wealth—and hence one's culture and social standing: "these useful ornaments . . . require no explanation; it is sufficient to point out their merits as elegant luxuries for the wealthy."

Fig. 32. The difficulty in understanding the taste of an earlier age strikes us at every turn in the 1851 Exhibition. Amid its "gorgeous" displays of ornament, we learn that elegance was "more often united to simplicity than allied with abundance."

Yet when we come upon an "elegant" design, we find the most surprising things, such as this piano.

32

Fig. 33. This gas lamp was criticized obliquely: "The only danger [in the use of foliage]—and it is one, we confess, we often see and regret—is the too free use of this ornamental adjunct." The only insurance against such indiscretion was "good taste."

33

praised, Josiah Wedgwood and the sculptor John Flaxman (who did some designs for Wedgwood) are the only familiar names. These beacons of "good design" were adrift in a sea of "endless specimens of the prevailing gorgeous taste of the present day, which gives the eye no resting place, and presents no idea to the mind, from the want of individuality in its gorged designs."[28]

The complaints as well as the praise of Wornum and others are easy enough to follow in the written word, but not so readily apparent when we can see the actual objects.[33] Ornament that was "suited to the task," for example, often seems irrelevant and excessive to the twentieth-century eye.[29] Leafing through the catalogue of the Great Exhibition, we are struck by a fact that would plague the reformers throughout the last half of the nineteenth century. To almost everyone but the reformers, ornament had come to symbolize Culture and Art in English society. It was the means of displaying wealth, with all the implications of social status and refinement that went with it. We frequently find the word "costly" used as an adjective of approbation. "The uses to which these useful ornaments are intended to be applied require no explanation; *it is sufficient to point out their merits as elegant luxuries for the wealthy*" (my emphasis).[30] This concern for the costly was a constant source of irritation to those who wished to educate the marketplace, and the Schools were continually hindered by "the vicious and vulgar admiration for what looks 'rich' and costly, rather than for what is artistic."[31]

The Causes of "Bad Design"

A number of explanations have been offered for the cause of what the reformers considered the "bad design" of the times. We are probably most familiar with those of John Ruskin and William Morris, who blamed the factory system's division of labor for having separated the act of designing an object from that of making it. Ruskin's description of the popular understanding of the division of labor reveals the extent to which notions of fine art philosophy had penetrated the popular consciousness. If a glassworker could "design beautifully," wrote Ruskin derisively, he should not be forced to remain in the factory: "Let him be taken away and made a gentleman, and have a studio, and design his glass there, and I will have it blown and cut for him by common workmen."[32]

But the "division of labor" (referring to the separation of conception from execution) would hardly seem sufficient reason to indict the factory system for the crime of "bad design." Architectural design, including the disposition of its ornament, has always been conceived by a master mason or overseer, while the actual ornament was executed by someone else. In some periods the ornament maker had considerable latitude in that execution. Building contracts from ancient Greece even show cases where one person was hired to build a building, another to decorate it.[33]

Nonarchitectural examples should also lead us to question those who blamed the state of the decorative arts on the method of production. The division of labor had existed in pottery production for thousands of years. Three centuries before Christ, Mediterranean potters devised molds for decorated lamps which were then manufactured by unskilled labor, taking advantage of this abundant resource in the same fashion as did nineteenth-century manufacturers.[34] And Josiah Wedgwood's renowned Jasperware was mass-produced with "applied" decoration—its relief sculptures being pressed from intaglio molds, wetted, and applied to thrown shapes before firing—a task which was certainly not executed by the artist who developed the original sketch.[35]

Another alleged cause of "bad design," and one which went hand in hand with the division of labor, was the substitution of machine-made for handmade ornament. Yet the majority of the goods displayed in the 1851 Exhibition, which marked a watershed in the criticism of "bad taste," were not made by machine but by hand.[36]

Whatever its real effects on the quality of ornamental design, mass production reinforced the barrier between fine and decorative art. The aestheticians had not permitted fine art any earthly function. Enveloped in such a rarefied atmosphere, fine art artists could hardly be expected to abide sustained contact with the banalities of everyday life with which the designer in industry dealt. Mere ornament had already become the province of lesser souls who lacked the sine qua non of art. That made it unthinkable for seers of truth to concern themselves with trifles, fixed higgledy-piggledy to the wares of merchants who anyway exhibited the most vulgar taste. To cap it all, the kind of discipline involved in designing for industrial production, with its technical and marketing restrictions, also placed intolerable restraints on the two qualities that had so recently proclaimed the artist's uniqueness: genius and originality.

Having escaped the ancient stigma of manual labor, artists were understandably uninterested in becoming involved in anything that might reestablish that association. Owen Jones even suggested that the decline of the decorative arts had been foreordained by the creation of the art academies centuries before, which had introduced the division of labor into art long before it came to industry. The academies emphasized specialization in the arts to the point where architects thought mainly of plan, section, and elevation, painters wanted to work more in their studios and less on buildings, "forgetting altogether the general decorative effect" of their work, while "high class" sculptors deserted ornamental work entirely in favor of more prestigious, free-standing pieces.[37][34] Many smaller art academies had sprung up in England in the middle of the eighteenth century, and it was shortly after the "invention" of fine art that the term "art" became limited to set pieces whose very subject matter was carefully defined by the academies.

To attribute "bad taste" in design to the means of production was to mistake a circumstance of the patient's daily life for the cause of the disease. The problem was not the means of production, but the taste of those who managed the means of production, and some critics did direct their disappointment in the quality of English goods at the "generally uneducated" taste of the producers. What was more, this argument continued, those few manufacturers who demonstrated some degree of refinement did so wholly under French domination—something the public approved of, but the reformers did not. An overwhelming proportion of exhibition space was given over to the styles of Louis Quinze and the French Renaissance, a vogue for that "interminable coquillage of the Rococo" which Wornum attributed to the great immigration of Frenchmen that had taken place after the Revolution.[38][35] Only one small area, that of the Medieval Court, was devoted to Gothic designs of English inspiration, and little was seen of Byzantine, Romanesque, Egyptian, or other styles.

The reformers' frustration was only increased by the manufacturers' custom of catering to market demand, which to the reformers meant

34

Fig. 34. Several causes were put forth to explain the "bad" design of English decorative arts around the time of the Great Exhibition of 1851. One of the more telling comments came from Owen Jones, superintendent of the exhibition, who felt that the elevation of fine art had so stigmatized the decorative arts that talented and ambitious artists were simply no longer interested in creating ornament.

35

Fig. 35. (*Left*) French goods, much admired by the English public for at least a century before the Great Exhibition, offered several prime examples of what some observers considered "proper taste." This sideboard was "beyond question one of the most meritorious articles of its class in the Exhibition, whether we regard the varied beauty of the design, or its execution." While this view probably reflected that of most of the public who attended the exhibition, it was not necessarily shared by those who had set out to reform the decorative arts, and to teach that public "good taste."

Fig. 36. (*Right*) In some cases, the mere presence of desirable ornament was enough to ensure approval of a design, even though it might make the object inconvenient or difficult to use: "We may, perhaps, be allowed to take an objection to the practical convenience of the bed, although we may unequivocally express approbation of its ornamental design"—*Art-Journal Catalogue*, p. 13.

36

accommodating the lowest common denominator of taste.[36] The great philosophies of fine art had been discussed in Germany for half a century by the time of the Great Exhibition, and disseminated among the learned classes of England through the efforts of Coleridge and Carlyle; furthermore, those who set out to "improve" taste were almost all artists in their own right, and never doubted the eighteenth-century assumption that the artist had superior judgment. Yet to their perpetual dismay, this appreciation of the value of the artists' vision had not filtered down to the "Public," and most Englishmen took it for granted that any opinion on the arts was purely a matter of taste.[39]

Other explanations relating to the rise of the middle classes and the deplorable democratization of taste were also put forth to account for the sad state of affairs. The profit ethic was said to have estranged decorative artists from their traditional sources of patronage, just as it had previously alienated the fine art artist. In his famous study of the youngest democracy, Alexis de Tocqueville showed how this affected the artisan in societies that permitted one to rise within their ranks:

> The men of whom [the aristocracy] is composed naturally derive from their superior and hereditary position a taste for what is extremely well-made and lasting. This affects the general way of thinking of the nation in relation to the arts. . . . In aristocracies, then, the handicraftsmen work for only a limited number of very fastidious customers: the profit they hope to make depends principally on the perfection of their workmanship.
>
> Such is no longer the case when, all privileges being abolished, ranks are intermingled, and men are for ever rising or sinking upon the ladder of society.[40]

Dissatisfied with the state of the decorative arts in both workmanship and design, and earnestly interested in improvement, the reformers repeatedly found themselves battling the kind of person Eastlake described in this charming vignette: "We may condemn a lady's opinion on politics—criticise her handwriting—correct her pronunciation of

Latin, and disparage her favorite author with a chance of escaping her displeasure. . . . But if we venture to question her taste—in the most ordinary sense of the word, we are sure to offend."[41] The lady's discomfort was understandable. The eighteenth-century assumption that taste could be refined through practice was still current, but it was a notion that people were more comfortable in applying to others than to themselves. A single characteristic consistently crops up in definitions of "bad" taste: *it is the other person who has it.* As early as the 1830s, "we meet with the belief that neither knowledge nor experience is necessary to criticize a work of art, and the 'impartial' middle class, with no tradition of culture, becomes final arbiters of taste."[42][37]

The reformers found this presumption of good taste intolerable. In their eyes, the middle class had no judgment whatsoever, and was completely at the mercy of the purveyors of fashion. Over the next decades, those who hoped to rectify this situation experienced a great and understandable sense of frustration, for they were dealing with a class of clients who, as a matter of self-preservation, refused to acknowledge a fundamental lack of "good taste" that was painfully evident to the reformers.

In surveying possible strategies for the war against "bad taste," decorative art reformers could not have failed to appreciate the mystical atmosphere that enveloped the fine arts once the philosophy of art effectively raised them above this untidy dilemma. By the beginning of the nineteenth century, most cultured observers assumed that an artist's creative freedom was hampered by catering to conventional taste: "Let [the artist] look upwards to his own dignity and to Law," wrote Schiller, "not downwards to fortune and to everyday needs."[43] "Genius," and its need for originality, had made the troublesome matter of who set the standard of taste a moot point. Artists were the only ones capable of defining beauty, therefore they should determine the rules of Art. If artists were slow to take up the tool that had been provided for them, it nevertheless cleared the path that led to freedom from the constraints imposed by popular taste (and by the academies).

37

Fig. 37. (*Right*) Although some critics decried the deceptive use of one material to imitate another, others viewed it as another sign of Progress: "The [papier-mâché] ELIZABETHAN CHAIR is a favourable specimen of the success which may attend the manufacturer who fearlessly carries out his conceptions in any material, however discouraging it may appear in the outset"—*Art-Journal Catalogue*, p. 66.

The road was not so simple for those who wanted to reform the arts of design; they had to conquer the fortress of personal taste, but had no offense with which to mount a siege.[38] The weapons of the fine arts were unavailable to them because most were fine art artists themselves, and did not question the qualitative difference that had separated fine from decorative art since the abbé Batteux. Therefore, they had nothing comparable to "genius" to spearhead their attack, and no battle cry like *l'art pour l'art* with which to blast complacent manufacturers, who insisted that "beautiful" was "whatever the public bought," or the bourgeois who "knew what he (or she) liked." The task was by no means easy, as at least one knowledgeable observer pointed out, for the English public could not tell good design from bad, and had no particular desire to inquire into principles.[44] Nevertheless, optimism ran high and benefits were seen for all:

> . . . to the artisan [the art schools] were invaluable, as giving him knowledge of drawing, which is, or ought to be, indispensable in every trade; to the manufacturer they were useful in the highest degree, as they tend to create in the minds of his workmen a correct perception of the beautiful in nature . . . to the shopkeeper they were advantageous, as they naturally draw much attention to those articles of taste and elegance which it is his particular province to dispose of; and to the middle and upper classes they ought to be instructive as shewing what may be done by that mighty engine, Education.[45]

To win the war that would decide who defined beauty, the reformers needed a weapon that would do for them what the new definitions of "genius" and "originality" had done for the fine art artist. Understanding how they went about this gives an insight into our present views of ornament, for the method of the last century's reformers formed our attitudes toward ornament and design.

Fig. 38. (*Facing page, bottom*) Some critics of the Great Exhibition were already invoking the principles of design for which the Modern movement of the twentieth century would become famous: "One of the great defects we have frequently noticed in decorative furniture is the inapplicability of ornament to the purpose of the object on which it appears . . . showing how little of the true principles of decoration have been acquired by the designer." No such charge was brought against this sideboard, however, for "the several details of which the ornaments are formed, at once declare its intended purpose."

Curing "Bad Design"

Before the Great Exhibition, attempts to improve the quality of English decorative art through the Schools of Design had been concentrated on improving the skill of the factory worker: providing him with greater knowledge of the principles of art offered the key to creating more beautiful manufactured goods, or so went the conventional wisdom.[46] Even the scheduling of classes, many of which were held in the evenings, was arranged to make it easier for the working person. From its inception, this view of training the craftsman was supplemented by a sister strategy, aimed at stimulating public interest in what was optimistically called the "progress of Art." The general improvement in the taste of the market-place was to be an important by-product of this "progress," to be accomplished through exposing the public to objects of high artistic quality in museums of ornamental art, which were to be founded in conjunction with the Schools, as well as by providing access to existing civic monuments.[47] It was noted with some optimism that workers had a "great desire" to have such public exhibits kept open in the evenings so they would be able to see them. "They have come for the cultivation of their taste," said one satisfied commentator, "for aid in the principles and general capabilities of ornamental Art."[48]

The full energies of reform were never focused on this broader field before the Great Exhibition, although it had always been in the background, a familiar chorus to the main theme of educating the "mechanic." After the 1851 Exhibition, however, it was apparent to a number of influential movers in the art world that educating the public at large was more important than had been imagined. In 1852, the Schools of Design were superseded by the Department of Practical Art, formed under the leadership of Henry Cole.[49] The premise upon which the new administration operated was stated succinctly in Cole's introductory address to the Science and Art Department of the South Kensington Museum: *The successful employment of highly skilled labour depends wholly on the demand of the market*" (my emphasis)."[50] The importance of the whole matter of taste now comes into focus. It was the taste of the marketplace which had brought on this desperate situation, and to correct the situation, reformers had to correct that taste.

To realize how that simple declaration influenced the approach to the decorative arts during the next half century, we must remember that these events took place at a time of unquestioned confidence in capitalism and the free-market economy. The frank assumption of many educated people of that day was that the fate of the arts was directly linked to the principles of commerce. When a committee of the House of Commons was established to examine the exclusive policies of the Royal Academy, some MPs who were unsympathetic to such an undemocratic institution voiced the hope "that the principle of free-competition in art (as in commerce) will ultimately triumph over all artificial institutions."[51]

In spite of their acknowledged subservience to commerce, the relationship between the decorative arts and the marketplace was plagued by the kind of ambiguities and contradictions one would expect to find when theories and ideals collide with the practical world. Like the fine art artists of a century before, decorative art reformers recoiled at the idea of permitting the standard of taste to be set by the "uneducated." On the other hand, their practical bent and economic disposition would not permit them to ignore the fact that manufacturers had no choice but to yield to this force of nature, and to accept the favorite commercial maxim: "Good taste" is what sells.[52]

The overriding belief in the rightness of the market economy was accompanied by an equally important article of faith, which also contributed to the decision to concentrate on mass art education to instill the market with the designers' "good taste." None of the reformers seem to have questioned the eighteenth-century premise that beauty could be universally perceived.[53] Put in terms that should be familiar to us from those earlier essays on taste, this implied a universal standard for recognizing "beauty," which people could be taught.[54]

Given a universal ability to perceive beauty, what was more

reasonable than to assume the market would recognize this commodity once they had been told what to look for? The projected sequence of events, based upon the inevitability of the manufacturer yielding to market demand and the universal recognition of beauty, went something like this:

- As the "operatives" learned the *principles* of "good design,"
- their creations would become more beautiful.
- As the general public became better educated in the principles of art, through massive art education programs, the beauty of the new designs would prove irresistible, and
- they would be snapped up by a public grateful for having been transported to the heights of the artistic Olympus on the gilded wings of the Principles of Art.

"Extending the love of arts" beyond the mere mechanic, to the masses, "cultivating and refining public taste," was a herculean task.[55] The new Schools of Art (as the Schools of Design were now called) proceeded along the lines of this grander vision and, in accord with the broad aim of stimulating a general love of art amongst the people, they undertook to develop the public's critical and perceptual faculties in order to make it "see correctly," as the headmaster of the National Art Training School put it a few years later.[56] A decade after the Schools of Art had come into being, Richard Redgrave echoed the initial hope, speaking of the great effort then under way to spread art education throughout Great Britain, to the poor as well as the middle and upper classes. This "must tell upon the rising generation," he wrote. "Once properly instructed, there is little doubt that the plain good sense, the energy of will, and this dislike of mere display of our countrymen will result in works of much higher excellence in decorative art than has yet been attained in this country."[57]

After Cole took over, the plan was expanded to include the establishment of self-supporting, provincial schools, whose purpose was to provide basic training to younger students. These would then become prospective candidates for the Schools of Art themselves. But to train these future students, they needed large numbers of art teachers, so a massive program was launched to teach people to be art teachers:

> The courses of instruction pursued in the School have for their object the systematic training of teachers, male and female, in the practice of [fine] Art and in the knowledge of its scientific principles, with a view of qualifying them to impart to others a careful Art-education, and to develop its application to the common uses of life, and its relation to the requirements of Trade and Manufactures.[58]

Some statistics help to show the scope of the program and the speed with which it was implemented:

1851: 3296 students were enrolled in the Schools of Design.

1864: 70,000 "poor" (the children of the working class) were being educated in the principles of art.[59]

1872: nearly 400 Art Night Classes were instructing over 13,600 students; 119 Schools of Art had an enrollment of 21,141; 1,796 Schools for the "poor" were inculcating the principles of art into 194,366 young boys and girls.[60]

1884: 177 Schools of Art had a grand total of 34,000 students studying the principles of art; 700,000 elementary students had undertaken the study of art.

1900: 300 Provincial Schools of Art had been established.[61]

It seemed like a sure way to flood the market with consumers of "good taste."

In addition to preparing potential students for the Schools of Art, the provincial schools had a more direct way of instructing the public. They had been established as self-supporting institutions, for neither politicians nor reformers were willing to subsidize private industry with public capital. Therefore, the provincial schools were expected to take in paying amateurs to supplement the earnings from regular students. The amateurs were ladies and gentlemen who sought to improve themselves by refining their sensibilities in the pursuit of the polite arts. According to John Sparkes's *History of the Schools of Art* (1884), the importance of these amateur classes in elevating the general level of public taste was not to be underestimated.[62]

But the war against "bad taste" was not left to the schools. It was waged on all fronts, and, considering the role of the Select Committees on the Arts, it is not surprising that legislation was enacted to further this kind of art education. Through a simple majority vote, the Public Libraries Act of 1855 enabled any town, parish, district, or union of parishes to levy a maximum of one penny per pound tax to establish or maintain libraries, museums, or Schools of Art.

Things did not turn out as planned, as we shall see shortly. The reformers made few converts from among the ranks of those whose taste ruled the marketplace, and out of their powerlessness grew a considerable hostility toward the values of the middle class. With its overt rejection of "progress," the English Arts and Crafts movement of the 1880s was an early sign of this malaise, and served as the inspiration for later art movements on the Continent. By the end of the century, the failure of designers to have any significant impact on the taste of the marketplace had helped to channel this frustration into a blatant rejection of all manifestations of conventional taste. Bourgeois values, epitomized by the taste for overdecoration, became the focus of a general revolution in the arts of design, which would eventually bring about the end of traditional ornament. But we are getting ahead of our story.

NOTES: CHAPTER V

1. Edward Bulwer-Lytton, *England and the English* (1833; reprint, Chicago: University of Chicago Press, 1970), p. 350.
2. Ibid., p. 339.
3. George Wallis, "Art, Science, and Manufacture, as an Unity," *Art-Journal,* 13 (1851):245.
4. Quentin Bell, *The Schools of Design* (London: Routledge & Kegan Paul, 1963), p. 46.
5. Ibid., p. 44.
6. Edward Edwards, *The Administrative Economy of the Fine Arts in England* (London: Saunders & Otley, 1840), p. 13.
7. The Schools of Design became Schools of Art after 1852.
8. *The Oxford Companion to Art,* s.v. "Art Education."
9. Bell, *Schools of Design,* p. 60.
10. Ralph Wornum, "The Government Schools of Design," *Art Union Journal,* 4 (1852):39.
11. William Dyce and Charles H. Wilson, "Letter to Lord Meadowbrook on the best means of ameliorating the arts and manufactures of Scotland in point of taste" (Edinburgh: T. Constable, 1837), p. 31. The place of "originality" and "novelty" in design would become a matter of great debate shortly, because it involved not only a matter of artistic prestige (originality being a sign of great gifts) but also a craving of the marketplace for ever-newer fashions. See also Edwards, *Economy of the Fine Arts,* pp. 101–2.
12. Bell, *Schools of Design,* pp. 101–2.
13. See ibid. for a detailed discussion of these battles.
14. William Dyce, "Reports of the Commons' Committee on the School of Design," *Journal of Design and Manufactures,* 2 (Sept. 1849, Feb. 1850):27.
15. John Sparkes, *The Schools of Art: Their Origin, History, Work, and Influence* (London, 1884), p. 106.
16. Bell, *Schools of Design,* pp. 224ff., 235, and 257.
17. Bell, *Schools of Design,* p. 230. See Michael Polanyi, *The Tacit Dimension* (Garden City, N.Y.: Doubleday, 1966), for a discussion of the difficulties of learning certain kinds of tasks without first-hand knowledge.
18. *Encyclopaedia Britannica,* 11th ed., "Exhibitions."
19. Ibid.
20. *Encyclopaedia Britannica,* 11th ed., "Albert."
21. Ibid.
22. *Encyclopaedia Britannica,* 11th ed., "Exhibitions."
23. *The Art-Journal Illustrated Catalogue: The Industry of All Nations, 1851* (London, 1851; reprint, New York: Dover Publications, 1970), p. 57.
24. Ralph Nicholson Wornum, "The Exhibition as a Lesson in Taste," in ibid., pp. I–XXII***.
25. Ibid., p. VI***. Like many interested in reform, Wornum began his career as a painter, giving that up in 1846 to become a critic for the *Art-Journal.* He published a catalogue of the National Gallery the next year, and began lecturing at the Schools of Design. In 1856, he published a best-selling book entitled *Analysis of Ornament,* which went through eight editions before the end of the century.

26. Wornum, "Government Schools of Design," p. 40.

27. Wornum, "Lesson in Taste," p. VII***.

28. Ibid., p. V***. The phrase "want of individuality" is particularly interesting in terms of later developments in the decorative arts, for until then, "individuality" (and the originality it implied) had been solely the province of the fine arts.

29. See *Art-Journal Illustrated Catalogue,* and all 6 volumes of the *Journal of Design and Manufactures,* edited by Henry Cole, 1849–52.

30. *Illustrated Catalogue,* p. 310.

31. Sparkes, *Schools of Art,* p. 121.

32. Ruskin, *The Stones of Venice* (3 vols., New York: John Wiley, 1851), 2:168. This approach has been sanctioned because of two misunderstandings, according to Ruskin: that one man's idea should be executed by another (the principle of the "division of labor," upon which the factory system was based), and that manual labor was "a degradation, when it is governed by the intellect."

   Of course, some degree of artistic specialization always existed, under the guild system —in painters' studios, for example, apprentices prepared surfaces, mixed colors, and painted backgrounds and figures of lesser importance. Yet this kind of specialization was not comparable to that introduced with the coming of factory production.

33. A. L. Frothingham, "Greek Architects, Contractors and Buildings Operations," *The Architectural Record,* 24 (1908):324. The same practice continues today. Any number of corporate headquarters skyscrapers have been designed by one firm of architects while the interiors have been done by another firm of decorators.

34. Cleo Rickman Fitch, "The Lamps of Cosa," *Scientific American,* 247 (1982):148–60.

35. In actuality the "grand principle of co-operation and division of labour—the fundamental source of modern wealth and social progress" went a long way toward creating the modern design profession. (Wornum, *Government Schools of Design,* p. 16.) Instead of being hurt by the creation of the factory system, it could be argued that the designers who took advantage of this kind of training found themselves in an unprecedentedly good position, for it became possible for the factory worker who laid out the pattern to separate himself from the demeaning, manual aspect of his trade, become interested in theory, and even devote himself to the study of fine art. All in all this made it much easier for designers to think of themselves as being closely aligned with fine rather than manual art, and for others to share this perception. (Wornum, p. 37.)

36. At the time of the Great Exhibition, the word "manufacture" meant to make "by art and labor; to form by workmanship," while "industrial artisan" described "every one engaged in handicraft"—*An Explanatory and Phonographic Pronouncing Dictionary of the English Language* (New London, Conn.: Bolles & Co., 1854); see also *Illustrated Catalogue,* p. 130.

37. Owen Jones, *Grammar of Ornament* (1856; reprint, New York: Van Nostrand Reinhold, 1972), p. 136.

38. Wornum, "Lesson in Taste," p. VIII***.

39. William Dyce, "Theory of the Fine Arts: An Introductory Lecture" (London: James Burns, 1844), p. 5.

40. Alexis de Tocqueville, *Democracy in America,* trans. John Stuart Mill (2 vols., New York: Schocken Books, 1961):57–8.

41. Charles Eastlake, *Hints on Household Taste* (1868; reprint, New York: Dover Publications, 1969), pp. 8–9. This problem was not limited to the nineteenth century. In the biography of Brunelleschi, Vasari complained that there were many people in Florence who claimed to know about art but few actually did—*Lives*, p. 146.

42. Kenneth Clark, *The Gothic Revival* (Baltimore: Penguin Books, 1964), p. 102.

43. Friedrich Schiller, *On the Aesthetic Education of Man, in a Series of Letters,* trans. Reginald Snell (New York: Frederick Ungar, 1965), Letter 9, p. 52.

44. Eastlake, *Hints on Household Taste,* p. 118.

45. "Birmingham and Wolverhampton—Effects of the Great Exhibition—Schools of Design," *Journal of Design and Manufactures,* 6, no. 31 (1852):151.

46. Edwards, *Administrative Economy,* pp. 12, 13–14.

47. Ibid., pp. 18, 101.

48. Wornum, "Government Schools of Design," 4:38. To this end, the Select Committee of the House of Commons (1837) expressed an interest in inquiring into "the best means of extending a knowledge of the Arts and the principles of Design among the people of this country, as well as into the constitution, management, and effects of Institutions connected with the arts" (see Edwards, *Administrative Economy,* pp. iii, 325).

49. Bell, *Schools of Design,* p. 253.

50. Henry Cole, "The Functions of the Science and Art Department," *Introductory Addresses on the Science and Art Department and the South Kensington Museum,* no. 1 (London: Chapman & Hall, 1857), p. 12.

51. "Report of the Select Committee of the House of Commons," 1835–6, p. viii, as quoted in Bell, *Schools of Design,* p. 57.

52. Richard Redgrave, "On the Necessities of Principles in Teaching Design: Being an address given at the opening session of the Department of Science and Art, Oct. 1853" (London: Chapman & Hall, 1853), p. 31. See also Bell, *Schools of Design,* p. 242.

53. In Kant's words, "The beautiful is that which pleases universally without [requiring] a concept"—*Critique of Judgment,* Div. 1, bk. 1, 2nd mom., para. 9.

54. The same belief would influence the English Arts and Crafts movement, founded in the mid-1880s, and become the basis for the German Werkbund and Bauhaus in our own century.

55. Edwards, *Administrative Economy,* pp. 13–14.

56. Richard Burchett, "The Central Training School for Art," *Introductory Addresses on the Science and Art Department and the South Kensington Museum,* no. 4 (London: Chapman & Hall, 1858), p. 6. The name of the schools changed from Schools of Design to Schools of Art after Henry Cole took over, in 1852.

57. Richard Redgrave, *Manual of Design* (New York, 1876), pp. 16–17.

58. "Prospectus of the National Art Training School," in *Art Directory* (London, 1872), p. 94.

59. Bell, *Schools of Design,* p. 256.

60. *Prospectus of the National Art Training School,* pp. 11ff.

61. Bell, *Schools of Design,* pp. 257–8.

62. Sparkes, *History of the Schools of Art,* pp. 105–6.

CHAPTER VI

Ornament and the Intellect

The Shift from Eye to Mind

We have just had a thumbnail sketch of the growth of a revolutionary art education system, the purpose of which was to elevate the taste of a new, consumer class. It was a grand scheme, well matched to the optimism of that time. It was also a unique approach to the knotty problem of "taste," which had already occupied sensitive art lovers for more than a century and a half. But its importance in terms of the future of ornament lay not in its novel aim, mass education, but in the means by which the masses were to be enlightened. Beauty was now to be judged by the *principles of art,* which marked a fundamental change in the rules that governed the arts of design. The change was crucial, for it transformed the final judgment of ornament from a matter of the eye into a matter of the intellect, which facilitated the eventual banishment of all ornament.

The principles first appeared well before the 1851 Exhibition, when Augustus Welby Northmore Pugin brought them forth as part of the effort to "revive" Christian (or Pointed) Architecture. Through various revisions and emendations, they have been carried proudly as the commandments of "good design" by every would-be Moses striving to lead his people out of the wilderness of "bad design."

A proselytizer for the Gothic Revival, Pugin's devotion to pre-Renaissance English architecture was a manifestation of his devotion to pre-Renaissance Catholicism, the faith that had ruled England before Henry VIII broke with Rome and established the Anglican Church.[39] In Pugin's eyes, the sad state of taste in the nineteenth century was but one indication of the nation's spiritual decline. His remedy for this condition was a stroke of political genius, and one that later designers—even in this century—intuitively recognized as the most convincing way to establish their judgment as the proper authority for setting the standard of public taste.

The eighteenth-century assumption that taste was an innate faculty was firmly lodged in the popular mind by Pugin's time; anyone could lay claim to taste, and few were willing to admit that theirs needed any refinement. Indeed, with this given, Pugin appears to have sensed the futility of continuing to approach the problem of "bad taste" from an aesthetic point of view.[1] That would only perpetuate the endless and indecisive bantering about whose taste was better. Instead, he spirited the aesthetic question away from the ill-defined, personalized precincts of taste, and lodged it safely behind the more defensible battlements of Christian morality.[2]

I have put Pugin's principles in their familiar, present-day formulations first, followed by passages from the two volumes in which Pugin originally espoused them:[3]

HONEST *EXPRESSION OF STRUCTURE:*[4] the structure of a building or an object should be emphasized not disguised.

PUGIN: Pointed Architecture does *not conceal her construction, but beautifies it.*
—*there should be no features about a building which are not necessary for convenience, construction, or propriety.*[5]

HONEST *EXPRESSION OF FUNCTION:* the purpose of the object or building should be apparent from looking at it; and deceptions,

such as three-dimensional patterns on two-dimensional surfaces, should not be permitted.

PUGIN: It will be readily admitted, that the great test of Architectural beauty is the fitness of the design to the purpose for which it is intended, and that the style of a building should so correspond with its use that the spectator may at once perceive the purpose for which it was erected.[6]

—*the external and internal appearance of an edifice should be illustrative of, and in accordance with the purpose for which it is destined.* —All really beautiful forms in architecture are based on the soundest principles of utility.—The severity of Christian architecture requires a *reasonable purpose for the introduction of the smallest detail.*[7]

HONEST *EXPRESSION OF MATERIALS:* one material should not pretend to be another; also known as being "true" to the nature of the material. The physical characteristics of a material should determine the techniques used to work it and the appearance of the final product.

PUGIN: . . . even the construction itself *should vary with the material employed,* and the designs should be adapted to the material in which they are executed.

—Moreover, the architects of the middle ages were the first who *turned the natural properties of the various materials to their full account,* and made *their mechanism a vehicle for their art.*[8]

HONEST *EXPRESSION OF THE SPIRIT OF THE TIMES:* the belief that the character of one's time can be captured in the design of an object or a building, and that the designer has an intuitive understanding of what that spirit is, which gives him or her the right to "capture" it for the rest of society.

PUGIN: Acting on this principle [that the style of a building should so correspond with its use], different nations have given birth to so

Fig. 39. (*Facing page*) The English architect A. W. N. Pugin was the first to advocate the principles that have allegedly governed design for the past 150 years. A fervent supporter of the Gothic Revival, Pugin deplored Renaissance architecture, with its pagan forms, seeing in it a sign of the decay of true Christian (Gothic) values. St. Peter's, Rome.

many various styles of Architecture, each suited to their climate, customs, and religion.—In new Buckingham Palace, whose marble gate cost an amount which would have erected a splendid church, there is not even a regular chapel provided for the divine office; so that both in appearance and arrangement it is utterly unsuited for a Christian residence.[9]

The novelty of this approach cannot be overemphasized. Beyond a general agreement on iconography, design had been guided primarily by *visual* premises before the principles were introduced. These visual premises were based upon stylistic conventions that had evolved over time, and which were periodically modified by various kinds of proportional systems, depending upon the fashion of the times. These proportional systems were based upon either purely *visual criteria* (the most pleasing column has a shaft that is x times its diameter; the most pleasing room has a height that is x times its breadth [40, 41]) or upon *arithmetic or geometric ratios,* which had metaphysical or other "significant" connotations, such as the Pythagorean ratios or the famous Canon of Polyclitus.[10]

Proportional determinants of design have been used as a guide to refining styles for a very long time, and have generally been seen as one of the most important tools designers have at their disposal for making beautiful buildings. Vitruvius hinted at the difference which such a system might make when he suggested that architects had something more to offer than builders:

> When it appears that a work has been carried out sumptuously, the owner will be the person to be praised for the great outlay which he has authorized; when delicately, the master workman will be approved for his execution; but when *proportions and symmetry* lend it an imposing effect, then the glory of it will belong to the architect. (my emphasis)[11]

The beauty and serenity of the architect's proportions did not come from an extraordinary, personal quality—our "artistic genius," for example. The "glory" that might accrue to an architect came from using

40

Fig. 40. (*Left*) In the final analysis, the rules governing traditional styles were based upon visual criteria—which proportions were most pleasing. Vitruvius gave simple, straightforward rules for determining each part of a building in his 1st-century B.C. treatise on architecture, from the width of door jamb (a specified fraction of the width of the doorway) to the height of column (a specified multiple of its diameter). Detail of the Roman Temple of Jupiter, Baalbek, 1st century A.D.

Fig. 41. (*Right*) Andrea Palladio's *Four Books of Architecture* (1570), modeled after Vitruvius, was the bible of architects for 350 years. He expressed the relationships between parts in proportions, which stressed the visual impact of the composition. "The rooms are either made with a vaulted or flat cieling [sic]. If with a flat cieling, the height from the floor to the cieling must be equal to their breadth; and the rooms above must be a sixth part less in height than those below. . . . The height of vaults in rooms that are square is a third part more than the breadth of the room"—"The Height of Rooms."

41

rules. Vitruvius turned the visual decisions of design (what we would call "aesthetic" choices) into what we might think of as formulas, guidelines similar to the technical tips he offered his fellow engineers on how to lay a proper Roman roadbed, orient a house, or build an aqueduct: "Doors should be constructed with the hingestiles one twelfth of the width of the whole aperture."[12] Or, again, as he described a proper Tuscan temple: "Let the thickness of the columns at the bottom be one seventh of their height, their height one third of the width of the temple, and the diminution of the top, one fourth of its thickness at the bottom."[13]

These rules were rooted, at least originally, in aesthetic preferences—a frame to opening ratio of 1:12 was preferred because it looked nice. Visual guidelines continued to exist after the introduction of the principles of design, of course, for designers still operated according to taste, certain aspects of which can be codified. But when it came to prevailing over popular taste, a design weapon of a different caliber now existed, which convinced not by the eye, but by moral authority. Because of the nature of its power, it seemed to guarantee the designer hegemony over the marketplace.[14]

We see evidence of the new weapon in the "lesson" which Ralph Wornum extracted from the Great Exhibition of 1851. The clearest traces are found in the way Wornum indicated his approval of the individual submissions: an object was worthy because of its "strict attention to natural truth," or the "skillful adjustment of the [ornament] to the situation or use of the object decorated," or because the ornament "expressed" the function.[15] And the universal "lesson" Wornum drew from those crystal corridors was shared by all the reformers: that "all those styles which have carried with them the feelings of ages, could not be otherwise than *based upon some fixed natural laws*" (my emphasis).[16]

Contemporary decorative arts were to be rejuvenated by applying those same "natural laws" to the circumstances of modern manufacture. Such "laws" were not the tangible *visual* rules of a Vitruvius or a Palladio, but intellectual abstractions. Because they acknowledged no formal debt to the eye, and therefore to taste, the reformers saw in them a true potential for controlling the "overloaded" ornamental displays about which Bulwer had spoken twenty years before.[17] If these principles also implied a rational approach to design, their ultimate claim to sovereignty lay in their moral underpinnings: "Now the severity of Christian architecture is *opposed to all deception.* We should never make a building erected to God appear better than it really is *by artificial means*" (my emphasis).[18]

Why was it necessary to invoke moral authority in art, when beautiful objects had been created for so many centuries without having to resort to such a ploy? The answer is that it seemed to offer the surest way to control "bad taste." The earl of Shaftesbury had written about the decline of taste a century and a half before the Crystal Palace Exposition, but neither his cure, reason, nor the later appeals of the philosophers to accept the spiritual authority of the artist-genius, had noticeably improved the public in this respect. The principles were intended to settle this matter once and for all. They were presented as *revealed truth, and their purpose was to cajole an unwilling public into adopting aesthetic values they would not otherwise have accepted.*

The invocation of the principles had several important consequences for the decorative arts. In the first place, the principles raised the prestige of the minor arts by giving them an intellectual cachet they had never before enjoyed. Secondly, their pseudo-moral foundations lent the shield of integrity to their cause. Both changes made the decorative arts less vulnerable to assaults based upon simple arguments of taste. Furthermore, by stating their criteria explicitly, the reformers' position automatically became more readily defensible than the rules of "popular" taste, which had no formal, systematic ideology beyond the historical copybooks.[19]

This completed the gentrification of all the arts of design. Their practitioners had backed away as far as they could from their menial beginnings in antiquity, short of ignoring the actual practice of their trade. In the terms of Plato and Aristotle, even ornamental art was now ruled by the more noble faculties, by the mind rather than hand and eye.

42   43

Figs. 42, 43. The legendary principles of design—expression of structure, function, material, and spirit of the times—supposedly *determined* the appearance of things, but have rationalized every kind of style from the Gothic Revival Grace Church, by James Renwick, Jr., of 1846 (42), to the Seagram Building, by Mies van der Rohe, of 1958 (43).

Anyone who has the slightest acquaintance with modern design will be quite at home with these nineteenth-century principles, for modernists copied them almost word for word. Only the designs were changed—historical styles rejected, technological forms embraced—in order to protect the need to be original. In the nineteenth and twentieth centuries, however, the overriding virtue of the new focus on morality and intellectualism in the arts was that the elite's objections to "bad taste" no longer had to be couched in terms of that disturbingly democratic commodity, "taste." By tying aesthetic choice to abstract principles, legitimized by links to culturally accepted ideals of reason, morality, and utility, artists were relieved of any responsibility for aesthetic choice. Hence they were no longer personally liable for their actions, that is to say, aesthetic choice no longer seemed to be a matter of personal taste.

As we know these principles intimately as the basis of modern design, many will find it difficult to see that they were really an afterthought. I do not mean to imply that those who said they were being guided by the principles were insincere. They surely believed that the principles actually *determined* the styles they chose—but this could hardly be the case. In fact, the great value of the principles over the decades has been their *ambiguity,* for it has enabled them to clothe the most disparate design choices in virtuous morality with equal ease. *The principles of design have been used to justify virtually every style of the past 150 years, from Gothic Revival to postmodernism.* [42, 43]

After the reorganization of the Schools, in 1852, the effort to root out the causes of "bad design" continued but was now directed toward disseminating these prescriptions for beauty to a vastly larger audience. Our particular interest in the principles is to show how, although they did not actually determine the forms of designed things, they were used to try to *control* the use of ornament—the most insistent indicator of "bad taste"—and it is from this point of view that we will examine them.

The Apotheosis of the Decorative Artist

The pathway was plainly marked: The principles had to reach as broad a public as possible, for it was only through their imposition that the decorative arts would realize their full commercial—and aesthetic—

value. We begin to see the direction the minor arts were to take from a lecture entitled "On the Necessities of Principles in Teaching Design," given in 1853 by Richard Redgrave, himself a painter. In the past, he wrote, the Schools had taught only the hand and the eye, neglecting the mind—that is, neglecting to teach the *theoretical* principles of art.[20] The fact was that the skills of the hand and the eye no longer sufficed, because the social controls that had once so closely governed the evolution of styles had been destroyed when the arts entered the marketplace.

The approach through which the reformers hoped to impose their principles on the marketplace was directly related to the experience of the fine arts a few short decades before. It is impossible to prove that the reformers consciously set out to duplicate that experience for the minor arts, but it is equally difficult to imagine that those men, all deeply committed to the furthering of fine as well as decorative art, could have been unaware of the dramatic change in status that had accompanied the great intellectualization of the fine arts. The reformers clearly understood that to place the decorative arts beyond the clutches of popular taste required that they be linked ever more closely to their more prestigious cousins, the fine arts.

If decoration was still on a lower plane than fine art, it was not to be thought of as a frivolous extravagance: "ornament is not a luxury, but, at a certain stage of the mind, an absolute necessity."[21] As fine art was a response to one kind of spiritual need, ornament was now thought to satisfy its own peculiar kind of intellectual craving. Like the fine art artist, the ornamentist now had access to the loftier regions of the intellect.

"Originality" Comes to the Decorative Arts

The nineteenth-century attitude toward originality (also called novelty) seems to have been the product of a slow reversal that took place over the course of the eighteenth century. Dr. Johnson, for example, spoke derogatorily of the mannerism of popular writers that led them to add a note of novelty to the commonplace in an effort to separate themselves from others in their trade—"to quit the beaten track," as he put it, "only because it is known, and take a new path, however crooked or rough, because the straight was found out before."[22] In the first part of the next century, the solid link that Kant forged between originality, art, and genius was reflected in the observation of Coleridge that "the highest and most useful prerogative of genius [is] to produce the strongest impressions of novelty."[23]

We should not be surprised, then, that originality, or novelty—the definitive quality of the artist-genius—also began to be seen as an important quality of artisans. The editors of the *Art-Journal's Catalogue* were quite explicit about this new relationship between the arts, as we see in this description of a French toilet table: "Whatever mind is brought to bear upon matter, so as to leave upon it the impress of *genius,* not mere mechanical ingenuity [craft skill] the result becomes entitled to the highest award that can be accorded to it" (my emphasis).[24] [44] And again, in this comment about a dessert service by Minton, which had been ordered by Queen Victoria: "The series (which is entirely original in the models, arrangement, and decoration), is one of exceeding beauty, designed with pure artistic skill, and exhibiting, in manipulation and finish, a degree of refinement that has rarely, if ever, been surpassed in modern art . . . nowhere do they seem crowded or overladen."[25] [45]

There were even the first hints that decorative art might affect viewers in the same way the great art of the past had, before it lost its usefulness with the coming of fine art:

> The highest value of the arts of design consists, not in their power to minister to the luxury and splendor of a few, but in their eminent capability to promote the fitting and cultural education of all—to contribute to what Milton calls "the inbreeding and cherishing into a people of the seeds of virtue and public civility."[26]

And, in one of the Juries' Reports on the 1851 Exhibition, Redgrave

Fig. 44. By linking the decorative arts to the fine arts, reformers hoped to give the former the prestige of the latter. The aim was to raise the status of the ornamentist to the glorified position of the fine art artist, who could in theory ignore the dictates of "taste" as defined by the marketplace. This process was well along by 1851. One critic spoke of this contribution to the Great Exhibition as a "work of Art," and went on to complain that "we are too apt to draw the line of distinction between the artisan and the artist, where none, in truth, should exist." Wrought-silver toilet table, French manufacture.

44

spoke of "[t]he desire evinced by the rudest as well as the most civilized nations for the decoration of their buildings, utensils, and clothing [which] almost raises ornament into a natural want,"[27] imputing to the decorative arts some of the characteristics of the natural force Kant had associated with the artist-genius.[28]

William Dyce was also quite clear in his assertions on behalf of improving the standing of the decorative arts. The new Schools of Art should teach artistic mastery to the same degree as the schools of fine arts; the only difference should be the objective of the education—the decoration of manufactured goods rather than the creation of set pieces of fine art.[29]

As the distinction between artist and artisan grew less and less clear, a lack of originality ceased to mark the difference between these two categories, and came to be interpreted, instead, as a sign of "bad" as

Fig. 45. A dessert setting manufactured by Minton & Co., and purchased by Queen Victoria was extolled for its beauty, and for the "pure artistic skill" that went into its design. It was also praised because it was "original in the models, arrangement, and decoration."

Fig. 46. This column capital was chastised for "exhibiting no originality in design."

45   46

opposed to "good" design. Thus the description of an acceptable (although far from extraordinary) column capital began with the phrase: "though exhibiting no originality in design,"[30] a phrase that occurred frequently in the *Catalogue,* always with a pejorative connotation.[46]

The term "novelty" also occurred often in these descriptions, and the objects it referred to were always assumed to be the better for having partaken of it: "We admire this as a deviation from the ordinary forms of such objects, as well as for its own intrinsic merit," wrote the editors of the *Art-Journal Catalogue,* about a flamboyant fish-carver.[31] [47] Too much novelty, however, could bring criticism, but this generally happened only when the demand for it had been imposed upon the designer —that is, when it had interfered with artistic freedom—as when the marketplace's fascination with the "charm of novelty" compelled designers "to produce, for the sake of change, and to please a public too exacting

Fig. 47. Novelty, or originality of conception, was the distinguishing characteristic of Kant's fine art artist; by mid-19th century, it was also attached to ornamental works. This bizarre fish-carver, for example, was applauded first for "its *deviation from the ordinary forms of such objects*" (my emphasis), and only then for its "own intrinsic merit"— *Art-Journal Catalogue*, p. 27.

on this point, that which his judgment and matured experience would impel him to withhold."[32]

"Originality," with its intimation of artistic creativity, acquired a near-irresistible appeal, and even its overzealous pursuit was not viewed as entirely negative. "Novel" forms were still expected to be beautiful, after all, and beauty—novel or not—sprang from the same source, for major and minor arts:

> Above all, the [decorative-art] designer should be taught that his principles [of beauty] are to be found only in the very highest art. The designer must, *in mental power, be raised to the level of the artist,* and must emulate him, not only in skill, but in range of information. (my emphasis)[33]

The critics' demands for a certain degree of originality in the decorative arts were virtually identical in tone to the directives of Kant and Schiller to the fine art artist: reject "convention" and search out your own, original artistic path. Under the strictures of the philosophies of art, the following passage could have described a piece of "fine" art but referred, instead, to a sideboard: "It shows a freedom from too great slavishness of idea, a determination to get rid of the trammels of conventional styles, which is very cheering to all who have felt its primary importance to native interests."[34] [48]

The qualitative differences between fine and un-fine art became more and more indistinct as the century wore on, and the reformers

Fig. 48. The virtue of this sideboard lay in its "freedom from too great slavishness of idea, [and] a determination to get rid of the trammels of conventional styles"—*Art-Journal Catalogue,* p. 203.

continued to search for ways to make the ornamentist less vulnerable to market pressure. Three decades after the Crystal Palace, William Morris would fly against a century of artistic theory, holding that nothing could be a work of art that was not useful—whether it soothed, amused, or elevated the mind.[35] This revolutionary assertion of the importance of decorative art virtually equated it with fine art.

By the 1860s or 1870s, it was increasingly difficult to find differences between the principles of fine and decorative art. The intent was clear. The lot of the artisan was to be improved in the same way as that of the fine art artist had been raised a century before, and for much the same reason: to place him beyond the reach of vulgar taste. It became as important for the designer of "art-manufactures" to express the principles of art, laboring in the grimy factories of England, as it had been for the *artiste*-painter, who struggled to express his personal genius in a tiny Parisian garret.

NOTES: CHAPTER VI

1. Whether Pugin arrived at his unique solution through religious conviction or aesthetic discontent is less important than the fact that he changed the rules when it came to deciding what was "beautiful."

2. In the ancient equation of "Truth and Beauty," the latter referred not to the lesser, physical beauty, but to philosophical beauty. While it could be argued that morality and art had always been linked in the Western mind, it must be remembered that morality was the end, not the means. The arts of antiquity encouraged a higher morality by instilling a sense of correct behavior in the citizenry. The nineteenth-century idea that morality should determine artistic form turned that cause-and-effect relationship topsy-turvy.

3. Augustus Welby Northmore Pugin, *Contrasts: or A Parallel Between the Noble Edifices of the Middle Ages and Corresponding Buildings of the Present Day; Shewing the Present Decay of Taste* (London: Charles Dolman, 1841), and *The True Principles of Pointed or Christian Architecture: set forth in Two Lectures delivered at St. Marie's, Oscott* (London: J. Weale, 1841). In some cases the modern understanding of the principles has diverged somewhat from Pugin's original intentions—as we shall see when we discuss these principles in detail—but the fundamental relationship is always clear. Note that the emphasis in the following quotations is Pugin's.

4. "Appropriate" was often substituted for "honest" by both nineteenth- and twentieth-century designers, but invariably carried a connotation of sincerity, guilelessness, directness, or lack of deception.

5. Pugin, *True Principles,* pp. 3, 1.

6. Pugin, *Contrasts,* pp. 1–2.

7. Pugin, *True Principles,* p. 42, 11, 18.

8. Ibid., pp. 1–2.

9. Pugin, *Contrasts,* pp. 1–2, 10.

10. H. Stuart Jones, ed. and trans., *Select Passages from Ancient Writers: Illustrations of the History of Greek Sculpture* (Rev. and enlarged ed. Chicago: Argonaut, 1966), p. xvii. The Canon of Polyclitus listed proportions that were felt to be beautiful when reproduced in the human figure. The only surviving fragment attempted a mathematical demonstration of those proportions, presumably an *ex post facto* mathematical proof that those *preferred* proportions were tied to significant mathematical relationships.

11. Vitruvius, *The Ten Books on Architecture,* trans. Morris Hicky Morgan (New York: Dover Publications, 1960), 6.8.

12. Ibid., 4.6, p. 118.

13. Ibid., 4.7, pp. 120–22.

14. I do not mean to imply that content played no role in how things were designed, only that the same content can find expression in many different forms—a Byzantine versus a contemporary Madonna, for example.

15. Ralph Wornum, "The Exhibition as a Lesson in Taste," in *The Art-Journal Illustrated Catalogue: The Industry of All Nations, 1851* (London, 1851; reprint, New York: Dover Publications, 1970), pp. IX***, XIII***.

16. Ibid., p. I***; see also XXII***.

17. See also E. H. Gombrich, *A Sense of Order* (Ithaca, N.Y.: Cornell University Press, 1979), p. 51.

18. *True Principles,* p. 44.

19. The inherent difficulties that dog "invisible" aesthetic standards have been pointed out by Herbert Gans in his *Popular Culture and High Culture* (New York: Basic Books, 1974), p. 116.

20. Richard Redgrave, "On the Necessities of Principles in Teaching Design" (London: Chapman & Hall, 1853), p. 7.

21. Wornum, "Lesson in Taste," p. XXI***.

22. *The Idler,* no. 36 (Dec. 23, 1758), reprinted in *Harrison's British Classicks,* vol. 8 (London: Harrison, 1787), p. 52. See also no. 85 (Dec. 1, 1759), pp. 121–22.

23. Coleridge, "Aids to Reflection," *Coleridge: Select Poetry, Prose, Letters,* ed. Stephen Potter (London: Nonesuch Press, 1971), p. 449.

24. *The Art-Journal Illustrated Catalogue,* pp. 130–31.

25. *Illustrated Catalogue,* p. 114.

26. Edwards, *Administrative Economy,* p. 340.

27. Richard Redgrave, "Supplementary Report on Design," in *Great Exhibition of the Works of Industry of All Nations, 1851, Reports by the Juries* (2 vols., London: Spicer Bros., 1852), 2:1588.

28. "Genius is the innate mental disposition *(ingenium)* through which nature gives rule to art" —Immanuel Kant, *Critique of Judgment,* trans. J. H. Bernard (New York: Hafner Publishing Company, 1951), Div. 1, bk. 2, para. 46.

29. William Dyce, "Lecture on Ornament Delivered to the Students of the London School of Design," *Journal of Design and Manufactures,* 1 (1849):26ff. See also Dyce, "Education of Artists and Designers," *Journal of Design and Manufactures,* 6 (1852):131–35; 165–67. Yet there was still an ambivalence in Dyce's attitude when he spoke of beauty with regard to the decorative arts. Beauty, as we learned from Kant, was an attribute of fine art; thus Dyce said that a vase decorated with painted or sculpted flowers might sometimes be beautiful, but then it would be judged a work of fine, not decorative art. (William Dyce, "Universal Infidelity in Principles of Design," *Journal of Design and Manufactures,* ed. Henry Cole, 6, no. 31 [London: Chapman & Hall, 1852]:1–6.) Yet in the same lecture he spoke of the "beauty" of the decorative arts, so he seemed to be saying that they too could partake of this exclusive commodity, implying only that it was modified somewhat. The fine artist imitated the beauty of nature, whereas for the decorative artist, beauty was a quality separate from the imitation of nature, "and he makes the separation in order to impress the cosmetic [beautifying powers] of nature on the production of human industry." (Dyce, "Universal Infidelity," *Design and Manufactures,* 6:2.) That is to say, machine-made and/or practical forms were distasteful, and had to be beautified by the decorative artist.

30. Ibid., p. 164.

31. Ibid., p. 27.

32. Ibid., p. 25.

33. Ibid.

34. Ibid., p. 203.

35. William Morris, *The Decorative Arts and Their Relation to Modern Life and Progress* (Boston, 1878), p. 3.

CHAPTER VII

Regulating Ornament

Rationalism and Science

The reformers looked everywhere to find support for the new rules. As an appropriate adjunct to the intellectualization of the decorative arts, a "scientific" approach to design was frequently advocated, and by the mid-nineteenth century the search was on to establish new connections between science and art.

At the basis of this search lay a belief that the miracles of science could somehow improve the production of contemporary decorative arts. In discovery after discovery, science had shown that natural events were founded on knowable "first principles." Now the decorative arts, too, had their first principles. Just as natural law had yielded its secrets to careful reasoning, so that they could be applied to mankind's quest for material progress, science would guide the reformers in applying the principles of the past to techniques of modern art manufacture. As faith in God was the rock on which one built one's life, so faith in Science became, for many, the basis for believing in the inevitable improvement of the "Art of Manufacture" through the application of the principles.[1]

The scientific analysis of nature became one of the prime concerns of the decorative artist, who was cast as a kind of artist-scientist, going about his task with a keen, objective eye:

Again, do we esteem highly the labours of men of science, who investigate one class of the phenomena of nature, for the purpose of applying natural principles to new uses in the economy of life, and shall we think lightly of the ornamentist, who studies *another class of natural phenomena* for an analogous purpose? . . . [The ornamentist's] purpose is to adorn the contrivances of mechanical and architectural skill by the application of those principles of decoration, and of those forms and modes of beauty, which nature herself has employed adorning the structure of the world. *Ornamental design is, in fact, a kind of practical science, which, like other kinds, investigates the phenomena of nature for the purpose of applying natural principles and results to some new end.* (my emphasis)[2]

The beauty offered by the ornamentist was even compared to that presented by the scientist, as both applied "[Nature's] operating and governing laws and the means and hints furnished by her to the accomplishment of new ends of convenience and utility; and the real position, accordingly, of ornamental design is side by side with practical science."[3]

The application of scientific principles to art became a familiar battle cry. Science came to the service of Richard Redgrave, when he argued in favor of more geometric, conventionalized decorative design, announcing that he had found a botanist who said that "[i]f the nature of vegetation is rightly considered, a symmetrical arrangement is almost inevitable."[4] [49] The French architect and theoretician, Viollet-le-Duc, declared that you could actually "classify the examples that had resulted from an unbroken [artistic] course of logical deduction" by cataloguing the past as a butterfly hunter would pin down his prey.[5]

The one serious obstacle that might have aborted these exuberant scientific expeditions into the decorative past was itself done away with by the application of science to art. The near-equation of ornamentist and artist[6] made reformers extremely sensitive to the need for originality, and the mere fact that they looked to the arts of the past for inspiration implied a sacrifice of the freedom and originality Kant had said was essential to creativity. This appearance of artistic impropriety was elimi-

49

Fig. 49. The reformers soon introduced science in defense of their efforts to influence taste in the marketplace. But the handmaid of Art was suspect. At various times, designers have claimed that the natural disposition of vegetation is both symmetrical (Richard Redgrave, in a speech to the Department of Science and Art in 1853) and asymmetrical (William Hogarth, *Analysis of Beauty,* 1753, p. 22). The eye finds symmetry or asymmetry, depending on how we choose to look. Each individual flower in this photograph is (roughly) symmetrical; the arrangement on the stem is distinctly asymmetrical.

nated by a little fancy ideological footwork. It was deemed acceptable to study history as long as it first passed through the purifying filter of science: "the thing to be deplored is the persistence of the belief that the study of the past is injurious [to artistic creativity] now that we can apply analytical methods to architecture as we do the sciences."[7]

Our view of their search for historical principles is distorted by the legacy of modernism—a firm distrust of anything artistic that relies on the past. Yet the distrust of history that is so intimately associated with modernism was born in the writings of these early reformers. In spite of conventional wisdom on the subject, with the exception of Pugin, few if any influential thinkers of the last century actually recommended copying from the past. Simple imitation—whether of the history or Nature—was as repugnant to reformers in 1850 as it was to those of 1920, and for precisely the same reason, which harks back to the new philosophy of art. Literal copying showed a meanness of creative spirit and a lack of that most important quality, *genius,* which was becoming more and more firmly attached to all the arts of design.

There may still be a few people who claim that the definitions of "good" and "bad" design—or the difference between beauty and ugliness—depend upon something other than personal taste, but such a delicate thing as taste was far too fragile a foundation to support such judgments in eras that worship science and the practical solution. Thus the nineteenth and twentieth centuries both asserted that rationality was the basis of all "good" design choices. Yet even Viollet-le-Duc, an austere, Gallic rationalist, decried the Roman Corinthian capital because a basket of vegetation was incapable of supporting anything, while in the same breath he approved the Egyptian lotus capital for the same purpose, not in the least disturbed by the incongruity of a lotus bud holding up tons of stone.[8]

Logic also seemed to fail the reformers when it came to denouncing hated styles, which was based purely upon arbitrary judgments of taste. "Do you suppose that any modern architect likes what he builds, or enjoys it? Not in the least. He builds because he has been told that such and such things are fine, and that he *should* like them," wrote John Ruskin about architects who build in the Renaissance style. "Do you seriously imagine, reader, that any living soul in London likes triglyphs?—or gets any hearty enjoyment out of pediments? You are mistaken. Greeks did: English people never did,—never will."[9] Where was the calm discussion of principles here, or even the idealistic appeal to honesty and candor? This was pure hostility, directed blindly at anyone who might thwart your goal. It was the zeal of a missionary which, by a quirk of history, was directed toward the world of art rather than the mysteries of religion.

Designing "rationally" only implies following a given set of criteria; the important thing is how you come to them. Making "rational" design choices (that is, adhering to your guidelines in a rationally verifiable way) means little when they have been chosen by whimsical, irrational "taste."

The "Honest" Expression of the Spirit of the Times

In *Contrasts,* Pugin stated that an architectural style constituted the physical embodiment of the virtues and the ills of the age that created it.[10] The beauty of a style, in other words, was a function of the moral fiber of the times. The superficial similarity to the modern idea that designers should express the "spirit of the times" is deceptive. Pugin was revolted by the expression of his own time, as he made clear in the subtitle of *Contrasts: A Parallel Between the Noble Edifices of the Middle Ages and Corresponding Buildings of the Present Day, Shewing the Present Decay of Taste.* Rather than expressing the degenerate spirit of his own time, he hoped to recapture the spirit and values of an earlier era by recreating its architectural style. Pugin proselytized for the revival of the Gothic style because he yearned to recreate virtues which he associated with those halcyon days, and proposed to bring about a spiritual regeneration through an architectural transfusion.

Other influential nineteenth-century designers and critics also spoke of creating a style appropriate to their time, but were dedicated to evolving a new one. Owen Jones, architect, author, and superintendent of the Crystal Palace Exposition, accepted Pugin's premise that a style could embody and convey the values of an era, but rejected Pugin's purpose, transplanting the spirit of one time into another.[11] Jones actively lobbied against the "unfortunate tendency of our time to be content with copying . . . the forms peculiar to any bygone age." He passionately studied the history of the decorative arts, but the information gleaned from those backward glances was not meant to provide grist for the copy-mills, but to be combined with new studies of nature, which would result in a unique *style of the times.* [12]

Jones's version of the "spirit of the times" seems quite familiar —even identical to the one adopted by modernists, while Pugin's seems backward. But this superficial similarity between our own notion and that of Jones is also deceptive; the style "of the times" was not to be a new kind of architecture but a new kind of *decoration,* for, in his eyes, decoration was the essence of style.[13]

If we analyze the principles Jones laid out in *Grammar of Ornament,* we find that their purpose was to convince the reader of the rightness of their author's taste. To see this we must first understand that, beyond any rules imposed by gravity and physics, few if any "universal" principles mold the designer's work.[14] Of Jones's 37 propositions[15] to guide the decorative designer, four (nos. 2, 3, 5, and 35) were variations on Pugin's moral laws of design.[16] The other thirty-three dealt either with matters of taste or the psychology of perception (for example, that primary colors are best used in small areas balanced by large masses of secondary or tertiary colors; or that the same color appears lighter on a dark background, darker on a light background). The four propositions for which Jones is indebted to Pugin have no direct connection to *visual* decisions, but merely provide the moral authority to police the taste mapped out by the others.

The "Honest" Expression of Structure

Close behind the "spirit of the times" came the demand for ornament that was in some way related to function—integrated with the structure, as the argument went, rather than "applied" willy-nilly. [50] Vitruvius has often been invoked to prove the ancient lineage and rational heritage of the "honesty of structure" principle. In *The Ten Books on Architecture,* the Roman author objected to a trend in mural painting, fashionable in the first century B.C., that used natural elements in ways nature would never permit—flower stalks as columns, for instance.[17] But his was a totally different emphasis from that which came with Pugin and later reformers. Vitruvius was not arguing for "honesty" of structure—in the sense of not "disguising" it. He was lobbying for verisimilitude, truth to nature, "the

50   Fig. 50.   Designed by Maderna and executed by Bernini, the false perspective of the windows of the Palazzo Barberini in Rome (1628–38) illustrates the kind of Renaissance "deceit" that was repugnant to 19th-century reformers of the decorative arts.

principles of reality," as he called them.[18] He objected to this fashion on the basis of its going against common sense. The reformers, on the other hand, were urging the application of a moralistic principle in support of one style (Gothic) over another (Renaissance), and for increasing abstraction rather than verisimilitude. This had nothing to do with Roman common sense, and everything to do with *taste*.

If one accepted the guideline of structure-based decoration, argued some critics, then Greek sculpture—while perfect in form—was not wholly satisfactory as ornament because it was often "applied," rather than being an integral part of the construction. It was a prejudice that clearly favored Gothic over Classical architecture. Islamic architecture was particularly favored, especially by Jones, because it was said to decorate the construction rather than construct the decoration—the great sin of Classical and Renaissance architecture in general, and of the Roman in particular.

Viollet-le-Duc, to name one, pointed out the dishonesty of Renaissance (as opposed to Gothic) architects, who were overly fond of using piers with decorative inserts, structurally irrelevant wall medallions, irrelevant objects over doorways, curved and triangular pediments, and oversized keystones.[19] Le-Duc felt that all of these things were completely unrelated to structure. [51] (It is difficult to understand why a curved pediment should be less "structural" than one which is straight, or an oversized keystone less a structural member than one which is "correctly" proportioned, unless one simply assumes a bias against Classical styles.)

Similarly, Gothic ornament was admired by many reformers because *it was assumed to adhere closely to the principle that structure should determine the placement of decoration.* "One of the chief merits of the Pointed style," wrote Eastlake about Gothic architecture, is "that the origin of every decorative feature may be traced to a constructive purpose."[20] [52] Thus the pinnacle was beloved because it was both ornamental and functional, its extra weight serving to deflect the outward thrust of the wall downward through the flying buttress. Needless to say, it oversimplified things somewhat to claim that all Gothic ornament was intimately connected to structural necessities. [53] While anything that is physically attached to a building could be said to be "related" to its construction, many Gothic decorations had a relationship to structure that was more coincidental than integral—painting, crockets, and crestings, for example. Nevertheless, as late as 1898, a well-known American writer on architecture could still claim that Gothic architecture was nothing if not sensible.[21]

Gravity demands that a building's structure follow a fairly obvious logic. Simple functions, too, can sometimes be clearly defined. But the decision to ally ornament with structure and function was completely serendipitous—purely a matter of taste.

Our familiarity with modern, structural exhibitionism could lead

52

Fig. 52. From our historical vantage point, it might seem as though 19th-century pleas for functional, rational design had as their aim the ultimate banishment of "useless" ornament. Far from it, as the contemporary assessment of the Albert Memorial indicated. Sir Gilbert Scott's delightful Victorian confection (1863–72) was not criticized for the exuberance of its embellishment, but because its vault was secured by concealed—and therefore dishonest—iron ties. (*Photograph courtesy of the British Tourist Authority, New York, N.Y.*)

Fig. 51. Viollet-le-Duc pointed with disdain at architects working in classical styles, who created decorative elements with no direct connection to the structure of the building. What was more, they frequently confused one's perception of structure, as does this strangely distorted pediment in Vienna.

Fig. 53.   Barge boards were generally approved of by the reformers, for they had
a practical as well as a decorative purpose: they protected the exposed ends of
cross-members running perpendicular to the rafters. Yet they were often elaborated
well beyond what was necessary, as in this cottage on Martha's Vineyard.

53

to another misunderstanding of nineteenth-century honesty of structure. This principle was not intended to eliminate ornament, in favor of revealing the bones of the buildings, as has happened in recent times. Naked structure was the epitome of ugliness to the sophisticated lover of architecture in the last century:

> We are all sensible, and we cannot help being so, that mechanical contrivances are like skeletons without skin, like birds without feathers, pieces of organization, in short, without the ingredient which renders natural productions objects of pleasure to the senses.[22]

The controlling principle of "honesty of structure" was intended to insure the creation of decoration that would clothe the ugliness of these naked structures: "*its* [decoration's] *real use is to hide, by a coating of beauty, the* skeleton like *contrivances of* [practical science], *and thus to bring them into a condition of the works of nature in which beauty and utility are always concomitant*" (his italics).[23]

The reformers' decision to link decoration and structure might seem to have been an effort to make ornament appear more practical or inevitable—something one would expect if designers had to make ornament appeal to clients who had grown skeptical of its worth. But decorative art reformers had precisely the opposite problem in the middle of the nineteenth century; neither clients nor designers doubted the value of ornament, though the former craved it in what the latter often considered unmanageable quantities. Ornament was not linked to structure in order to make it more palatable to the public. It was tied to these aspects of building as part of the overall effort of the reformers to *control its use,* to impose their taste on the marketplace. The surest way to restrain a public clamoring for rich and flamboyant decoration was to begin to place restrictions on how it could be used; to declare that it must "honestly" express a rational structural system, for instance, or the practical demands of use. "Good" ornament (related to structure) versus "bad" ornament (unrelated to structure) was an arbitrary dichotomy with its own peculiarly Victorian purpose: to inject morality into the decorative

arts in support of the designer, with the hope that this would bring to
an end the dominance of the market-pleasing fashions which these men
found so displeasing. As with all the honesties of design, the benefits of
linking ornament to structure and function lay mainly on the side of
designers.

As we would expect, the petit bourgeois were among the chief
sinners against the honest expression of structure, for they persisted in
decking out their houses and stores with fraudulent, pretentious architectural trappings: "As long as people of humble means will insist on
assuming the semblance of luxuries which they cannot really afford,"
wrote Eastlake, "vulgarities of design and structural deceits must prevail
in this direction."[24] These vulgarities and deceits included relatively
harmless things such as using Italianate moldings that were said to look
fine under sunny southern skies, but were thought to be less purposeful
in the duller English climate.[25]

Ironically, the goal of expressing structure honestly through
decoration was pursued more to purge the world of deceptive ornament
than to insure structural soundness. When structural concerns were mentioned it was almost always in reference to poorly made stucco copies of
stonework columns, parapets, balusters and the like, the worst of which,
it was said, could endanger life and limb. Yet for all the alleged logic
of the principles, the solution proposed for the one real structural problem
associated with this "honesty" was emotional, not rational. There was no
talk about making better stucco ornament, although at the time there
were examples of sixteenth-century stucco work that were still in fine
condition. There was only a vile denunciation: "In an evil hour *stucco*
was invented," cried Eastlake, so banish it![26]

The "Honest" Expression of Function

The matter-of-fact emphasis on physical necessity, or "function," as the
primary generating force in design is a relatively recent historical development. The Renaissance biographer of Brunelleschi provided a capsule

history of the evolution of society which hardly supported this point of view: "With wealth and principalities came the ceremonial uses: for splendor, for displaying magnificence, to command admiration, and to provide ease and comfort. They then progressed to the [practical] construction of enclosures and defenses for kingdoms and treasures."[27] Most of the reformers, however, including Pugin, Eastlake, Morris and Crane, among others, never seem to have questioned the assumption that the utilitarian needs of life had always been the prime movers in matters of design. Most assumed, as did Crane, that "the first arts are, of course, those of pure utility, which spring from the primal physical necessities of man."[28] First came the necessities of construction, according to this argument, and only then the niceties of ornament.

"The great test of Architectural beauty is the fitness of the design to the purpose for which it is intended, and that the style of a building should so correspond with its use that the spectator may at once perceive the purpose for which it was erected."[29] This sounds like the 1920s Bauhaus, but it was 1840s Pugin, championing one of several views which eventually found their way into the ideological heart of modern design. After the honest expression of structure came the principle that "fitness" (or "propriety" or "appropriateness") and "utility" should determine the form of a building and the character and disposition of its decoration.

Pugin followed this thoroughly modern-sounding declaration with a functional litany with which we feel quite at home, urging that buildings should be made responsive to the needs of climate, customs, living habits, and so on. Ornament was part of this amalgam of forms-fitting-functions because decorations also had functions, being "emblems of [the] philosophy and mythology" of nations.[30] But take care to put the correct emblems on the correct buildings, because functions were to be expressed accurately.

The link between beauty and utility, which Pugin proclaimed so loudly, had been an unquestioned aspect of the design arts throughout much of the eighteenth century, and was frequently pointed out by analogies to nature:

The truth or beauty of every figure or statue is measured from the perfection of Nature in her just adapting of every limb and proportion to the activity, strength, dexterity, life and vigour of the particular species or animal designed.

Thus *beauty and truth are plainly joined with the notion of utility and convenience,* even in the apprehension of every ingenious artist, the architect, the statuary, or the painter. (my emphasis)[31]

Some decades after these remarks of the earl of Shaftesbury, the English painter William Hogarth still spoke of fitness as "of the greatest consequence to the beauty of the whole."[32] But with the acceptance of the abbé Batteux's new classification of the arts, it became impossible for beauty and usefulness to coexist. Schopenhauer, for example, declared that architecture could not be art because it served useful ends.[33]

Pugin's formulation—that ornament should express structure and function—amounted to a return to the pre–fine-art assumption of a direct link between utility and beauty—particularly the notion of revealing *function* through ornament—an attitude universally adopted by later decorative-art reformers, including Charles Eastlake:

If that which appeals to the eye—if that which charms the ear—if that which appeals to the more imaginative faculties of the human mind have no direct and practical result for our benefit [i.e. no utility], then poets, painters, and musicians have, indeed, lived and wrought for us in vain. . . . No decorative feature can legitimately claim our admiration without revealing by its very nature the purpose of the object which it adorns.[34]

Most advocates of "functional" design have at some time turned to Vitruvius, citing his references to "fitness" or "propriety" as a sign that utility was always a prerequisite of beauty (at least before the creation of fine art placed beauty above such worldly concerns). His far-reaching influence can be seen in the Renaissance in Alberti's *Ten Books on Architecture*—where the proper decoration for town houses was said to be grave, while country houses, intended for pleasure, should have the gayest and most licentious decoration.[35] And the ancient influence was still strong in the eighteenth century, when philosophers like Alexander Gerard continued to pay homage to Vitruvius, speaking of wrongly applied ornaments which displeased because of the "impropriety of [their] position."[36]

The antique idea of "fitness" or "propriety" was based upon a practical, no-nonsense view of the world that befitted a Roman engineer. Vitruvius had none of the moral hyperbole of Pugin, who consistently called forth images of a struggle between architectural good and evil: "Let then the Beautiful and the True be our watchword for future exertions in the overthrow of modern paltry taste and paganism (the Renaissance), and the revival of Catholic art and dignity."[37] [54]

There is also another subtle but important difference between the antique notion of "fitness" or "utility" and that which became current in the last century. The root of the nineteenth-century idea did come from Vitruvius' view that architectural elements should have some common-sense relationship to experience. But while fitness was a necessary quality of antique works of art, it was never considered either an organizing principle of design or a guarantor of beauty.[38] [55, 56] Pugin's concept of "utility" as the focus of ornament represented a remarkably modern point of view. His passionately Catholic view went well beyond Vitruvius' modest demand for propriety or appropriateness, and has the ring of Puritanical modernism to it:

> The severity of Christian architecture requires a *reasonable purpose for the introduction of the smallest detail,* and daily experience proves that those who attempt this glorious style without any fixed idea of its unalterable rules, are certain to end in miserable failures.[39]

With the advent of the principles of design it was no longer enough that a building or an object simply serve the utilitarian purpose for which it had been intended—knives should cut, castles be impregnable, pitchers pour, etc. Such things also had to look as if they were doing what they were doing. [57, 58] They had to "express" their functions, a new variation on Vitruvius' propriety. In trying to understand the

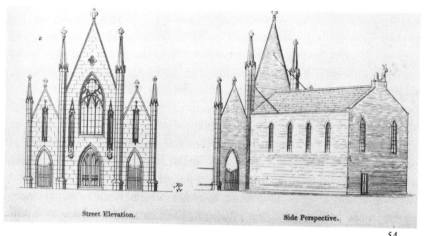

Street Elevation.   Side Perspective.

54

Fig. 54. While common wisdom suggests putting one's "best foot forward" in good society, such traditional architectural gestures as making the front of a building more impressive than the back were pilloried as *immoral* and *deceitful:* "the severity of Christian architecture is opposed to all deception. We should never make a building erected to God appear better than it really is by artificial means." The quotation and illustration come from Pugin's *Contrasts*.

55

56

Figs. 55, 56. The "expression of function" became an exercise in a personal interpretation of the spirit of the times, that mythic—and useful—force which has allegedly guided designers for a century and a half. The poetic nature of expressing a function becomes clear when we see that even so utilitarian an item as a clock can function perfectly well in any stylistic skin: in this case, one Gothic (55), the other Art Deco (56).

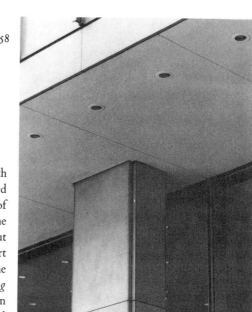

58

Figs. 57, 58. Design reformers of both the nineteenth and twentieth century urged the abstraction, or conventionalization of ornament, in order to better express the function. Yet there is little doubt about which form "expresses" the support function better—the telamon (57) (the male counterpart of the caryatid), (*facing page*) or the modern column, first clad in concrete, then sheathed in stainless steel (58). Discussions about "expressing" this or that are verbal smokescreens, designed to obscure the fact that design is a matter of taste.

nineteenth-century concept of "expressing" utility in decorative design it is best not to be too literal. The placement and character of the ornament could be determined by something so casual as the form "suggested" to the designer by the function. As Eastlake put it, in words very close to those of Pugin: "Every article of manufacture which is capable of decorative treatment should indicate, by its general design, the purpose to which it will be applied, and should never be allowed to convey a false notion of that purpose."[40]

The "Honest" Expression of Materials

Virtually every nineteenth-century observer who wrote about design registered outrage at the commonplace custom of disguising inferior materials as finer ones.[41] But what they complained about, and the fact that they refused to recognize certain perfectly reasonable alternatives, leads one to suspect another motivation. I have already mentioned East-lake's disgust at shoddy stucco fakeries, and his failure to suggest using better made fakes. Viollet-le-Duc's reaction was similar. He claimed to be outraged at plaster ornaments made to look like stone, while admitting that, in reality, no one could tell the difference between the fake and the original: "What advantage is there in cutting an ornament in solid stone if it looks exactly like one that is moulded and stuck on?"[42]

Others, influenced by Pugin's rhetoric about the virtue of this principle, felt that design truly mirrored the moral condition of society. Consequently, the very integrity of English culture was threatened when wood carvers painted their work realistically rather than allowing the natural grain of the material to show. The moral appliqué attached to this view tended to obscure its inherent social and economic bias. [59, 60, 61] Underlying the ideal of "honesty of materials" was a rejection of the taste of those who accepted the "faked" goods and of the social and economic values which motivated them. In addition, from the Arts and Crafts Movement to modernism, "good design" has almost always been an expensive affair. "Fake" materials were all that most of the buying public could afford. To take a modern-day example, choosing between a high-style, $200 kitchen chair and one that sells for $18 is not a choice for anyone but the wealthy. [62] The economic and sociological implications of pursuing the principles of honesty of material to its logical conclusion were seldom discussed by the reformers of either century.

Oddly enough, although last century's reformers continually looked to historical precedent to determine their principles, they consistently overlooked the cases in which their design forefathers used materials "dishonestly." (This is just one example of how we see history—and nature—selectively, finding only what we want to find to support our point of view.) [63] In one of many such cases Pausanias, author of a second-century-A.D. guidebook to Hellenistic Greece, remarked that it was hard to tell whether the statues of mythical birds on the roof of a temple in Stymphelos, Arcadia, were wood or plaster. His best guess was that they were wooden. He was not scolding sculptors for the attempted deception, but accurately describing what he saw. It is doubtful that he

59

Figs. 59, 60.   The wall at the right of this
photograph (59) is farther away than that on
the left, and its wood paneling is absolutely
flat. The appearance of low relief has been
achieved through the art of intarsia, which
uses different shades of wood give the illusion
of shadows. Santa Maria del Carmine,
Florence. The "back" wall of the Fisher
Building in Detroit (60) uses a simple kind of
deceitful decoration to make a potentially
boring facade more lively. Bricks of different
colors are laid in patterns that give the
impression of shadows, making it seem as
though the wall is not flat.

60

149

61

Fig. 61. Desire frequently outstripped the means to acquire, and the real materials associated with wealth and status were beyond the reach of most of the new middle class. They then resorted, in time-honored fashion, to imitating rare materials with less rare ones. Here the "marble" of the abbey of Ottobeuren, Bavaria, is concocted of painted stucco. Architect, Johann-Michael Fischer; stuccoes and statues by Johann-Michael Feichtmayr, begun 1748.

Fig. 62. (*Right*) In 1924, the French architect Robert Mallet-Stevens wrote that "ornaments are expensive and these days economy is an important factor for builders." "High-style" design carries its own costly ornament, that of status, which adds a very tangible price to such items. The same Robert Mallet-Stevens who claimed that ornament was doomed by the need for frugality designed a modest kitchen chair of sheet and tubular metal which can be purchased today for $200. (*Courtesy of Turpan Sanders, Inc., New York City*)

Fig. 63. (*Below*) Certain effects are easier to achieve in one material than another. Relatively deep undercuts, yielding dark shadows, are easier to make in clay than marble, yet the notion that the "nature" of marble should circumscribe the artisan's vocabulary did not inhibit antique sculptors. The stonecutters of classical Greece translated the character of the clay models of Phidias, including those for the Panathenaic frieze, into the gleaming, Pentellic marble. (*Photograph by Brent C. Brolin. Courtesy of The British Museum, London*)

62

would have been offended even if he had found that the birds were made of cheaper plaster rather than more expensive wood, for why should a temple be stripped naked just because its builder had limited resources? And it is likely that most if not all medieval sculpture and architecture was painted or gilded, including moldings, columns, colonnettes, doors, rosettes, brackets, walls, vaults, crockets, and virtually all of the "honest" Gothic details beloved by Pugin and others. [64, 65, 66] The wall paintings, patterned floor tiles, banners, and hangings of these sacred edifices were all awash in the candy-colored light of stained glass, creating a shimmering glaze of hues that, combined with the delicacy of the stonework, would have effectively denied the solidity of these solid, "honest" stone structures, in much the same way that faceted mirrorwork dematerializes the vaults and domes of nineteenth-century Persian shrines. Yet disguising the "true" nature of these materials by painting them had already become a practice detested by the arbiters of art in the nineteenth century.

One spin-off of the notion of being "honest" in one's use of materials was the idea that each material had a discernible "nature," which determined the way it could be worked and therefore its ultimate appearance. If designers were true to these combined principles, the form and decoration of their constructions would be defined by the physical properties of the materials and the techniques used to shape them. There was some truth to the notion to be sure; a glass-blower can achieve a thinness of wall that is almost beyond the imagining of a potter. But the idea could not survive the dogmatic application which these reformers tried to give it.

Eastlake once said that "all cast-iron ornament, except under rare conditions [the low relief ornament of old Sussex stoves], is bad in style,

66

Fig. 64, 65. (*Top right & below*) The pervasive grayness of most Gothic cathedrals is quite misleading. The facade of Wells Cathedral (ca. 1180–ca. 1425) originally held hundreds of painted statues, and must have looked like a gaily colored peasant shawl (64). Ancient Greek temples would probably have seemed equally flashy, for they, too, had boldly colored sculpture and ornamental details. The original appearance of these festive facades was probably closer to that of a contemporary Indian temple (65), covered with multicolored gods, than the vision most of us have of dark, weathered limestone, or marble bleached to a blinding white by the Aegean sun.

65

Fig. 66. (*Facing page*) This painted rood screen, from a parish church in Devon, England, has upward of half a dozen colors, and presents an extraordinarily lively image compared to the somber browns of the old wood carvings normally associated with Gothic architecture. The moldings, columns, colonettes, rosettes, brackets, vaults, crockets, and other details of the "honest" Gothic structures so beloved by Pugin would all have been painted or gilded—finances permitting—permanently disguising the nature of whatever material was involved.

Fig. 67. Called "true examples of Art," these remarkably delicate bracelets are made of cast iron. Often reviled because of its crudeness—a quality generally associated with the lack of handworkmanship—the ultimate character of most materials in fact depends more on the worker's skill, his or her aesthetic aims, and the refinement of the techniques used, than on the nature of the material.

67

Fig. 68. The assumption that the nature of a material defines the form it must take ignores the skilled craftsman's compulsion to triumph over intractable materials, to make marble domes fill with air and billow like silk. Mosque, New Delhi.

68

Fig. 69. The "principles" of design did not determine form, but provided a rationale for convincing others to accept the designers' taste. Thus, while trying to convince the reader that the material and the technique of fabrication should determine the appearance of the final product, Sir Charles Eastlake could argue that flat rugs should have flat patterns rather than the illusion of three-dimensions, even though both patterns would have been made on the identical machine.

69

and when employed to represent wrought work, must be detestable in the eyes of a true artist."[43] It was a seductively simple approach to a complicated question. While cast iron may never be as fine as the most delicate wrought work, it is possible to do remarkably finely cast work. [67] The line cannot be drawn as clearly and absolutely as Eastlake and others would have liked because, to a remarkable extent, the delicacy of decorative work in any material depends upon the aesthetic aims and technical virtuosity of the designer and/or maker.

Few materials have only one "nature." What is the "nature" of clay, for instance? To be cast? Built up in slabs? Thrown? Carved? Should wood be turned? Carved? Glued and built-up? Laminated and bent under steam and pressure? Most materials can be worked in a variety of different and equally "natural" ways. Whatever the limitations that may be imposed by materials and techniques, they permit much more flexibility than the proponents of this principle ever chose to let on. You cannot "blow" stone, as you blow glass, to cite just one example, yet you can make a stone structure look as light as a silken veil filled by the wind. [68] The idea that the "nature" of a material or technique actually *determined* the form of an object or a building has always ignored the most important ingredient in the creative process: the compulsion of skilled artisans to push a material or technique to the outer limit in an effort to achieve a "triumph over intractable materials."

Like most such assertions of principle, Eastlake was stating an aesthetic preference rather than revealing a design "truth." The true motivation behind this came out when he arbitrarily remarked that it was "natural" to hammer iron on a forge and unnatural to cast it.[44] It may be "natural" to shape this material by hammering when it is in a plastic state, but what is more "natural" than to pour liquid iron into a mold? Eastlake's decree had nothing to do with the "dishonesty" of making cast work look like wrought or vice-versa. He simply seems to have disliked the entire genre of cast iron and to have recognized that the "principles" were an effective means of enforcing this preference.

Fig. 70. The more restrictions there are, the easier it is to design, because the number of choices is reduced. The "principles" provided restrictions at a time when new manufacturing techniques were presenting designers with an unprecedented range of choices. Papier-mâché chair from the 1851 Exhibition.

The frailty of this principle is most apparent when it is misapplied by the very people who touted it. Shortly after he had declared the importance of being *true* to the nature of the material and technique, Eastlake stated that carpets should not have three-dimensional designs because these threaten to trip up the unsuspecting pedestrian by deceiving him into thinking a flat floor has depth.[45] [69] Unless the Victorians were much more gullible than I think, this is a patently silly argument which has nothing to do with any principle. Carpets with two- and three-dimensional designs were produced with equal ease using precisely the same materials and techniques.

When he wrote that "every material used in art manufacture is obviously restricted by the nature of its substance to certain conditions of form,"[46] Eastlake ignored the many different ways in which things can be made. [70] Yet the pseudo-scientific, pseudo-rational sound of this pompous postulate—plus its convenient ambiguity—insured that it would be invoked by generations of designers who continued to attack popular styles, and it retains a place in the pantheon of design dogma to this day. The origins of this principle of design lay in the combined effect of the invention of new manufacturing techniques, which offered many new ways to make things, and the growth of the popular art marketplace.

Perhaps the most telling point is that the "nature" of materials only became an important design concern after harsh market demands had wrenched artistic control from the artisans' and artists' hands, and new methods of manufacture had proven that many materials in fact had several "natures."

The Virtue of Simplicity

Most of the European objects displayed at the Great Exhibition were covered with clouds of putti, acres of acanthus, and cornucopiate harvests from the vegetable kingdom. Repelled by the endless appetite of *nouveau riche* taste for all types of ornament, these earnest reformers found the perfect counter to cluttered middle-class indulgences in yet another "honest" virtue: simplicity. Like his contemporaries, Charles Eastlake's design morality was founded upon a profound disgust for the "lust of profusion" which violated "artistic propriety."[47] Yet it is hard to believe that he was espousing a relatively Spartan approach to ornament when we look at the illustrations in his *Hints on Household Taste*. [71]

Simplicity is obviously a relative term. Walter Crane spoke of the extreme simplicity and spare severity of Greek temple ornament, at the same time acknowledging that it would have been "heightened" with color.[48] Crane's image evokes the familiar vision of gleaming whiteness under an Aegean sun, touched up here and there with a few spots of color —like the ubiquitous "accent cushions" in stark, white modern interiors. In reality the effect would have been far richer than many purists of the Classical "simplicity" could have stomached.[49] Even those gleaming icons of pure pentellic that graced the Parthenon's sacred pediments were probably painted in what would today seem garish colors.

Part of the appeal of simplicity came from its alleged connection to the domestic equivalent of Rousseau's "noble savage." Peasant craftsmen were supposed to possess all the virtues lacked by the middle classes,

71

Fig. 71. Sir Charles Eastlake preached the virtues of "simple" ornament, although, from our vantage point, the simplicity of the style of ornament to which he gave his name is not so apparent. Ornament in the Eastlake style, New York City.

and the term "simple" was often employed when reformers spoke about folk arts. "Art was not born in a palace," said Morris, "rather she fell sick there."[50] Crane went so far as to say that when Japanese goods were beautiful, it was because Japan was still a medieval (pre–bourgeois) culture (a viewpoint that would be difficult to maintain today). Traditional designs, which had never been intended for wealthy homes, were regularly characterized as "deftly and honestly made."[51] In their folk wisdom, humble craftsmen had allegedly turned out these simple, honest objects because they knew better than to harbor unnatural aspirations to the unattainable extravagances of the aristocracy, and were blessed with enough common sense not to covet the tacky imitations that satisfied the middle classes.

In actuality, those who believed in "simplicity" were fighting middle-class pretensions with some equally pretentious notions of their own. For better or for worse, many "humble" folk were only biding their time until they had the means to indulge in bourgeois excesses. In their passionate attempts to restrict the use of ornament, English reformers frequently assumed that the simplicity often (but by no means always) marking the life of the poor was a matter of choice. When men like Ruskin, Morris, and Crane eventually turned to socialism, this supposed peasant virtue took on an even more pointed meaning, the simpler folk crafts becoming tangible proof of the uprightness, practicality, and natural wisdom of the poor, as contrasted with the degenerate taste of their social "betters."

Avant-garde artists in Russia made a similar misjudgment after the Revolution, when they scorned stylistic anachronisms in order to get on with the creation of new art for the new society. The disconcerting reality was that the Russian peasant and proletarian longed for the same patterned china and needlework settees that had graced the salons of the banished bourgeois. The teapot shown here was part of a set of china designed in Russia seventeen years after the Revolution by Eva Zeisel. It was produced with a variety of traditional ornaments, and one modern decoration by the Suprematist, Nikolai Suetin. Needless to say, the ornament with traditional roots had far greater sales appeal. [72, 73]

Nor were the political revolutionaries of the new Russia prone to "avant gardism" in the arts. Leon Trotsky, writing about Tatlin's proposed tower for the meeting of the Communist International, asked some hard-nosed questions about the usefulness of this poem to the new era, as well as making some astute observations about the architect's failure to realize his aim: "The props and piles which are to support the glass cylinder and the pyramid—and they are there for no other purpose —are so cumbersome and heavy that they look like unremoved scaffolding. One cannot think what they are for. They say: They are there to support the rotating cylinder in which the meetings will take place. But one answers: Meetings are not necessarily held in a cylinder and the cylinder does not necessarily have to rotate."[52]

The virtues of simplicity had been romanticized since the eighteenth century, and the simple and often beautiful artifacts which were part of the daily life of the "simple" peasant were frequently turned into symbols of the latter's pure and noble condition, generally by those whose

Figs. 72, 73. (*Above and top right, facing page*) The decorated teapot in this photo (72) was produced by the Dulevo factory, outside Moscow, in 1935, and proved far more appealing to the market than the one decorated by the Suprematist Nikolai Suetin. (Form of teapots by Eva Zeisel; traditional ornament by Protopopova.) Vladimir Tatlin's proposed tower (73) for the Communist International was attacked, on curiously bourgeois, practical grounds, by none other than Leon Trotsky.

purpose was to rebel against the ruling bourgeois taste. Having first-hand experience of the simplicity imposed by poverty, the peasants of both eras rarely seemed to hesitate at choosing the symbols of luxury characterized by the extravagant taste of the upper classes. De Tocqueville, on the other hand, did not miss the point. He noted that the simple tradesman partook of the same "passions" for the appearance of wealth as did the bourgeoisie.[53]

It seems to have been a generally held assumption that the masses would choose the simpler design if only they were given the choice, based on the observed "close alliance of *utility* and *simplicity*" which characterized the English race.[54] In spite of the reformer's near-universal emphasis on "simplicity," however, if it came in the wrong style-package, it, too, ceased to be a virtue. "No one would call these members beautiful," wrote John Ruskin about the stern lines of a Doric cornice. [74] If they had a certain emotional impact, it was because of their "severity and simplicity," not their beauty.[55]

Fig. 74. (*Below*) The most beautiful forms for decorative inspiration were to be found in nature, according to John Ruskin. Architectural styles that excluded natural shapes, therefore, did not qualify for his highest accolade. No one found the cornice of a Doric temple beautiful, said Ruskin. It might have an emotional impact, he admitted grudgingly, but this was due to its extreme "severity and simplicity," not because it was beautiful. St. Joseph's Church, New York City.

The Sanctity of Nature

In an effort to save designers the embarrassment of having to haggle about taste, no dictum was more frequently and earnestly put forth than the one that said "good design" follows the principles of growth seen in nature. (Frequently mentioned in the nineteenth century, the demand for abstraction in our own century meant that faith in observable principles of nature necessarily took a back seat. But the analogy to the usefulness of natural forms has always been implicit in the contemporary notion of functionalism.)

Virtually everyone who wrote about decoration cited some natural precursor for what they considered good ornament. A simple, Christian logic seemed to be at the heart of this reasoning; without nature's example (and through nature, God's), man was incapable of creating beauty.[56] [75] Ironically, in the light of later events, this religious angle was reinforced by the assumption that natural forms were inherently utilitarian, a view that received its sanction through the writings of Charles Darwin and Herbert Spencer.

The logic by which ornamental forms were judged "fit," however, was far less rigorous than the allusion to nature implied. A Renaissance festoon could be a beautiful natural form in itself, for example, but turned into an inappropriate bit of "luscious ugliness" when tacked onto a flat wall.[57] [76] The author of this view, John Ruskin, also strained the bounds of logic by categorically stating that decorative lines were only beautiful if they were adaptations of the most common natural lines.[58] The opposite also held true, of course, that forms "*not* taken from natural objects must be ugly."[59] [77]

Natural forms varied in their degree of beauty, said Ruskin, depending upon how often they occurred in the world around us, and the ease with which they could be seen. Reasoning with arbitrary and

Fig. 75.   (*Facing page*) Ruskin created a hierarchy of natural forms for ornamental use based upon how frequently they were seen in nature, and their position on the evolutionary ladder. Human and animal forms, like those in this fountain by Bernini in the Piazza Navona, Rome, occupied the upper end of Ruskin's scale. Crystalline, mineral forms were the least visible and hence least desirable natural forms for ornamental purposes.

Fig. 76. "Expressing" structure, in 19th-century terminology, meant connecting the ornament somehow to structure. Festoons or garlands might be beautiful in themselves, but, in the words of Ruskin, became inappropriate bits of "luscious ugliness" when tacked onto a flat wall, as Sir Christopher Wren did on St. Paul's Cathedral. If properly located, however—attached to a capital, for instance—they were perfectly acceptable.

absolute rigidity, Ruskin stated: "From Frequency to Beauty, and vice versa; that knowing a thing to be frequent, we may assume it to be beautiful."[60] Sinuous vegetation was always visible, and consequently a thousandfold more beautiful than geometric mineral forms buried in the bowels of the earth.

In an age that favored Gothic, it was predictable that the Renaissance would suffer, and that era was constantly accused of using unnatural and "ugly" elements such as arabesques, armor, meaningless scrolls, curled shields, and other "fancies."[61] Inscriptions, another Renaissance favorite, were also frowned upon. One could use them if absolutely necessary, but they should not be mistaken for ornament. On the contrary, they were "obstinate offenses to the eye."[62]

Ruskin held that Eastlake had first set down the correct principle for creating a hierarchy of ornamental usage: The more noble the subject, the more closely nature could be imitated, although complete imitation was never really sanctioned.[63] The four levels of architectural ornament, ranging from most to least noble, were defined by Ruskin as follows:

Fig. 77. The color of architectural ornament, like its form, should imitate nature, said Ruskin, which meant that materials should be used in their natural state, made decorative by contrasting their colors and arranging them in patterns such as those on the facade of the Doges' Palace, in Venice, 1309–1424.

ORGANIC FORM DOMINANT: Free-standing sculpture, rich capitals and moldings, high relief.

ORGANIC FORM SUBDOMINANT: "To be more abstract in proportion to the reduction of depth," and more rigid and simple in contour.

ORGANIC FORM ABSTRACTED TO AN OUTLINE: Monochrome design, simpler contours; this is the first level at which color can follow the outline of the form.

ORGANIC FORM DISAPPEARS ENTIRELY: "Geometrical patterns or variable cloudings [variegated patterns] in the most vivid color."[64]

Examples of the first order of decorative art were not to be placed where they would be subject to wear and tear, as "on domestic utensils, or armour, and weapons, and dress." Those locations were more appropriate for "forms of inferior art," ornaments that by virtue of their simplicity were less likely to suffer damage or, by virtue of their complexity and repetitiveness, were able to show to advantage regardless of the complexity of the form they adorn.[65]

In spite of the air of finality that accompanied this kind of pronouncement, the line between realism and abstraction was not so clearly drawn, even for Ruskin. True, this great moralist of nineteenth-century criticism had declared that higher forms of decorative art always imitated, but with *discretion*[66]—that is to say, the goal was never simple copying. Thus, primitive art always showed incomplete imitation of nature, and increasing skill in imitation was a sign of higher culture. But absolute imitation, as in Greek art, was generally a sign of decline.[67] In a typically vague formulation, the essence of architectural decoration was said to be "Proportion and Abstraction," and its goal, a harmonious relationship to Natural Law. Deciding how to achieve that goal was described, with equal vagueness, as a matter "of much nicety."[68]

Given such imprecision, it was not surprising that reformers could agree on a sweeping principle, such as taking inspiration from nature, but frequently parted company when it came to the details of its application. The first victim of Ruskin's pro-nature stance, for example, was the Greek fret. [78] Nothing about the fret was natural, he swore (although rectangular crystals occur in nature), and "on this ground, then, I allege that ornament to be ugly; or, in the literal sense of the word, monstrous."[69] Yet Owen Jones and others found nothing wrong with this modest geometric ornament. [79]

Realistic ornament had already begun to meet with opposition at the time of the Great Exhibition. China and pottery, in particular, came under attack; although the eye can compensate for considerable surface distortion on a plate or dish, and still interpret a "realistic" perspective scene correctly, Eastlake himself argued point blank against three-dimensional illusions on two-dimensional surfaces, arbitrarily declaring that "[t]he representation of perspective, of aerial effect, and of chiaroscuro would be impossible on surfaces which . . . are liable to every variety of contour."[70] [80]

However, within a few short years after Ruskin laid out his neat hierarchy (the version quoted appeared in *The Seven Lamps of Architecture* in 1848), a divergence of views became much more apparent. The preference of most reformers, including Eastlake, whose definitions had formed the basis of Ruskin's hierarchy, was shifting toward greater abstraction at all levels of ornament. Indeed, in the continuing search for controlling principles, "good taste" began to be associated not only with lesser quantities of ornament, but also with greater abstraction.

Therefore, although nature remained the obvious choice for ornamental inspiration, if it was too naturalistic—that is to say, if the sensitive eye of the ornamentist had not modified it—it was ornamentally unfit. Its variety, it was decided, was too overwhelming, and the delicacy of its detail too fine to be appreciated. Even when accurately represented natural forms produced decoration that was acknowledged to be attractive, it was disliked. Ornament could be "ingenious, amusing, attractive for the moment, but [did not] lie within the legitimate province of [decorative] art" if it was imitative.[71]

Eastlake's irrationally based preference for two-dimensional carpet designs reflected an aspect of the reformers' approach that would take over by the end of the century. [81, 82, 83] It was blatantly elitist. Virtually anyone can understand or develop an appreciation for an art when the criterion for judgment is directly related to experience. But the

78

79

Fig. 78. (*Top left*) Nature was to be the source of all ornamental motifs, said Ruskin. The first victims of this dictum were the geometric, man-made ornaments such as this fret, from the Roman temple complex at Baalbek. Nothing about this form of decoration was natural, declared Ruskin, which made it ugly by definition.

Fig. 79. (*Top right*) The line of reasoning that rejected the geometric fret because it had no obvious precursor in nature, embraced the egg and dart molding, this one from a fallen entablature in the Forum in Rome.

Fig. 80. (*Middle*) Being in favor of abstraction in decorative art meant opposing realism, which included, of course, all those true-to-life details and scenes even the uneducated could understand. "Landscape and pictures are almost always out of place in pottery," wrote Richard Redgrave, in a "Supplementary Report on Design," in *Reports by the Juries,* 2:1647. *Joseph Receiving His Brothers in Egypt. (Photograph by Brent C. Brolin. Courtesy of The Metropolitan Museum of Art, New York)*

80

82

83

Figs. 82, 83. As the search continued for new ways to control the proliferation of ornament, "good taste" came to be linked with less ornament, and with greater abstraction of that ornament. Patterns based upon the strawberry and daisy pattern, F. E. Hulme, *Suggestions in Floral Design,* 1880.

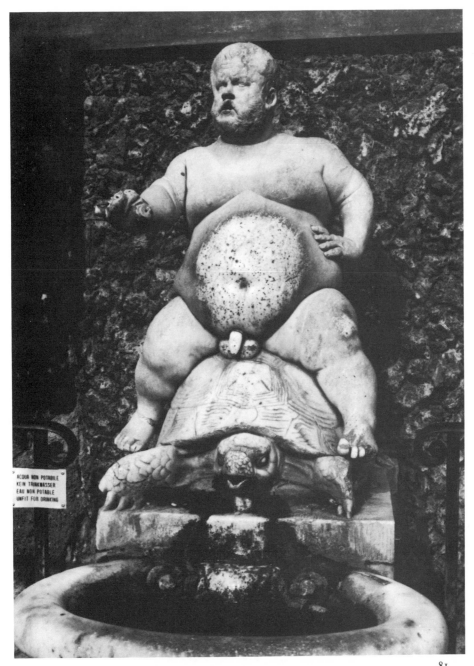

81

Fig. 81. The opposition to representational ornament eventually led reformers to forbid shading even conventionalized forms, for fear of "dishonestly" implying the third dimension. In a preview of 20th-century attitudes, Viollet-le-Duc equated Abstract with Rational (the Good) and Realistic with Irrational (the Bad). An ornament might be amusing and attractive, but if it was also realistic, like this fountain in the grounds of the Pitti Palace, Florence, it was not within the legitimate province of decorative art.

Fig. 84. The Roman acanthus and scroll imitated nature too exactly for Owen Jones, becoming graphically confusing and therefore less decorative.

84

steady march toward abstraction, and away from popular realism, meant that the most comprehensible ornaments—those most readily appreciated by the general public—suffered the greatest criticism. By the last decade of that century, virtually all semblance to nature was abandoned by "progressive" designers, and abstract form itself became the vehicle of ornament and art. [84, 85, 86]

Although hindsight may indicate a fairly direct line from realism, to abstraction, to the banishment of ornament, its elimination was the farthest thing from the minds of these men. [87, 88] In spite of decades of rejection in the marketplace, the ornament of these nineteenth-century reformers did no great violence to traditional expectations; it generally retained a flavor of the historical styles, as well as being naturalistic enough so that its sources would have been apparent to even the unsophisticated viewer. Perhaps the most extreme position was held by Viollet-le-Duc, who seems to have presaged Adolf Loos's famous link between ornament and barbarism by equating Abstraction with Rational (Good) and Realism with Irrational (Bad).[72] When we think of abstraction in art, however, the images that automatically flash before our mind's eye are far more extreme than anything these artists or critics could have imagined. Morris could not abide forms that had been sucked dry of meaning through abstraction. And Ruskin only envisioned its selective use; a hierarchy ranging from realism in the highest ornamental forms, to complete abstraction in the lowest. The reformers never intended to banish ornament, nor did they consciously consider obliterating the past. They only wanted to educate the market.

85

Fig. 85. "It will be noted," wrote Walter Crane, "that those primitive sources to which we may trace motives in ornament design [are] afterwards developed on purely ornamental [i.e., nonnaturalistic] lines, and because of their ornamental value." This Nuristani grave ornament derives from a horse's head. Horses were feared and respected by the mountain tribesmen of Nuristan, whose native terrain was too high and rugged for them, and whose only contact with the animals came from battling mounted plainsmen. 20th-century gravemarker, Kunar River Valley, northeastern Afghanistan.

86

Fig. 86. Most Middle Eastern and Oriental decorative art was admired by 19th-century observers in part because it was abstract. Ironically, some Middle Eastern ornament that appears to be a frank expression of structure is not honest at all. The pattern of brick joints on this vault is painted on mud plaster, and, as close examination will show, has little or nothing to do with their structure. Bazaar, Shiraz, Iran.

87

88

Figs. 87, 88. Modernism has taught us to be wary of history, which leads us to focus on pedigrees of ornament—is it Louis XIV, Greek, Chinoiserie?—rather than on how that ornament influences the way we see things. In purely visual terms, ornament generally operates in one of two ways. It can set something apart from its context: as a "jewel," which becomes a focal point (87); or it can unify an entire composition, as an edge ornament, which defines the boundaries of a facade composition (88).

The Visual Factor

The principles of design bathed aesthetic matters in the beatific light of Truth, providing a useful tool with which to bring the importance of the designer's taste to the attention of an often inattentive audience. The earnestness with which these principles were presented does not alter the use to which they were put: they served as a diversion, to shift attention away from the arena of *taste* in which design choices continued to be made.

Precisely because these choices continued to be matters of taste, designers continued to base them upon visual criteria. Consequently the craft of design—the guidelines by which designers disposed form, color, and texture to achieve effects that pleased their taste—was still necessary, and continued to be explored and refined. [89, 90] It should not come as a surprise, therefore, to find that discussions about design morality were frequently interwoven with thoughtful observations on how to achieve a particular visual effect, frequently including detailed descriptions of the proper disposition of colors, the superiority of certain kinds of lines or forms, etc. These were *visual* solutions to a *visual* problem: How to achieve "beautiful" effects—that is, effects *pleasing to one's own taste.* This involved principles of *craft* rather than *ideology,* and continued a line of craft literature going back to Vitruvius and beyond.

It is in these practical accompaniments to the principles of design that we find the beginning of a new way of seeing the visual problems designers have always faced. Toward the end of the century, these writings began to take on a novel aspect, an assumption that designers could succeed using abstract motifs, where before they had relied on the inspiration of either nature or the historical styles. This revolutionary approach to the craft of design complemented the moral principles by providing the technical means to accomplish what the latter had come to advocate: the rejection of popular taste in the arts of design.

One example of this new approach is found in Franz Sales Meyer's *Handbook of Ornament* (1894). In the introduction to the first English edition, a lecturer at the National Art School noted that personal

89

Fig. 89. All ornament, whether geometric, curvilinear, flat, or three-dimensional, conveys some kind of feeling. Walter Crane's notion of "expressive line" (as opposed to expressive content) suggested that feeling could be evoked by abstractions, as well as by the more realistic, traditional styles. This encouraged the idea that popular styles could be abandoned without losing any of the communicative power of decoration. Hence the iron support of Otto Wagner's Karlsplatz Station, in Vienna, does not rely on historical precedent to convey its message. Indeed, unlike traditional supports, it does not even "push up." It is "heavy," but its weightiness is unrelated to the task at hand; the support actually sags, as though it had been heated to a plastic state, cooling only after it began to flow.

90

Fig. 90. This twisted column, from the Russian Church on the Matildenhöhe Hill in Darmstadt, conveys a different feeling. Its crisp profile is tailored—almost machinelike—and it is appropriately rigid in its role as support.

experience had already proven this book to be a valuable teaching aid.[73] The most interesting aspect of the *Handbook,* and the source of its real value to designers, lay in its unique organization: "No other book, published either in England or abroad, can compare with it, for the amount of illustration it contains, or for the order with which its contents are arranged." Unlike earlier tomes, such as Jones's *Grammar,* Meyer's relatively modest volume was not sub-divided into historical cubbyholes. Instead, it catalogued ornament according to its visual characteristics ("curvilinear" versus "geometric," for example) and/or the visual uses to which these various categories could be put (borders, panels, center ornaments, etc.). [91–104] The first section of the book was devoted to Geometric Elements, Natural Objects, and Artificial Elements; the second examined Bands, Supports, Enclosed Ornaments or Panels, Repeating Ornaments, and Free Ornaments (designs that ended repetitive patterns); the third included Utensils, Weapons, Furniture, Jewelry, and similar objects, all of which were illustrated in groupings of type rather than style. The effect of this arrangement was to steer readers away from thinking of ornament in terms of the conventional, historical styles, and to emphasize the way individual elements were perceived.[74] [105, 106]

A few years after the English edition of Meyer's *Handbook* appeared, Walter Crane's *Line and Form* (1921) marked a revolutionary expansion of the designer's horizon along these same lines. This fascinating and visually perceptive volume implied that the power to move the viewer emotionally, which had always resided in the associative aspects of traditional, representational ornament, could as well be assumed by *abstract, content-less* line and form. Crane did not advocate the rejection of either history or nature, but the implications of his ideas for attitudes toward ornament were remarkably far-reaching in this respect. Until then, the ability to evoke emotion had been associated, by both public and designer, with the "styles": sober, Doric strength, effusive Rococo, austere, Romanesque power, etc. Now this reservoir of communicative power could be tapped by the simple manipulation of line and form. Historical and nature-based forms, so beloved by the middle classes, were now no longer necessary.

91

92

Figs. 91, 92.   With or without specific cultural associations, ornament can change our perception of a form. A tower of stone can be a gossamer affair, almost seeming to soar (91) Cologne Cathedral (1248); or it can be a phlegmatic, immovable presence (92) Worms Cathedral (1110–81). It all depends on the treatment of the decoration.

93

Fig. 93.   A building can appear longer and lower than it is by the careful emphasis of horizontals. Robie House, by Frank Lloyd Wright, 1908–9. (*Photograph by Eva Zeisel*)

Fig. 97. The densest stone turns to taffy under the mason's chisel. English parish church, Countisbury, North Devon.

Fig. 94. The weight of a marble column is denied as the shadows cast by its fluting eat away at its solidity.

Figs. 95, 96. A container can sag under the weight of its contents (95), or actively contest the forces of inertia, which try to keep it in place (96).

Fig. 98. A perfectly stable structure conveys a sense of rhythmic movement through the repetition of the arch and the shadow lines of the moldings that compose it.

Fig. 99. Heavy bricks become heavier when grouped in large, make-believe rustications. If the mortar between their courses is recessed, to make horizontal striations, they become lighter; and they are still less weighty when they are turned into a paper-thin plane.

Figs. 100, 101. The shape of a pot is negated by a calligraphic ornament which runs from edge to edge (100), reinforced by a similar ornament which follows the rim (101).

102

103

101

Figs. 102, 103.   A wall plane can be reinforced by a repetitive geometric pattern (102), or dissolved by faceted mirror work or mosaic (103) 19th-century shrine, Shiraz, Iran.

104   Fig. 104.   Roof cresting, pinnacles, crockets, and other devices break up the silhouette of Amiens Cathedral, and reduce the apparent bulk of this huge structure by feathering its mass into the sky.

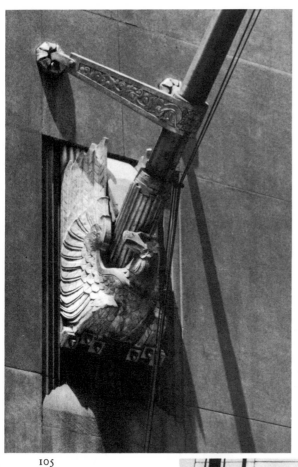

105

Figs. 105, 106. Ornament can express an emotion or sentiment through association: the American eagle, for example (105). Or it can evoke a visceral response through our anthropomorphic association with the implied movement or gesture of a line, as Geoffrey Scott pointed out so eloquently in *The Architecture of Humanism*. There is a sense of agitation and excitement in the movement implied by this Art Nouveau pattern (106). All ornaments are capable of speaking to us in this way; some are simply more articulate than others. Entrance to apartment building at Linke Wienzeile 38, by Otto Wagner, 1898–9.

106

The potential of abstract forms to convey emotion had been noted at least as early as the eighteenth century. In *The Analysis of Beauty* (1753), the painter William Hogarth suggested that the serpentine line might be the key to pictorial beauty (although the "S" curve of the serpentine line was directly associated with natural forms). And most nineteenth-century designers took it for granted that agitated forms were exciting, while broad, smooth ones were calming. But Crane's book came after a half-century of failure at trying to influence taste, and his message presented itself to eyes that were ready for a new way of seeing.

The notion that abstract form was capable of transporting the onlooker without the aid of historical associations added another weapon to the designer's arsenal in the battle against conventional taste. Like the principles, the ability of abstract form to evoke emotion held the promise of release from an intolerable situation: escape from the demands placed upon designers by the market. Crane's "expressive line" offered a tailor-made tool which seemed to enable designers to reach the public in the same way the "styles" always had, but without resorting to debased, decorative vocabularies that had been vulgarized by commercialism. One of the great decorative artists of his time, and a lover of fine ornament of all periods and styles, Crane had made an unwitting and invaluable contribution to the banishment of all traditional ornament by diverting attention from the real problem designers faced: the market's intractable love affair with historical styles and naturalistic ornament.[75]

With a few, rare exceptions, the will of the artist had always been subordinated to the will of the patron in the history of art. If this did not create as much strain as we might expect, it was largely because they and their patrons had similar artistic values. This mutually supportive arrangement disintegrated with the emergence of a vast and relatively uneducated mass market of art consumers—yet the subordinate position of the artist remained the same. The invention of a formal philosophy of art, at the end of the eighteenth century, changed this situation dramatically. The artist—in theory, at least—was now in charge; the burden of accommodation lay with the public. They had the opportunity to improve themselves through the experience of Art as defined by the values of the artist/genius; if they did not take advantage of it, well, what could one expect of the boorish bourgeois?

There is no question that decorative art reformers profited from observing how the fine arts had been extricated from the thicket of the marketplace. In sympathetic resonance with their prestigious sister arts, the reformers adopted a similar approach, and went about trying to accomplish their aim through the adoption of the "principles," which amounted to a streamlined philosophy of design for the "lesser" arts. As esoteric as they sounded, the principles served a very practical purpose. If the market refused to accept your taste on its aesthetic merit, the only alternative was to present it in less easily rejectable terms. The "honesty" and "dishonesty" that came to be so closely associated with the principles did double duty. Superficially, these characterizations established the relative "virtue" of a design (in non-visual terms), while in reality they were codewords for "aesthetically pleasing" and "aesthetically displeasing."

The principles of design provided an intellectual foundation for the decorative arts, lending them a prestige these lesser arts had never enjoyed before. By the middle of the nineteenth century, qualities that had previously been the jealously guarded attributes of painters and sculptors began to be assigned to artisans. In a process remarkably similar to that undergone a century earlier by the fine arts, the function of the "baser" senses in the appreciation of the ornamental arts was slowly reassessed and found to be of secondary importance. "Beauty" was no longer dependent solely upon the skill of the hand and eye. Although visual considerations could never be totally ignored, they could be relegated to a position of lesser importance. The redeeming value of ornament, it was said, lay not in the way it teased and pleased the eye, nor even in its literal or symbolic message. If an object, or a building, displeased, according to William Morris, the most famous reformer-artist of the last century, the ultimate blame fell not on the designer's inadequate aesthetic sensibilities—a lack of feeling for color, or a bad "eye" for proportion—but on his or her ignoble motivation. Goods fabricated for commerce or war rather than for the purer pleasure of artistic creation were, in Morris's terms, "dishonest," and therefore incapable of being beautiful."[76] In a curious turn, those who sought to elevate the design arts had once again reaffirmed the ancient idea that appearance was but a pale reflection of more significant forces.

Never, before Pugin, had this kind of morally-based, nonvisual principle been employed as a guide in matters of taste. And for good reason. Nonvisual rules had not been needed as long as those whose opinions mattered could come to some general agreement about what was "beautiful." Once that became impossible—that is, once the market had been taken over by a public whose taste differed significantly from that of the design elite—the "principles" became the only means by which the reformers could try to convince the consumer that theirs was the "correct" taste. The increasing reliance on moral and intellectual premises in the minor arts was perhaps the clearest measure of the degree of difficulty the reformers encountered. As the ultimate weapon of an embattled minority, the priceless value of the principles lay in the appearance of reason and morality that they lent to personal aesthetic preferences. They were, in short, the primary means of shoring up the professionals' faltering defenses in a self-proclaimed holy war against the taste of an indifferent, often hostile public. The rich harvest of nineteenth-century principles provided ample seed for the art ideologies that have proliferated in our own time, and we are so accustomed to hearing intellectual justifications for visual preferences that it is difficult for us to see the novelty of that approach.[77]

Commonly held up to the public as rules which, when followed carefully, almost automatically yielded "good" design, the principles were actually *ex post facto* rationalizations. They have invariably been invoked to impose a style, not to create one. While generations of nineteenth- and twentieth-century designers have sworn that a sacred and indissoluble link existed between ideology and form, between principles and practice, that relationship has been little more than a marriage of

Fig. 107. One must not take 19th- or 20th-century ideas of utility or functionalism at their word. They never actually determined the appearance of a building or an object. The principles have been used in poetical and suggestive ways by various reformers of the past two centuries in an effort to cajole an uncooperative, often disinterested public into accepting the designers' idea of beauty. By now nearly everyone will admit that the physical requirements of any design program —whether a hospital or a teapot— can be clothed in an infinite variety of different skins. The Woolworth Building, by Cass Gilbert (1913), shown with a more recent neighbor.

convenience. The principles have been ritualistically invoked to rational- ize the birth of every chosen style from Gothic Revival to postmodern- ism. They were intended to reassure the more conservative world outside the design elite that there were, in fact, sensible, logical, even scientific, reasons which explained why the familiar objects of everyday life now had to look different. [107]

Fig. 108. Once an ideology, or set of principles, is attached to a particular style, it tends to become identified with the characteristics of that style, whether it be Art Nouveau or Miesian modern. A contemporary architectural journal described the Singer Building (New York, 1907; architect Ernest Flagg) as an Art Nouveau structure, whose form was the logical outcome of a rational interest in purely functional concerns, while the purveyors of modernism (also labeled "rational" and "functional") would more likely have thought of it as an embodiment of sentimental expressionism.

In only one sense did the principles have a real effect on the way things looked. Because they offered a new category of rules, whose authority came from morality rather than from traditional visual judgments, they made it possible to consider challenging the traditional rules —the historical styles. And this presented designers with an option that had been unimaginable before, to abandon history, and therefore ornament.

By using a cloth woven of moral and intellectual dogma to camouflage their revulsion at bourgeois taste, nineteenth- and twentieth-century designers could sustain the remarkable illusion that taste—an elusive commodity molded by a complex mixture of social and aesthetic values—played no role whatsoever in their design decisions. [108] That assumption, in turn, eventually made it possible to argue for something so universally unpopular as the abolition of all ornament, without ever touching upon taste.

Today, we are far enough removed from the pronouncements of the early modernists to understand their predicament. Popular styles such as Art Deco needed no ideological phalanx to force their way into people's hearts and homes. But the various offshoots of modern design, from the International style on, have not been wholeheartedly embraced by the "Public." Like Pugin a century before, modernists were well aware of their position, and intuitively recognized that they would do well to remove the matter of aesthetic preferences from the realm of aesthetics. Without impugning the sincerity of their beliefs, we can see how the proponents of that anti-traditional style—genuinely convinced of the rightness of their cause and the moral superiority of their approach to design—could fervently believe that they had little choice but to use ideology to coerce nonbelievers into submission.

The Middle-Class Connection

The taste of the middle classes, despised by the artistic elite, brought on the creation of "principles of design." It is not surprising, therefore, that the nineteenth-century reform movement began in England, then the most powerful commercial and industrial nation in the world, with the most formidable middle class. William Makepeace Thackeray succinctly pointed out the problem faced by English artists when he compared their position to that of their French counterparts:

> These young men [French art students] (together with the students of sciences) comport themselves towards the sober citizen pretty much as the German *bursch* toward the *philister,* or as the military man, during the empire, did to the *pékin*—from the height of their poverty they look down upon him with the greatest imaginable scorn—a scorn, I think, by which the citizen seems dazzled, for his respect for the arts is intense. The case is very different in England, where a grocer's daughter would think she made a mésalliance by marrying a painter, and where a literary man (in spite of all we can say against it) ranks

below that class of gentry composed of the apothecary, the attorney, the wine-merchant, whose positions, in country towns at least, are so equivocal.[78]

De Tocqueville analyzed the impact of this newly powerful middle class on the design arts, and his insight laid bare the raw core of the problem that faced reformers. In aristocracies, said de Tocqueville, the artisan had a limited but fairly dependable market for his goods, and was therefore interested in preserving his reputation through the high quality of his work. The concern for quality of design and workmanship became strained in democratic societies, because there were always

a large number of men whose fortune is upon the increase, but whose desires grow much faster than their fortunes: and who gloat upon the gifts of wealth in anticipation, long before they have the means to command them. Such men are eager to find some short cut to these gratifications, already within their reach. . . . *The artisan readily understands these passions, for he himself partakes in them.* (my emphasis)[79]

Although this new class was eager to possess the symbols of high social standing, their means were relatively limited. To meet the demand, therefore, artisans lowered the prices of their goods either by "ingenious" methods of production, or by making products that were "nearly similar" in quality and design, but actually of less value: "Thus the democratic principle not only tends to direct the human mind to the useful arts, but it *induces the artisan to produce with great rapidity a quantity of imperfect commodities, and the consumer to content himself with these commodities"* (my emphasis).[80]

If they did not put it so concisely, the reformers did recognize that the problem lay in the makers' greed and the ignorance and impatience of the buyer. The ineffectiveness of their efforts to change this was laid to various causes: uneducated people were forced to buy cheap goods because nothing better was offered; manufacturers had failed in their societal duties by not hiring the most talented, best-trained designers; and those who had been trained in the design schools refused to go into industry because the life of the fine art artist offered a chance for greater fame and wealth. Another explanation might also have been offered, namely, that the goods produced by the Arts and Crafts movement were quite expensive compared to mass-produced products. Hermann Muthesius, who later helped to found the German Werkbund, noted that English craft pieces often cost as much as ten times more than mass-produced versions of the same item—because they were produced as though they were works of art.[81]

As the market steadfastly refused to have its taste "improved," the reformers' wrath focused increasingly on ornament because ornament had "become the metaphor of Art, and of Art as the symbol or visible token of wealth."[82] The object of their concern was plain from the way the reformers wielded their prime weapon, the principles. These were fixed in a hierarchy with the clear-cut aim of minimizing the importance of traditional ornament. *Structure* was to be the primary determinant of design. As structure implied "purpose," *utility,* or function, was next in line. Then came the necessity of being *true to materials and techniques.* At the nether end of this chain of command came *ornament*—the glaringly obvious cause of the designers' displeasure, and the market's pleasure.

If this hierarchy sounds logical, it is probably because we have been taught to think this way, not because the progression has anything to do with the way buildings are perceived. It is the mind, not the eye, that analyzes a style into hierarchical elements. [109, 110]

Toward the end of the nineteenth century, even one of the most famous generals of the war against "bad taste" knew that the enemy still held the high ground in the marketplace. The principles of design had been touted for over fifty years when William Morris acknowledged the failure of the Arts and Crafts movement. "The world is everywhere growing uglier and more commonplace," he wrote, "in spite of the conscious and very strenuous efforts of a small group of people toward the revival of art, which are so obviously out of joint with the tendency of the age that, while the uncultivated have not even heard of them, the

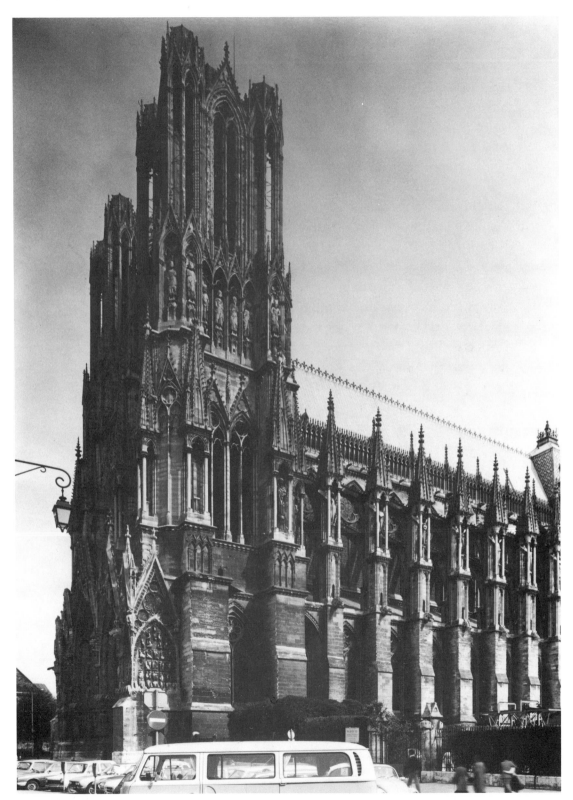

110

Figs. 109, 110. Those who wanted to control the use of ornament lodged it at the bottom of the hierarchy of elements to be considered when designing. But a building, regardless of style, is perceived as a whole, a combination of elements that includes massing, plan, structure, color, materials, *and ornament.* Different aspects dominate, depending upon the vantage point. The massing of Reims Cathedral is most important when seen from some distance; the closer you come, the more its decorative sculpture and other small-scale details take precedence.

mass of the cultivated look upon them as a joke, and even that they are now beginning to get tired of."[83]

The artist as giver of rules rather than follower of popular artistic convention became a familiar image in the arts of design. The stigma that had already marked "Popular" art in the eighteenth century had now become so obtrusive that artists who achieved popular success came away with the uneasy feeling they had somehow betrayed their own kind. Instant popularity, commented Oscar Wilde, invariably made the artist question whether "in its creation he had really been himself at all."[84] The ever present fear of being "conventional"—of pandering to middle-class taste rather than being "true" to one's own creative genius—encouraged the annoyingly persistent, self-serving, and fallacious myth which E. H. Gombrich has called "the romantic fairytale that great artists were always derided and rejected by their contemporaries."[85]

As the century drew to a close the rebellion against middle-class values—what sociologist Herbert Gans has called the "marked disdain for ordinary people and their aesthetic capacities"—became the artistic norm.[86] And, according to Wilde, artists gained prestige in almost direct proportion to the violence of the public's denunciation of their work.[87]

Under these circumstances, it was hardly possible that the economic system responsible for degrading art could have escaped direct criticism for long, not to speak of the middle classes which had grown fat on that system. It is understandable that many important figures in the English arts found a congenial philosophical haven in socialism: Ruskin, Morris, Shaw, and Wilde, among others. "The tap-root of all this mischief," wrote John Ruskin about design education in England, "is in the endeavor to produce some ability in the student to make money by designing for manufacture."[88] Socialism seemed to offer a plausible alternative to an economic system that had proven its baseness by undermining both the beauty and the virtue of the arts. Society's power over artists, which denied them the all-important freedom of creativity, was proof enough of the uncivilized state of affairs.[89] The only reason there was good poetry in England, quipped Wilde, was because the public had no interest in it.[90] The arts needed only to await the golden age of socialism to blossom again. Once that had happened, society could not fail to recognize the importance of freedom in the arts, and artists would be released from the iron grip of the marketplace.[91]

The Reversal

By the beginning of this century, vitriolic anti-middle-class sentiment had boiled to the surface in all the arts—"an [artists'] army of propagandists" composed of a "galaxy of exuberant young men" was occupied with the overthrow of the values by which bourgeois society was governed.[92] Their strategy: Breach its formidable battlements by shock attack; ridicule its values by inverting inviolable conventions. [111, 112] Jacques Barzun describes the battle plan as carried out in the literature of the time: Ibsen showed that truth was really murderous, a flimsy disguise for selfishness; Nietzsche called for the Transvaluation of All Values; and, wrote Shaw, "Do not do unto others as you would have them do unto you; you may not have the same tastes."[93]

The salvos of artistic wrath that were aimed at popular taste in the design arts were guided by the same tactic of inversion, and offer dramatic confirmation of the deep hostility toward middle-class values, for they amounted to nothing less than a frontal assault on the popular understanding of "Beauty." Nineteenth-century art lovers had either ignored technical forms (bridges, railroad stations, etc.), considering these manifestations of progress to be beneath the realm of art, or had condemned them as outright abominations. Indeed, one of the main purposes of ornament had been to cover them up, to clothe their bare bones in "beauty" the way feathers disguise the awkward skeleton of a bird. At the turn of the century, the artistic elite confounded convention by reversing the definition of "good taste." Between roughly 1890 and 1910, "beauty" became "ugliness" and "ugliness" became "beauty." History and nature, the wellsprings of beauty for cultured Victorian gentlemen and ladies, became synonymous with ugliness—symbols of aesthetic degeneracy—while industrial and technological forms, which had been non-art at best, the epitome of ugliness at worst, were transformed into the very measure of beauty.

DEEPDALE VIADUCT, ON THE SOUTH DURHAM AND LANCASHIRE UNION RAILWAY —SEE PRECEDING PAGE

112

All those who set out along this new course navigated according to charts sketched out by the English Arts and Crafts movement. The guiding principle was that the "spirit of the times" would create an architecture "of the times," and that this would develop of its own accord, if only designers would abide by the principles rather than catering to convention. The indifference to accepted models offered a "virgin-birth" view of design, which naturally and irresistibly led to the rejection of traditional ornament.

The realization of an inevitable, "modern" style was linked to the rational, functionally based process of design by which engineers were presumed to have created the technical marvels of their day. If mere technicians could achieve such glorious results, why not architects? Simply lay out the functional requirements of a given problem and accommodate them. This virtually autonomous process implied a guarantee of success, the final result being "truth instead of [traditional] beauty."[94]

Figs. 111, 112. In the final hostile gesture toward the middle class, the artistic elite reversed the definition of "beauty" 180 degrees. What had been beautiful for the 19th-century art lover—historical styles and natural forms (111)—became symbols of degeneracy; and the forms of technology and industry (112), considered non-art by the cultured of the last century, became the embodiment of beauty.

Fig. 113.   Conventional ornament was abandoned by some designers at the beginning of this century, but ornament per se was not. Otto Wagner began his professional life in the early 1860s, and for decades used the popular historical styles as his guide. This Viennese apartment house at Universitätsstrasse 12, complete with rustication, scrolls, and shields, was built in 1889. Within a few years of its completion, Wagner, like many of his contemporaries, had abandoned conventional decoration, while continuing to design highly ornamented buildings.

113

By the turn of the century, those who continued to advocate a style that would be free of historical contamination had come to view the engineer's work differently from the early reformers. Bathrooms and kitchens, not to speak of factories—all of which had been passed over as non-art—now became objects of great beauty by virtue of their utility.[95]

Although the shift in the definition of "beauty" was masked by moralistic and rationalistic rhetoric, the objective of this stunningly bold attack was clear enough. By making popular artistic conventions anathema to designers, the problem that had dogged reformers for fifty years was eradicated in a single stroke.[96]

Such a remarkable turn about cannot be passed off as the by-product of an infatuation with technology or even a fanatical faith in Progress. An active and quintessentially negative element was involved here, almost a sore-loser perverseness in thumbing the collective artistic nose so flagrantly at accepted canons of taste.

The metamorphosis was most dramatic in those designers whose style changed in mid-career. Otto Wagner (1841–1918) is one of the clearest examples of a designer who abandoned traditional styles of decoration, but whose work remained highly ornamented. [113–128]

Fig. 114.   Built in 1898–9, the Majolica House (Linke Wienzeile 40) abounds in ornament based upon nature forms, but which is used in decidedly untraditional ways. While a gesture is made to create the traditional attic story and ground floor, the traditional division of the facade into base, shaft, and capital (according to the form of the classical orders) is seriously threatened here—literally overgrown with ornament.

114

115

Figs. 115–117.   The Majolica House (Linke Wienzeile 40). The bulk of the facade
(115) is engulfed by ornamental tentacles following their own idiosyncratic rule
rather than abiding by traditional norms. Blossoms and tendrils are splashed across
its face (116), creeping from two into three dimensions as they slide onto the
window sills, and intensifying in richness as they pool in the shadows of the
recessed balconies (117).

116

117

118

Fig. 118. (*Above*) The apartment house at Linke Wienzeile 38, completed at the same time as the Majolica House, has more conventional decorative elements, including palm fronds and medallions, but they are also used in unconventional ways. The medallions are fixed onto a band that weaves in and out between the windows. The body of the fronds slides behind this band, and a few leaves fall over it, giving an untidy impression of great immediacy. The beading, above the band and below the guttae of the sills, hints at the mechanistic ornament that will characterize Wagner's later buildings.

120

Figs. 119, 120, and 121. The Karlsplatz Station of the subway (1898–9) is rich in the new ornament of Art Nouveau, and prominently sports the sunflower, symbol of the Aesthetic movement in England.

121

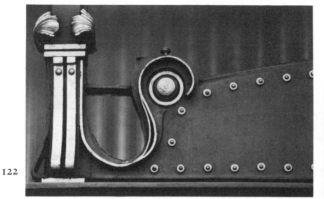

122

Fig. 122. (*Above*) The "pediment" above the entrance to the Karlsplatz Station combines naturalistic tendrils, characteristic of Art Nouveau, with decoration based literally on the nuts and bolts of construction.

Figs. 123, 124. (*Below, and right*) In the Post Office Savings Bank in Vienna (1904–6), traditional ornamental vocabularies have been exchanged by Wagner for a "modern," mechanistic one, but one that still goes about its task of embellishing in familiar ways. It changes in character as it goes from the top to the bottom of the facade, and from the outer edges to its central entrance. This is a traditional ornamental disposition, but the decorative vocabulary is anything but conventional, consisting of abstract patterns made up of aluminum bolt heads and the like.

123

125

126

127

Figs. 125, 126, and 127. In the church of Am Steinhof in Vienna (1905–7), Wagner also substituted original for traditional kinds of ornament. The "wreaths" around the attic story of the main body of the building (125), and the "swags" and their supports at the base of the dome (126), are abstract recollections of historical forerunners. The coffered soffit has a similarly innovative variation on the classical mutule, part of the Doric order. Only the angels over the main entrance (127) (by Othmar Schimkowitz), and the saints crowning its flanking towers (by Richard Luksch), although abstracted, are recognizably traditional.

Fig. 128. The fascination with nontraditional, geometric ornament extended to all aspects of Wagner's work, as we can see in this detail of a chair back, designed in 1898. (*Photograph by Brent C. Brolin. Courtesy of Galerie Metropol, New York*)

128

The defiant disregard for middle-class values, made plain by the new definition of "Beauty," was reinforced by other attitudes and events, to be sure.

- First and foremost, the moralistic, Puritanical bias inherent in Western society worked to ensure that any principles which were for "honesty" and opposed to "deception" would be given a serious and respectful audience.
- The idea of evolution—of a never-ending movement toward Progress—was already current in the early nineteenth century. Herbert Spencer, an indefatigable popularizer, applied evolutionary theory to almost every aspect of life, and the essence of evolution implicitly invalidated the past with a promise of inevitable Progress.
- Machines and other technical triumphs, which promised this material progress, became objects of an ever-increasing fascination as the century drew to a close.
- Finally, there was the designers' own personal deus ex machina: the "spirit of the times." When it was combined with the popular assumption that artists were compelled to create by an uncontrollable, inner force called *genius,* (a notion which had filtered down from the philosophies of art), it placed the responsibility for choice conveniently beyond the artist's conscious will.

Each of these factors encouraged those who hoped to undermine the foundation of legitimacy that supported tradition as the appropriate generator of new styles. But the longest-standing source of aggravation, and the prime catalyst, was the revulsion of the artistic elite at the taste and values of the middle class—the focus of English decorative art reform for over half a century. By hindsight we can see that the threat to traditional ornament was growing over the decades; but without this fundamental disrespect for middle-class values, the final banishment of traditional ornament could never have happened.

Designers of this century chose an ironic weapon to finish off traditional forms of decoration. The same sensitive souls who were horrified at the continuing plight of art at the hands of commerce chose to embrace the philistine's own prime tenet. They created a "functional style," an artistic vision of the same utilitarian ethic that had created the very factories, machines, and middle-class art-marketplace that had precipitated the disastrous decline of the design arts.

NOTES: CHAPTER VII

1. Redgrave, "On the Necessities of Principles in Teaching Design, Being an address given at the opening session of the Department of Science and Art, Oct. 1853" (London: Chapman and Hall, 1853), pp. 10–12. As was often the case, in linking science and art the reformers were following an eighteenth-century precedent. (See Gerard, *Essay on Taste,* 3rd ed., intro. by Walter J. Hipple, Jr., Scholars' Facsimiles & Reprints [1780; facsimile ed., Gainesville, Fla., 1963], p. 266.)
2. William Dyce, "Lecture on Ornament Delivered to the Students of the London School of Design, *Journal of Design and Manufacturers,* 1 (1849):65.
3. William Dyce, "Universal Infidelity in Principles of Design," *Journal of Design and Manufactures,* 6, no. 31 (1852):1.

4. Richard Redgrave, "Necessities of Principles," p. 26.

5. Eugene Emmanuel Viollet-Le-Duc, *Lectures on Architecture,* trans. by Benjamin Bucknall (1889; reprint of 1st American ed., New York, 1956), p. 208.

6. The Arts and Crafts movement, begun in the 1880s, marked perhaps the first formal attack on the classification of the arts that the abbé Batteux had put forth in 1747, and a clear breach of the line separating artist from artisan.

7. Viollet-le-Duc, *Lectures,* p. 207.

8. Ibid., pp. 182, 176.

9. Ruskin, *The Stones of Venice,* 3 vols. (New York: John Wiley, 1851), 1:44.

10. David Hume had spoken of "the spirit of the age" as affecting all the arts (using "arts" in its broader, traditional sense) but not as a tool which, once identified, could be used by the designer to determine forms. (See David Hume, *Of the Standard of Taste and Other Essays* [Indianapolis: Bobbs-Merrill, 1965], p. 50.)

11. Pugin, who tolerated only Gothic, and only a small portion of that, would hardly have condoned Jones's great admiration for Egyptian art (see Owen Jones, *Grammar of Ornament* [1856; reprint ed., New York: Van Nostrand Reinhold, 1972] chap. 2).

12. Jones, *Grammar,* pp. 1–2.

13. Ibid., p. 155ff.

14. Jones refers to his principles as "general laws," which "reign independently of the individual peculiarities of each [style]." (Jones, *Grammar,* p. 1.)

15. "PROPOSITION, *n.* In logic, one of the three parts of a regular argument. A sentence in which any thing is decreed or affirmed." From *An Explanatory and Phonographic Pronouncing Dictionary of the English Language* (New London, 1854).

16. The propositions of Owen Jones included: "2. Architecture is the material expression of the wants, the faculties, and the sentiments, of the age in which it is created. 3. As Architecture, so all works of the Decorative Arts, should possess fitness, proportion, harmony, the result of all which is repose." "5. Construction should be decorated. Decoration should never be purposely constructed." "35. Imitations, such as the graining of woods, and of the various coloured marbles, allowable only, when the employment of the thing imitated would not have been inconsistent." In the last one Jones goes farther than the "severity" of Pugin's Pointed Architecture would have permitted. (Jones, *Grammar,* pp. 5ff.)

17. Vitruvius, *The Ten Books on Architecture,* trans. Morris Hicky Morgan (reprint, New York: Dover Publications, 1960), 8.5.3–4.

18. Ibid., 8.5.4.

19. Viollet-Le-Duc, *Lectures,* p. 201.

20. Eastlake, *Hints on Household Taste* (1868, reprint ed., New York: Dover Publications, 1969), p. 36.

21. Barr Ferree, "Utility in Architecture," *Popular Science,* 37 (1890):206.

22. William Dyce, "Lecture on Ornament Delivered to the Students of the London School of Design." *Journal of Design and Manufactures,* 1 (1849):65.

23. Dyce, "Universal Infidelity," in *Journal of Design and Manufactures,* 6 (1852):2.

24. Eastlake, *Hints,* p. 19.

25. Ibid., pp. 19–20.

26. Ibid., p. 27. Although many reformers became socialists, notably Ruskin and Morris, their approach to design was distinctly aristocratic. One should not aspire to the trappings of the

rich unless, like the designers themselves, one could afford them.

27. Antonio di Tuccio Manetti, *The Life of Brunelleschi*, trans. Catherine Enggass (University Park, PA: Penn. State University Press, 1970), p. 56.

28. Walter Crane, *The Bases of Design* (London: George Bell and Sons, 1904), pp. 2.

29. Augustus Welby Northmore Pugin, *Contrasts: or A Parallel between the Noble Edifices of the Middle Ages and Corresponding Buildings of the Present Day, Shewing The Present Decay of Taste,* 2nd ed. (London: Charles Dolman, 1841), p. 1.

30. Ibid., p. 2.

31. Shaftesbury, *Miscellany,* III, in Albert Hofstadter and Richard Kuhns, eds, *Philosophies of Art & Beauty: Selected Readings in Aesthetics from Plato to Heidegger,* various trans. (Chicago: University of Chicago Press, 1976), p. 262.

32. William Hogarth, *The Analysis of Beauty: Written with a view of fixing the fluctuating ideas of taste* (London, 1752), p. 13.

33. Schopenhauer, *The World as Will and Idea,* Third Book, 2nd Aspect, Para. 43; in Hofstadter and Kuhns, *Philosophies of Art & Beauty,* p. 469.

34. Eastlake, *Hints,* pp. 166–167.

35. Alberti, *Ten Books on Architecture,* trans. Leoni (1755; reprint ed., London, 1955), p. 108.

36. Gerard, *Essay on Taste,* p. 38.

37. Pugin, *The True Principles of Pointed or Christian Architecture* (London: J. Weale, 1841), p. 67.

38. Harold Osborne, *Aesthetics and Art Theory: An Historical Introduction* (New York: Dutton, 1970), p. 45ff. Utility plays a role in the appreciation of art through the eighteenth century. As late as the 1780s, Alexander Gerard could remark that "proportion" (by which he meant the relationship of parts) "as in the general aptitude of the structure to the end proposed" had a direct influence on our perception of beauty. (Gerard, *Essay on Taste,* p. 33.)

39. Pugin, *True Principles,* p. 18. See also p. 21, where he speaks of ancient Gothic artists who rendered "the useful a vehicle for the beautiful."

40. Eastlake, *Hints,* p. 91.

41. Only Ralph Wornum, who supported the government Schools of Design against the criticism after the Great Exhibition, held a view that seemed to disregard this tenet of design. "Beauty depends on the arrangement, not on the materials. . . ." (Ralph Wornum, "The Government Schools of Design," *Art Union Journal* 4 [London, Jan., Feb. 1852]:37.)

42. Viollet-le-Duc, *Lectures,* p. 202. Ironically Pugin, one of the main proponents of honesty of materials, was so taken by the emotionalism of his beloved Gothic architecture that he lost sight of his own principles and "was content to have thin walls and plaster vaults and ornaments." (*Encyclopaedia Britannica,* 11th ed., s.v. "Augustus Welby Northmore Pugin.")

43. Eastlake, *Hints,* p. 46.

44. Ibid., p. 244.

45. Ibid., pp. 47–48.

46. Ibid., pp. 46–47.

47. Ibid., p. 22.

48. Crane, *Bases of Design,* p. 6.

49. "M. Beule on Greek Polychromy," *American Architect* 1 (1877) pp. 271–272, 278–280. Condensed from *A History of Greek Art Before Pericles.*

50. Morris, *Hopes and Fears for Art,* 5th ed. (New York: Longman, Green & Co., 1898), p. 162.

51. Eastlake, *Hints,* p. 295.
52. Leon Trotsky, *Literature and Revolution, Tatlin's Monument, 1924,* in *Architecture and Design,* pp. 101–102. Collection, The Museum of Modern Art, New York.
53. de Tocqueville, *Democracy in America,* trans. John Stuart Mill, 2 vols. (New York: Schocken Books, 1961), 2:58.
54. Dyce, "Which direction is ornamental art likely to take in this country, toward elaboration or simplicity?" *Journal of Design and Manufactures,* 6, no. 31 (1852):135.
55. Ruskin, *The Seven Lamps of Architecture* (1848; reprint, New York: The Noonday Press, 1961), p. 101.
56. Ibid., p. 102.
57. Ibid., pp. 110, 111.
58. Ibid., p. 100.
59. Ibid., p. 101.
60. Ibid., pp. 103, 112.
61. Ibid., p. 131.
62. Ibid., p. 107.
63. Ibid., pp. 129, 126.
64. Ibid., p. 137.
65. Ibid., p. 127–131.
66. Ibid., p. 126.
67. Ibid.
68. Ibid.
69. Ibid., p. 103.
70. Eastlake, *Hints,* p. 234.
71. Ibid., pp. 68, 114.
72. Viollet-Le-Duc, *Lectures,* pp. 174ff.
73. Franz Sales Meyer, *Handbook of Ornament,* ed. Hugh Stannus, 8th ed. (Montreal, Que., 1894), *pref.
74. These purely visual discussions are rare in the twentieth century. They occur seldom, if ever, in architecture—until Robert Venturi; perhaps more frequently in painting, as in the *Pedagogical Sketchbook* of Paul Klee (New York: Praeger, 1960).
75. The emphasis on form versus content would be intensified in the early decades of the 20th century by Clive Bell's theory of "significant form" (*Art* [New York: Capricorn Books, 1958]), and the writings of Roger Fry (*Vision and Design* [1924, reprint, New York: P. Smith, 1947]), whose criticism emphasized the pre-eminence of formal relations and plastic qualities in art.
76. Morris, *Hopes and Fears,* p. 60. "Commerce" equaled profit, in Morris's equation, and we are once again reminded of Aristotle's admonition against the ungentlemanly pursuit of gain.
    William Blake made a similar equation of profit and war almost a century earlier. These are a few of the inscriptions on his engraving of the *Laocoön Group* (1820), taken from Jacques Barzun, *The Use and Abuse of Art,* Bollingen Series XXXV· 22 (Princeton: Princeton University Press, 1974), pp. 35–6:

    The Eternal Body of Man is The Imagination, that is, God himself. . . . It manifests itself in his [man's] Works of Art.

Good and Evil are Riches and Poverty. Where any view of Money exists, Art cannot be carried on, but War only. . . .

A Poet, a Painter, a Musician, an Architect: the Man or Woman who is not one of these is not a Christian.

Christianity is Art and not Money. Money is its Curse.

The Whole Business of Man Is the Arts, and All Things Common. . . .

Art is the Tree of Life . . . Science is the Tree of Death.

77. The past few decades have seen the growth of "conceptual art," in which the artist merely writes about the idea, and does not need to execute the work.

78. William Makepeace Thackeray, "On the French School of Painting," *The Paris Sketch Book* . . . (Boston: Lee & Shepard, 1888), p. 44.

79. De Tocqueville, *Democracy in America,* 2:58.

80. Ibid., 2:59.

81. Hermann Muthesius, "The Development of the English House" (1904–5), in Tim Benton, Charlotte Benton, and Dennis Sharp, eds., *Architecture and Design: 1890–1939* (New York: Whitney Library of Design, 1975), pp. 34, 35.

82. E. H. Gombrich, "Visual Metaphors of Value in Art," *Meditations on a Hobby Horse: And Other Essays on the Theory of Art* (3rd ed. New York: Phaidon Press, 1978), p. 19.

83. William Morris, *The Aims of Art* (London: Strangeways & Sons, 1887), p. 14.

84. Oscar Wilde, *The Soul of Man Under Socialism* (Portland, Me.: Thomas B. Mosher, 1909), p. 51.

85. Gombrich, "Art and Scholarship," *Meditations on a Hobby Horse,* p. 108.

86. Herbert Gans, *Popular Culture and High Culture* (New York: Basic Books, 1974), p. 61.

87. Wilde, *Soul of Man,* p. 52.

88. Ruskin, *Laws of Fiesole,* in *The Works of John Ruskin,* ed. E. T. Cook and A. Wedderburn (39 vols., London: George Allen, 1903–12), 15:344.

89. Wilde, *Soul of Man,* p. 64.

90. Ibid., p. 45.

91. Ibid., pp. 7, 64. The attraction of socialism for men so different as Morris and Wilde does not mean they necessarily had similar views of the role of the artist in society. Morris, for example, had a loathing for the elite avant garde who "communicated only with one another as though they were the possessors of some sacred mystery." Quoted in Barzun, *Use and Abuse of Art,* pp. 83–4.

92. Barzun, *Use and Abuse of Art,* pp. 49–50.

93. Ibid., p. 50.

94. Theo Van Doesburg, "The Will to Style," in Benton, Benton, and Sharp, eds., *Architecture and Design,* pp. 34, 35, and 94.

95. Muthesius, "The Development of the English House," in Benton, Benton, and Sharp, eds., *Architecture and Design,* p. 35.

96. Artistic problems are frequently solved by avoiding them. When I was a student, John Hedjuk pointed out to me that one of the most difficult design problems the architect faces—again and again—is that of breaking into the facade of a building to create an entrance. Le Corbusier often solved this problem by not breaking the facade at all but lifting the building on his famous *piloti* and entering from underneath.

CHAPTER VIII

Ornament in Disguise:
The Twentieth Century

Pre-"Modernist" Modern Ornament

Because we think of the 1920s as a seminal era—the time when the
ornamental past was eclipsed by the birth of the new style—we tend to
see the preceding decades as having led directly to that watershed, a time
when decoration was slowly but inevitably being exorcised. That was not
the case. Although designers of the late nineteenth and early twentieth
centuries were frequently revolted by the public's seemingly unqualified
love of ornament, their wrath was not directed at all ornament (at least
not at first) but at popular preferences for the traditional, ornamented
styles.

To see that ornament was not abandoned when our "modern,"
nontraditional styles first came on the scene at the turn of this century,
we need only look at the most famous of them. Known as *Art Nouveau*
in France, Liberty in England, and *Jugendstil* in Austria and Germany, it
flourished from the 1880s to World War I. The style was an original
approach to decoration in that it abandoned the more literal historical
precedents of the traditional decorative styles, and, in the hands of some,
stretched the image of nature almost beyond the limits of recognition.

The existence of Art Nouveau is critical to our discussion because it was an avowedly modern style that was also enthusiastically ornamental. In this sense, its tendrils were firmly attached to the world of the nineteenth-century reformers, who only objected to decoration that displayed "bad" (i.e., middle-class) taste. [129, 130]

But there is a more subtle point that is equally important. When we approach Art Nouveau from our side of history, so to speak, its originality seems to lie in its whiplash violence and ornamental abandon. While these qualities did not go unnoticed in its day, we tend to overemphasize them, for we view that explosion of decorative energy over the ornamentally barren plain of modernism. Had our initial sighting come via a different route—through the more taxing foothills of decorative Victoriana, for example—the flamboyance of Art Nouveau would surely have seemed less startling. From that hypothetical vantage point, its most revolutionary aspect would not have been its extraordinary exuberance, for much of the ornament of that era was exuberantly rich, but its lack of mass. The German architect Gottfried Semper expressed the typical mid-nineteenth-century view of the correct nature of architecture when he remarked on the impossibility of making it out of iron—There would be nothing there! It would be transparent! Just space![1] We are so accustomed to seeing massively solid buildings magically dissolved by steel and glass that it is difficult for us to appreciate this most surprising aspect of Art Nouveau: the dissolution of mass by the supreme celebration of line.

Despite the impression many of us received from courses in the history of early modern architecture, decoration continued to flourish—even among leaders in the field—well into our century. Louis Sullivan was known to my generation of architecture students primarily as the author of the phrase "Form follows function." He was also a consummate ornamentist. [131] And Frank Lloyd Wright's decorative work compares favorably with the finest examples of earlier periods, although this was hardly mentioned in polite artistic circles until quite recently. [132]

129

Figs. 129, 130.   Art Nouveau was the first modern ornament—that is to say, the first ornament not easily identified with an earlier, historical style. Like most other styles, it was based upon an infatuation with certain lines and forms, and was indulged in with a noticeable lack of interest in the "nature" of the material being used. These stone balconies look as though they could be made of fabric stretched over wire frames. The nearby railing shows the same curves—in wrought iron.

131

132

Fig. 131.   (*Above left*) Although the rhetoric of the day opposed traditional styles, virtually all the work of the most respected and avant-garde architects before World War I looks remarkably traditional in its use of ornament. Bayard Building, New York; architect Louis Sullivan,   .

Fig. 132.   (*Above right*) Frank Lloyd Wright was also a consummate ornamentist, who used his original two-dimensional surface decoration in traditional ways.

Fig. 133.   (*Facing page*) In modern design circles, Peter Behrens is better known for his factories than his houses. The fluted, if capital-less, shafts flanking the main entrance to this house show his interest in creating a new kind of ornament, but one which unself-consciously acknowledges a debt to tradition. Artists' colony, Darmstadt, 1901.

Notwithstanding the turn-of-the-century rhetoric about beautiful industrial forms, imperative functionalism, and the need for rational, scientific design, the pleasures of ornament continued to be part of virtually every designer's vocabulary. But there were some interesting changes relative to traditional approaches toward ornament. [133] For one thing, the more avant-garde designers—those to whom hindsight has accorded the title "visionary"—proceeded much farther along the pathway blazed by English reformers, rejecting ornament based on historical styles and/or nature in favor of a more geometric variety. We have already seen samples of the geometric decoration of Otto Wagner. The remarkable Josef Hoffmann (1870–1956) had a relentless love affair with the right angle and straight line, a passion that earned him the label "*Quadratl Hoffmann* (Hoffmann of the Squares)" in Viennese art circles. [134–137]

134

135

136

137

Figs. 134–137. The public's continuing indifference to the "good taste" of the designer made the rejection of all traditional ornament virtually inevitable. It became a reality in the turn-of-the-century work of Josef Hoffmann, who created an abstract ornament free of historical references. The plywood and bentwood deck chair (134) dated 1905 is ornamented with simple, square cutouts. The oak dining chair (135) of 1904 has been rubbed with white stain, bringing out its graining. The settee (136), part of a group including chairs and a table dated 1903–4, uses repetitive bentwood rounds to create abstract patterns like those the modernists would make twenty-five years later with steel pipe railings. These small metal pieces from 1904–5 (137) capture the "graph paper" feeling of the modern office building facade fifty years before it was invented. (*Photographs by Brent C. Brolin. Courtesy of Galerie Metropol, New York*)

138

Figs. 138, 139, and 140.   Josef Olbrich's Sezession Building, Vienna (1898), combined realistic and abstract decoration. He used the new fashion for pure geometry in a dramatic way, suspending a transparent sphere of gilded leaves between four cubic pylons.

Josef Olbrich's work also offers an instructive example of the interest in creating nontraditional yet ornamented styles.[138, 139, 140] Olbrich had an opportunity to pursue his interests in a grand manner when, around the turn of the century, the grand duke Ernst-Ludwig invited a number of artists to settle in Darmstadt to explore what was known as "total art." That very expression gives an indication of the distance traveled by the decorative artist in the one hundred or so years since "fine" art came upon the scene, for it referred to a unified style for all the arts, both fine and decorative.

139

140

141

Olbrich designed most of the buildings in the artists' colony located on a hill overlooking the small town of Darmstadt. These comprised a number of houses and a few larger structures, including the famous Wedding Tower (1908). [141–144] From our circumscribed point of view, the most interesting aspect of the then-modern Darmstadt buildings is, of course, that they were quite unself-consciously decorative. Ornament was still an unquestioned and essential ingredient in any artistic scheme that purported to be all-encompassing, although it was no longer to be tied so closely to conventions. Olbrich's work actually shows a surprising mixture of tradition and the ornamental world to come, previewing certain decorative motifs that would only be fully explored by the modernists, several decades later.

142

Fig. 141. (*Facing page*) The Olbrich houses at Darmstadt were all completed around 1901, and elements of the fashionable Art Nouveau are immediately apparent—the chimney of the Habich House (1901), for example. These are not unexpected, as the Darmstadt experiment was established as a *Jugendstil* colony. The appearance of decorative elements that would only be fully explored by modernists a quarter of a century later is more surprising (see captions 142–144).

Fig. 142. Olbrich's own house at Darmstadt has ceramic tile panels set between the windows. They imply a horizontal band continuing around the corners, which "breaks" the edges of the traditional facade—something modernists would later do with the ribbon window.

143

144

Figs. 143, 144.   Josef Olbrich's "Wedding Tower" in the Darmstadt artists' colony
(1908) mixed traditional and new ornamental approaches. The cascading tower
roof, with its concentric moldings, gives a traditional sense of symmetry—the
tower seems to have a "front," a "back," and two "sides." But this reassuring
familiarity is contradicted by a decorative device quickly identified as modernistic:
asymmetrical windows, which break around the corners of the tower, much like
the ribbon windows of the 1920s.

Modernism and the Nineteenth-Century Reformers

There were unquestionable and dramatic differences between design at the turn of the century and design in the 1920s: the turbulent curves and rich modeling of the fin de siècle subsided into calm, planar surfaces, organic forms straightened into crystalline geometry, and hues of the most delicate nuance erupted into bold primaries. These changes have often been explained by a gastronomic analogy: Like a greedy child who sickens at the sight of another chocolate sundae, designers began to gag at yet another cornice, cartouche, or gargoyle. [145]

On the face of it, this might seem a satisfactory explanation, but it only accounts for a symptom, not the illness. The irony of the matter is that, although they would have been outraged had anyone called their work "ornamental," the modernists of the 1920s did not eradicate the desire to ornament; by hindsight, we see that they simply restricted its theater of operations.

Modernists declared *traditional* ornament obsolete because, they preached, the principles of modern design would not tolerate it.[2] Nothing could be farther from the mark, as we have seen. The tenets that were supposed to have guided designers in the 1930s were identical to those that were supposed to have guided them in the 1830s. This should prompt an observation that has already been made but which bears repeating: Although presented as rules that *determined the appearance* of a design, the principles actually had no effect on what designed objects looked like, for the same ones gave us Queen Anne of the 1870s, new Brutalism of the 1950s, and virtually all styles in between. The inescapable conclusion from this observation is that designers have used these precepts to justify and rationalize preexisting style preferences rather than as a method for "determining form." Dramatic changes in the appearance of "designed" buildings and objects between, say, the 1890s and the 1920s did not happen because of new wisdom revealed by these principles, but because

145. The final rejection of traditional ornament as a symbol of middle-class society cannot be separated from the ghastly trauma of the Great War. The earnest social programs that underlay the most important art movements of the postwar decades were aimed at reforming the society that had brought on that terrible catastrophe. Karl Marx Hof, Karl Ehn, architects, Vienna, 1927–30.

of *a change in taste* that occurred for reasons that have been the object of our discussion up to this point.[3] It is not only the words which remained the same as in decades past; even certain characteristics we now associate with modernism were merely continuations of earlier practices.

While we think twentieth-century buildings look different because they use "new" materials, in many cases nineteenth- and twentieth-century designers worked with the same materials, and frequently used them in similar ways. In praising the virtues of new materials—concrete

146

Figs. 146, 147. Said Antonio Sant'Elia; "Modern constructional materials [including reinforced concrete] and the scientific idea absolutely do not lend themselves to the discipline of historical styles"—Tim Benton, Charlotte Benton, and Dennis Sharp, eds., *Architecture and Design: 1890–1939,* p. 71. But the "nature" of these new materials was never as clear-cut as modernists led the public to believe. This neo-Byzantine monastery in Washington, D.C., (146) was constructed around the same time Le Corbusier was being "true" to the nature of reinforced concrete in creating the revolutionary Villa Stein, at Garches, France (147). The monastery used rare and colorful aggregates, which were cast in place, serving as a facing for the thoroughly modern reinforced-concrete structure. (*Photograph of Villa Stein. Collection, The Museum of Modern Art, New York*)

147

and steel, for example—modernists invariably spoke of the radical new forms they "demanded"; and yet much ornament-less modern architecture was built of the same stuccoed brick that had been the mainstay of European architecture for millennia. It is true that concrete and steel were used, but they did not "demand" new forms. They adapted themselves to traditional forms as easily as to new ones. [146, 147]

The glass wall is a hallmark of modernism, yet three decades before its floor-to-ceiling plate glass became fashionable, William Morris complained that there was too much glass in the modern architecture of his own time. It was impossible to appreciate any subtlety of color in that glaring light, and providing curtains to make such rooms habitable was quite costly.

Another similarity between nineteenth- and twentieth-century designers is found in the attitudes they took toward the public at large. The paternalism of the nineteenth-century reformers is patently clear in the literature of modernism over the past eighty years; the sense of knowing what was right for everyone—if only the rest of the world was clever enough to see it too. And the reformers of both the nineteenth and twentieth centuries saw literal copying as a sign of artistic failure.

Perhaps the clearest parallel is that critics and professionals of both centuries sincerely believed they were responding rationally to the "spirit of the times," with the inescapable implication that the designer was the only one capable of discerning that spirit:

Sir Charles Eastlake, 1878: It remained for the rising generation of architects to profit by the labours of those able apologists [Ruskin and Pugin], and to show their patrons that the prevailing taste had not been called forth by the whims of a clique or the blind passion of an antiquary, but that, while based on the sound artistic principles of early tradition, it might be adapted to the social habits and requirements of the present age.[4]

Walter Gropius, 1935: . . . [the forms of the new architecture] are not the personal whims of a handful of architects avid for innovation, at all cost, but simply the inevitable logical product of the intellectual, social and technical conditions of our age.[5]

The Ornament of Modernism

A Broad Definition

Skeptics will ask, What could possibly have been ornamental about barebones modernism? The decorative palette was reduced, to be sure, but there were still ample possibilities. To begin to see the decorative elements of modernism, however, we must recognize that our definition of ornament is loaded. To imply that a "functional" form is unornamented because it is simple and geometric, for example, or because it mimics "functional" machine forms, is to fall victim to a semantic trick of the modern movement. Designs based on technical form could not be "ornamental," it was said, because they were inspired by nonornamental machines—although "functionalism" had been rationalizing ornamented styles for nearly a century by that time. [148]

Fig. 148.   Because the "machine aesthetic" was associated with unornamented machines, the highly ornamental qualities exhibited by many artifacts of that style have often been overlooked. Turntable, David Gammon, 1968; polished aluminum parts, black finish. (*Photograph by Brent C. Brolin. Courtesy of The Museum of Modern Art, New York*)

148

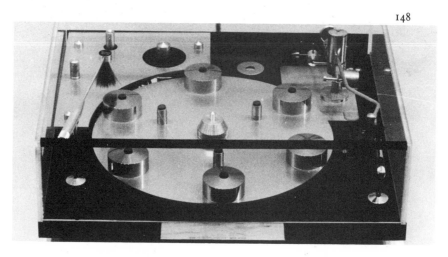

As much as definitions of ornament may vary, most people agree on a few points. In the first place, ornament is intentional; it is created on purpose, not to be confused with for a purpose. It also embellishes something. Thus a statue in a museum is not an ornament; but place it in a plaza, and it "ornaments" the space. Most people will also agree that ornament imposes visual order on the thing it embellishes. [149–152]

Beyond these rudimentary parameters lie territories virtually unexplored in our century; as a result, most contemporary views about the nature and purpose of ornament are based on ideas that are 150 years old. The most frequently encountered attitude holds that there is a difference between ornament and decoration: The former is organically related to structure, the latter is not.[6] The term "decoration" includes embellishments that relate "dishonestly" to structure; that is, which in some way could be construed as misinforming the viewer about how something was built. The folk tradition of house-painting falls under this heading, as would the sophisticated trompe l'oeil murals now in fashion. [153, 154] Such differentiation has an obvious appeal to those who cut their teeth on modernism, for it gives ornament an air of respectability by linking it to practical (i.e., functional) demands.[7]

This relatively rigid connection between "good" ornament and the system of construction seems unrealistically restrictive. Much beautiful embellishment is only coincidentally related to structure. The gorgeous mosaics of San Vitale, in Ravenna, are undeniably beautiful and ornamental. But do they "express" the structure as nineteenth-century critics felt ornament should, or is that relationship coincidental? These mosaics are populated with recognizable forms, which hover on shimmering gold backgrounds that have nothing to do with the bricks and mortar underneath. They do not reinforce the structure. They *dissolve* it. The craftsmen-artists of San Vitale were surely not instructed to "integrate" their work with the structure. Had they been given such an instruction, I am sure it would only have befuddled them. Their task was simple: to illustrate a biblical story or contemporary political reality by covering surfaces with tiny pieces of colored glass and stone. [155]

149

Fig. 149. The urge to ornament is rarely if ever suppressed in traditional societies. In a remote section of northeastern Afghanistan, some discarded batteries, the refuse of civilization, have already become the beginning of a contemporary mosaic.

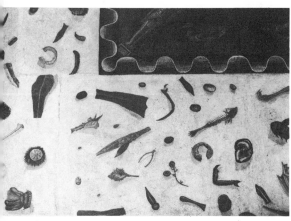

151

Figs. 150, 151, and 152. Ornament is always planned. The random lines on the side of this building—cracks in the brickwork filled by caulking—are not ornamental (150). Other kinds of contained or controlled "randomness," the seafood border around this Roman mosaic (151), or the Mondrianlike pavement from the Forum (152), are quite ornamental. (*Photograph of "shell" mosaic by Brent C. Brolin. Courtesy of The Vatican Museum*)

150

152

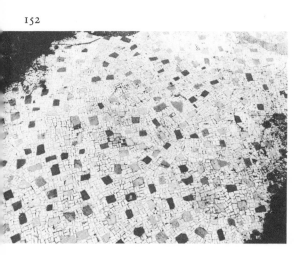

Figs. 153, 154.   Although the murals of Richard Haas are thoroughly dishonest, in 19th- and 20th-century terms, they are so beautifully done that some argue they are "art." Their country cousins, on the other hand, are generally referred to derogatorily as "decoration." Mural at exit of Lincoln Tunnel, Richard Haas, New York City, 1979; Grand pilaster and window ornament, near Wies Church, Bavaria.

Fig. 155.   (*Facing page*) The Byzantine mosaics of San Vitale do follow the compound curves of apses and the underside of arches. But does their inevitable compliance with that geometry mean the mosaicists wanted to "express" the building's structure? What else could they do? And although their decorative skin describes these surfaces precisely, it yields no information about the structure beneath. Is it brick or concrete, a welded steel armature or molded Styrofoam? And are they any less beautiful for camouflaging the structure? San Vitale, Ravenna, A.D. 526–47.

The same observation could be made about other ornamentists of the past. Was Phidias "expressing" the roof structure in the pediment sculptures that ornament the Parthenon, or was he simply filling in the leftover space with exquisitely beautiful figures rich in meaning for Athenian citizens?

Definitions of ornament that rely on a predefined relationship to one or another part of a building take too little account of the most important use of decoration, its visual effect. The quality of an ornament —is it well done or not?—should be determined by what you feel when you see it. If it delights your eye, that is sign enough of its "appropriateness." Rather than filtering our perceptions of ornament through the principles of design (almost a knee-jerk reaction by now), it would be more to the point to ask if the intention to express structure or purpose through ornament really ends up with more beautiful ornament. From the evidence of the last century, and much of the work of the present "transitional" period of postmodernism, the answer is a resounding No. Ideological approaches do not guarantee a skillful ornamentist. The most they can do is impose rules that restrict certain kinds of decoration.

As I emphasize this *visual* nature of architectural embellishment, my definition is probably broader than most. It also has no relation to the pseudomoral, pseudorational principles. My definition relies on a source rarely cited when discussing the vague ideologies of style, Noah Webster:

DECORATION: . . . that which decorates or adorns; an ornament.
ORNAMENT: . . . anything serving to adorn; decoration; embellishment.

Webster says "ornament" and "decoration" mean the same thing. For ideological reasons that originated in the nineteenth century, this definition is rarely accepted today. I take my cue from Webster, however, and use these terms interchangeably.

If you accept the dictionary definition, a curious thing happens to decoration, which some will surely find disturbing. As the criteria for judging decoration become *visual* rather than *ideological,* the moral connotations attached to decoration by both nineteenth- and twentieth-century reformers become irrelevant. Consequently, the maker of ornament is freed to do a number of things that have been frowned upon in the past century or so, such as:

- to obscure the method of construction, rather than explain how an object is made;
- to disguise the nature of the material and the techniques used to work it, rather than reinforce the "inherent" nature of a material and the techniques used to work it.

The breadth of Webster's definition has the virtue of common sense, which one often finds in the observations of the amateur. That is to say, it leaves the decision about what constitutes proper ornament to the eye, as that is the proper organ with which to make visual judgments. What William Morris once said about painting could apply as well to ornament: "A picture's either jolly well painted or it's not, and that's all there is to it."

This broad view of ornament also reflects the more flexible, traditional attitude, which assumed that virtually any object could be decorative. [156] If little was written on this vital aspect of visual life in the course of several thousand years, it was undoubtedly because no one felt the need to discuss it. As late as the nineteenth century, no less an authority than John Ruskin wrote that

the only essential distinction between Decorative and other art is in the being fitted for a fixed place; and in that place, related either in subordination or in command, to the effect of other pieces of art. And all the greatest art which the world has produced is then fitted for a place, and subordinated to a purpose. There is no existing highest-order art but is decorative. The best sculpture yet produced has been the decoration of a temple front—the best painting, the decoration of a room. Raphael's best doing is merely the wall-colouring of a suite of apartments in the Vatican, and his cartoons were made for tapestries. Correggio's best doing is the decoration of two small church cupolas at Parma; Michael Angelo's, a ceiling in the Pope's private chapel.[8]

Sharing this traditional outlook by no means limits us to traditional decorative forms. It does encourage a synthetic, rather than analytic view, however, which might eventually help reconnect the fine and decorative arts, and allow us to acknowledge the inherently ornamental character of murals, statues, bas-reliefs, and other artistic elements that we would otherwise be forced into thinking of as "works of art." It also makes it possible to confess that many of the more modest accouterments of buildings, things that seem "minimal" or "merely functional," can be used in highly ornamental ways.

In short, adopting a more flexible view of the nature of embellishment will make us aware of the variety of elements that can be a "decorative" part of architecture and design. Railings, for example, are routinely elaborated beyond simple necessity—even by modernists—and therefore, according to my definition, become "decorative." The ostensible purpose of a railing is to steady the climber, and/or to prevent falls from balconies, roofs, and stairs. The simplest, most "functional" way to accomplish this humane task would be to place a continuous horizontal bar at a "comfortable" height, with vertical supports—if warranted by the span—at the fewest possible points. Yet railings are rarely reduced to the barest "minimum," but to the minimum considered beautiful given the aesthetic canon in force. The decorative potential of their lines and shadows has rarely been ignored by sensitive designers. [157–160]

The fallacy of the view that modern design is an unornamented style becomes apparent as soon as one accepts anything broader than the

156

Fig. 156. The juxtaposition of "fine" versus "un-fine" art obscures the fact that any of the visual arts can be decorative. "The best painting," wrote John Ruskin, "[was] the decoration of a room. Raphael's best doing is merely the wall-colouring of a suite of apartments in the Vatican"—"The Two Paths." in *Works* 16:310.

most restrictive definition of ornament, particularly if that definition is based upon visual rather than ideological criteria. To take a prime example, hundreds, perhaps thousands, of miles of decorative mullions have been stuck onto steel and glass skyscrapers over the past thirty years, a new species of *applied* decoration that accomplished, in a modern vocabulary, what moldings had in the traditional styles.

157

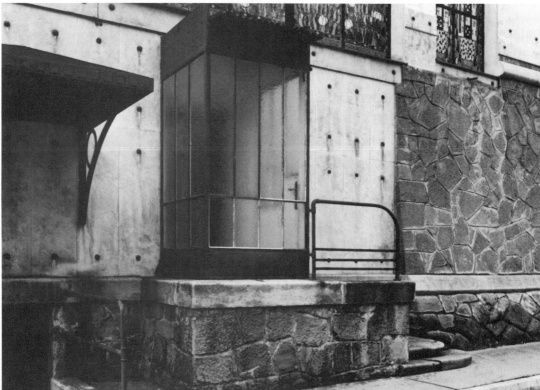

158

Figs. 157–160. Design choices are rarely limited to "ornamented" versus "not ornamented." There is, instead, a decorative continuum, encompassing objects that are more or less ornamental. The traditional ironwork of Nuremberg's *Schoner Brunnen* (Beautiful Fountain) (157), which was designed by Paulus Kuhn in 1587, renewed in 1902–13 and again after World War II, would be universally recognized as "decorative." Yet the carefully attenuated lines of the modern pipe railing (shown here in three different versions spanning eighty years) is no less decorative in intent: Otto Wagner's Am Steinhof Church, Vienna (158); Walter Gropius's Student Wing of the Bauhaus, Dessau (159); and Richard Meier's Atheneum, New Harmony, Indiana (160). (*Bauhaus Student Wing, by Walter Gropius, Collection, The Museum of Modern Art, New York; The Atheneum, Photograph by Ezra Stoller: Esto. Courtesy of The Atheneum*)

159

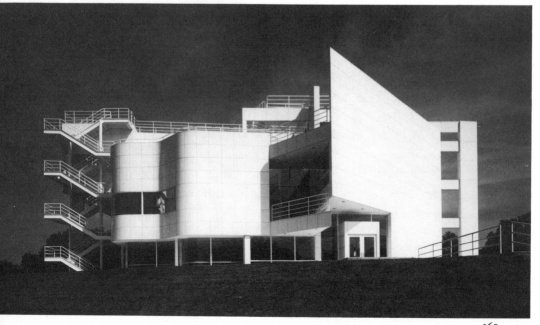

160

A few perceptive modernists were aware of the ornamental qualities of the new style from the beginning. Theo Van Doesburg, advocate of De Stijl, noted that one of the major differences between traditional styles and the "new style" was that the latter used "plastic form instead of imitation and decorative ornamentation."[9] As early as 1924, the French architect Robert Mallet-Stevens declared that applied decoration was no longer needed, because architects could now play with "monolithic cubes."[10] Instead of sculptural moldings, cartouches, and garlands, they should sculpt entire houses, which themselves became ornament.

Hans Poelzig also reflected on the continuing ornamental urge when he observed that, as traditional decoration was now forbidden, architects quite naturally relied upon the interplay of visually rich (and expensive) surfaces to become the replacement for traditional ornament.[11] [161, 162] He showed a remarkable insight for the time when he called attention to the elaboration of structure and other elements of construction for their ornamental value—the unnecessarily long spans, startling cantilevers, and large windows for which the movement was already famous in the 1920s. [163, 164, 165]

These perceptive, refreshingly candid contemporary observations went unacknowledged for decades, largely, we must assume, because (1) in the popular view, as well as that of most professionals, the word "ornament" was inextricably tied to "tradition," and therefore to traditional styles; and (2) such observations pointed up an embarrassing fact that was impossible for the faithful to accept: theirs, too, was an "ornamental" style. [166, 167]

It was understandably difficult for most modernists to admit to this new kind of ornament. The claim of a rational, ornament-less functionalism was essential if they were to present a convincing case for the health of their spartan new style, in contrast to the decaying degeneracy of the old. To admit that a strain of that dread contagion had contaminated the sterile laboratories in which this new style was produced would have been embarrassing to say the least, and would have exposed the fundamental premises of their program to fatal scrutiny.

162

161

Figs. 161, 162.   The relative simplicity of modern decoration is often coupled with expensive materials—the polished marble and chromium steel of Schullin's Jewelry Shop (161), by Hans Hollein, 1974—and the costly hand craftsmanship needed to create details like this one (162) from Mies van der Rohe's Barcelona chair. Such luscious displays of materials and workmanship became the ornament of modernism, and proclaim, as E. H. Gombrich writes, that "discriminating simplicity is a matter of choice and has nothing to do with lack of means"—*The Sense of Order,* pp. 30–31. (*Photograph Brent C. Brolin. Courtesy of Knoll International*)

164

Figs. 163, 164, and 165.   With few other options, modern architects turned to "playing" with structure for its ornamental value. These girders, screened through traditional ornamental metalwork, are the direct descendents of the exposed ribs and flying buttresses of Gothic cathedrals.

165

166

167

Figs. 166, 167.   The forms of modernism were chosen because designers found beauty in them and pleasure in the affront they offered to conventional taste. They then rationalized their choices by claiming that they were, for example, more functional than traditional forms. Le Corbusier's overstuffed chair (166), of the mid-1920s, is comfortable, to be sure, but no more so than the so-called Morris chair, manufactured at the same time by Sears-Roebuck (167). In addition to being relatively expensive, Le Corbusier's chair uses its "honestly" exposed chromium steel structure for the same decorative purpose as the floral upholstery on the Sears chair. Le Corbusier, *"Fauteuil Grand Confort, Petit Model,"* designed 1928, manufactured by Heidi Weber, Switzerland, 1959. (*Photograph by Brent C. Brolin. Collection, The Museum of Modern Art, New York*)

Having been weaned on the fiction that modern design is un-decorated, we are also prone to gloss over the obvious fact that there are *degrees of ornamental elaboration*. Everyone knows the Parthenon was decorated. And few would object if I said that the frosting-coated orna-ment of Dominikus Zimmermann's Wies Church, in Bavaria, is closely related to that of Pericles' monument—just much more exuberant.

The familial relationship between the decoration of the Parthe-non and that of Wies Church is hardly controversial. If we ignore the cubbyholes called "styles" for a moment, we can even locate these two buildings on a continuous line labeled "decorated architecture"—one toward the "less" end, the other toward the "more." But modern-ism's categorical *"ornament = history"* has made it difficult to take the logical next step: to see that the decoration of Mies van der Rohe's Barcelona Pavilion can be plotted along that same ornamental continuum. [168, 169]

Why should the invented marble of Zimmermann's interior be decoration, and the real marble of the Barcelona Pavilion not? I was once told that the decorative qualities of Mies's building were "inherent" in the "nature" of the material, and so he had come by them "honestly"—the implicit slur being that the extravagances of the Wies Church were the ignoble result of shameless Bavarian craftsmen bent on deception. Deceptive or not, Mies's decorative intention is no less apparent than that of Zimmermann. The grain and color of the Pavilion's natural marble may have been "built in," so to speak, but the choice of that kind of marble (presumably because of the beauty of its color and veining), the decision to cut it into simple, precise, geometric forms and to polish their flat planes to a silken, machinelike finish, was no more "natural" than the virtuoso performance of the plasterworker's *scagliola*. If we filter out the influence of decades of ornament-phobia and look at these two buildings with an unprejudiced eye, we can see that their architects took much the same kind of pleasure in embellishment.

In addition to varying in degree, different kinds of embellish-ments (traditional or modern) symbolize different things. The details of

168

Figs. 168, 169.   The faked marble of the church of the Jesuits (168), in Vienna, (1628–31, renovated in the 18th century), and the real marble of Mies van der Rohe's Barcelona Pavilion (169), in Spain, are both "decorative." The difference is one of degree, not intent. *(German Pavilion, 1929. Collection, The Museum of Modern Art, New York, Mies van der Rohe Archive)*

169

a Renaissance palazzo may be grand, robust, and generous, to convey an image of wealth and social position. The details of early modern buildings, on the other hand—the spare, attenuated pipe railing, for example —mimic the much-admired fittings of ocean liners and factories, and symbolize the unemotional objectivity and cool calculation of the engineer. [170, 171] The functional requirements are incidental to this decorative expressiveness, as a given function can be clothed in a variety of stylistic skins. The symbolic or expressive aim did not change when the historical content was extracted from the modern style. Designers simply had to rely on more limited means—"pure" form—to achieve that end.[12] To "see" these different emotions helps us become attuned to the ornamental message of modern design. There is no reason to question the sincerity of those who labeled traditional ornament a sin and a waste, but we can see how the urge to create it was not suppressed, only diverted into nontraditional methods. [172]

Although modernists continued to pursue the decorative tradition, their efforts obviously did not look "ornamental" to a public accustomed to traditional styles.[13] Modernists changed the nature of ornament, emphasizing broad, smooth surfaces at the expense of small-scale detail.[14] The essence of traditional ornament lay in its variety of scale, ranging from small and delicate (refined moldings and rosettes, for example) to monumental (entablatures, frescos, tympanums). Each feature depended upon a combination of many scales of ornament working in concert, offering much to interest the eye from close up as well as far away. The adamant opposition to historical styles, beginning at the turn of the century and culminating with the Modern movement, encouraged designers to disregard this important characteristic of traditional styles. The new style tended to glorify the sweep of uncluttered surfaces. A few designers earned a reputation for refinement in detailing—the meeting of glass and stone of Marcel Breuer's houses and the sculptured mullions of Mies come to mind—yet few modern works have used ornamental details over the range of scales that characterizes the styles of the past. [173, 174]

170

Figs. 170, 171.   The richness of the facade
of Linderhof, a small retreat of King
Ludwig of Bavaria built in 1874–9,
conveys a sense of grandeur that is
comfortable in its reliance on the past
(170). The carefully restrained delineation
of the modern office building (171) sends
another message, of the conservatism and
rigidity of the limited liability corporation.

171

172

Fig. 172. The "cost" of modern ornament has often been overlooked because it seldom looks like what most people think of as "decoration." Nevertheless, the client also pays for such gee-gaws as this "Sword-of-Damocles" cantilever, which threatens those who enter the new IBM Headquarters Building in New York City. Architect Edward Larrabee Barnes, 1983.

Figs. 173, 174. The modern romance with speed—recall Le Corbusier's grand renderings of giant buildings glimpsed from speeding automobiles traveling yet-to-be-built superhighways—encouraged designers to deal with the grosser aspects of their trade. While it is physically impossible to eliminate all small-scale detail, this emphasis on speed, combined with a thorough dislike of bourgeois "fussiness," dictated that much less attention be paid to the kind of detail the pedestrian can appreciate.

73

174

In addition to rejecting traditional vocabularies of decorative art, modern designers chose to use their new kind of decoration in *nontraditional* ways. Rarely is anything completely new, however, and while they did invent a new ornamental vocabulary, those new forms often recreated the feeling of traditional styles:

- The De Stijl group created an ornamental vocabulary of complex forms, constructed of simple geometric shapes and liberally colored with primary hues that rivaled the richness of Baroque. [175, 176]
- The complexity and intricacy traditionally associated with naturalistic ornament was simulated, if crudely, by exposed plumbing pipes, heating ducts, and electrical conduits. A contemporary description of the Vienna Postal Savings Bank, by Otto Wagner (1904–5), noted that the heating and plumbing pipes were carefully exposed in the hallways as one had come to expect even at that early date. The apotheosis of the "expose" approach came three quarters of a century later, when the Pompidou Center, with its gloriously decorative innards, exploded in Paris. [177, 178]
- Ornament frequently bore a close relation to structure and joints in traditional architecture; however, it was generally used to disguise the joints. Early modernists chose, instead, to elevate such rudimentary elements as the bolt (securing the marble facing of Wagner's Vienna Postal Savings Bank) [179] and the screw head ("honestly" exposed on Josef Hoffmann's deck chair and the Wiener Werkstatte's hat rack). [180, 181]
- In place of refined, classical moldings, which cast their shadows by standing out from the walls, modernists used an "anti-molding," the reveal, which casts its shadows by being cut into the wall. [182, 183]
- In place of the Rococo exuberance of Wies Church came the brutal geometric richness of the Secretariat Building at Chandigarh. [184, 185]
- Modernists used the same traditional ornamental devices to create a sense of lightness, changing only the means by which the effect was achieved: classical fluting and the clustered colonnettes of Gothic were exchanged for the vertical striations of alternating window and wall panels, and projecting mullions. [186, 187]

175

Figs. 175, 176. De Stijl created a complex vocabulary of form and color which, in its own way, rivaled the Baroque. Schroder House (175), Gerrit Rietveld, Utrecht, Holland, 1924. (Collection, The Museum of Modern Art, New York). San Carlino, Rome, (176), Francesco Borromini, 1665–67.

176

177

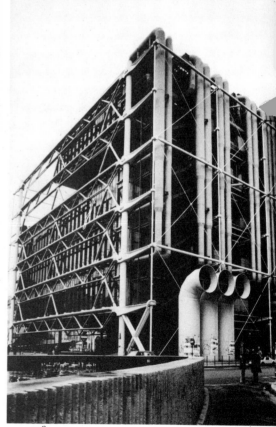

Figs. 177, 178. The notion of exposing mechanical services for their decorative effect has been around for some time. After seeing the interior of Wagner's Vienna Postal Savings Bank (1904–5), a contemporary critic reported that the "heating pipes run, as is taken for granted today, in full view along the walls"—Peter Vergo, *Art in Vienna, 1898–1918,* p. 106. The same principle, carried to a rather more exuberant extreme, envelops Pompidou Center in a carnival of structure and services.

178

179

180

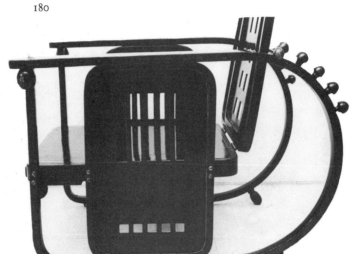

Figs. 179, 180, and 181.
Ornament has often been used to
disguise construction joints. Once
the "honesties" took hold—and
while decoration was still
acceptable—ornament became a
way to glorify the means of
construction. In Wagner's Vienna
Postal Savings Bank (179), the
heads of aluminum bolts, which
attach the marble facing to the
structural frame, became part of
the ornamental treatment.
Hoffmann's deck chair of 1905
(180), and a hat rack by the
Wiener Werkstätte (181), both
use screw heads as decorative
accents, where Biedermeier inlays
or Eastlake carvings would have
embellished before. (*Photographs
by Brent C. Brolin. Courtesy of
Galerie Metropol, New York*)

181

182

Figs. 182, 183. In place of traditional moldings, which stand out from the wall to cast a shadow (182), modern architecture perfected the reveal, an anti-molding cut into the wall to cast a shadow (183). St. Agnese, Rome, 1652–66; the Dresdner Bank Headquarters, Beckert, Becker & Partners, with H. D. Scheid, Frankfurt, 1978.

183

Figs. 184, 185. (*Facing page*) The modern, decorative vocabulary replaced the Rococo effusiveness of the Pilgrimage Church (184), Die Wies, Bavaria, 1746–54, with its own ornamental eruptions (185)—Le Corbusier, Secretariat Building, Chandigarh, N. India, 1953.

186

Figs. 186, 187. Each of these design devices—traditional and modern—creates a sense of lightness by splintering the solid plane.

187

188

Figs. 188, 189. Medieval cathedral-builders used stained glass to dematerialize structure as in the Chapter House, Wells Cathedral ca. 1319 (188). Modern architects have found another use for glass, letting it return the world to us in millions of liquid reflections (189).

189

- There is even a modern ornament that dissolves the wall as stained glass does in medieval cathedrals. The reflectivity of the glass curtain wall seems to have been an accidental by-product of the search for an "honest" expression of the non-bearing skin of modern skyscrapers. [188, 189] Once its decorative potential was realized, however, it was exploited with a vengeance, leading to acres of mirror glass and gigantic, varicolored prismatic buildings.

By asserting their independence from the visual past, modernists were able to employ the "principles of design" much more effectively than their nineteenth-century precursors. As the revolutionary forms of modern design relied on neither history nor nature, the claim that theirs was not an "ornamented" style at all seemed just.[15] And the illusion was easily maintained by the popular equation of "decoration" with nature forms and the familiar historical styles. As it was plainly both abstract and antihistorical, modern design could not also be "ornamental"—or so it seemed. Yet, as we have seen, modernists did invent an ornamented style. They did not "borrow," in the traditional, design sense of that word; that is, they did not go to the traditional sources of artistic inspiration, which have periodically refreshed the arts through the ages. *But they borrowed all the same.*[16] They simply took from the forms of industry and technology, sources that were artistically unacceptable to the vast majority whose buying power dominated the marketplace. The modernity of these forms and the imperative of "Progress" they symbolized struck the same kind of emotional chord in modernists that Josiah Wedgwood's diminutive bas-reliefs had in eighteenth-century classicists, and the great medieval cathedrals had in nineteenth-century Revivalists. In short, the romance of antiquity and the Middle Ages was replaced by the romance of the machine.

Decorative Structure and Function

We can easily confuse the nineteenth century's notion of "honesty of structure" with our own. The version put forth by most reformers, from Viollet-le-Duc to John Ruskin, was blatantly pro-Gothic and anti-

Renaissance. But that nineteenth-century principle also specified a relationship between ornament and structure: it was to be placed at joints and prominent structural members. So while the structure of Gothic Revival churches may have been visible, it was also carved, painted, and gilded, its interstices crammed with quatrefoils, crockets, and other paraphernalia of the style—a joyous celebration that had nothing to do with our idea of "honesty of structure." Modernists took the first part of the dictum (Don't disguise the structure) and ignored the second (Decorate it). Instead, they substituted the revolutionary notion that *naked* structure was enough in itself.

Of the many strange shapes to which the public has been treated since the beginning of modernism, most are efforts to treat an ailment for which there was no known cure once historical ornament had been banished, the longing to embellish. The desire persisted, but the familiar means of satisfying it—looking to history and to nature for ornamental inspiration—had been taken away. The only prescription was to push, pull, stretch, poke, bend, and carve the "significant form."

To this end, specific "functions" were exploited for their decorative effect, and the stair tower, elevator shaft, utility core, and so on became favorite devices for enlivening a building. Complicated corners and dramatic cantilevers strained to make the relatively simple, geometric "box" of early modernism "interesting." This exercise came to be referred to, within the profession, as "breaking the box." [190–195] By the 1960s, the tortuously intricate "insy-outsy" approach to design had become the accepted way to ornament a modern building. [196–200]

The effects were ornamental, to be sure, but they were unsatisfying in at least two important respects. (1) Their intentional obscurity (the demand for "originality" has been interpreted by three generations of architects as meaning, "Do anything but something that might be construed as pandering to popular taste"). And (2) this negative impetus— "Don't be traditional"—has destroyed the qualities of humanity and visual continuity–with–variety that make most premodernist cities delightful places to live in.

190

191

192

193

194

195

Figs. 190–195.   Most traditional ornament consists of a few elements repeated in relatively easily recognizable patterns (the egg and dart, for example, or the relatively simple curves which make up a molding). The variety of traditional ornament comes from combining these elements to make larger, ornamental features —cornices, pediments, window frames, and so on. Because the placement of traditional ornaments was generally the same, regardless of the style, the mere location of an ornament often gives the feeling of a traditional style. All historical styles decorated column capitals, for example, as well as window and door frames, and moldings were used to divide facades into the desired proportions. As modernists did not want to ornament in the traditional manner, they could not place ornament as it had been placed in the past. So they frequently relied on the weakest, least flavorful kind of ornament, uniform texture.

196

197

198

Figs. 196–200. "Building-as-ornament" was another alternative open to modern architects who had the urge to ornament, but who had been denied the traditional tools with which to do it. So buildings were pushed and pulled, bent and twisted, cut and pasted into all manner of "interesting" shapes. (196) Art and Architecture Building, New Haven, Paul Rudolph, 1963; (197) Salk Institute, La Jolla, California, Louis I. Kahn, 1959–67; (198) Gund Hall, Cambridge, Mass., Anderson/Baldwin, 1971; (199) Faculty Club, University of California, Santa Barbara, Moore and Turnbull, 1968; (200) Pacific Design Center, Los Angeles, Cesar Pelli, 1976.

Modernism Popularized: Mechanistic Decoration

Art Deco and the streamlined style offer the final proof that the "spirit" of modern times never mandated the banishment of ornament. Both were, like modernism, children of the fascination with the Machine Age, but both styles were also *ornamented* and *popular.* Their very popularity made them unacceptable to an elite which, by Kant's definition, was obligated to rise above popular taste. Art Deco designers are never mentioned in the same breath with the purists of modernism, and neither Art Deco nor the streamlined style merited a mention in the bible of modern architectural history, Siegfried Giedion's *Space, Time and Architecture* (1941).

201

Figs. 201, 202   Fortunately, Art Deco designers remained unaware of the modernist dictum that the "spirit of the times" demands the end of the ornamental tradition. Instead, they created new ornamental motifs using contemporary artifacts —the paraphernalia of the car, from an auto repair shop in Chicago (201), and, shown in a bas relief from Rockefeller Center (202), the very factories that had inspired modernists to discard decoration.

202

203

Fig. 203   Rather than sounding the death knell of ornament, the machine age inspired an ornamental style of "geometrized" or "mechanized" forms, as in this bas relief cataloging the means of modern communication, from Rockefeller Center. But the new, mechanized forms took *traditional* forms, offering eloquent testimony that the spirit of the industrial age was as compatible with the decorative tradition as the "spirits" of earlier times.

The ornamental vocabulary of Art Deco could be likened to a folk interpretation of the forms revered by modernists; a mixture of mechanistic abstractions—so dear to the elite—and popular, naturalistic, and historical motifs, all of which were "mechanized" by smoothing out and "geometrizing" the forms. The result of this process was "modernistic," to be sure, but it was a direct continuation of the traditional philosophy and method of ornamentation, as we see when we compare the ancient Greek anthemion (derived from palm or the honeysuckle blossom) to its mechanical, Art Deco cousin. [201, 202, 203]

NOTES: CHAPTER VIII

1. Hermann Muthesius, "The Problem of Form in Engineering" (1913), in Tim Benton, Charlotte Benton, and Dennis Sharp, eds., *Architecture and Design: 1890–1939* (New York: Whitney Library of Design, 1975), p. 116.

2. "The history of Architecture unfolds itself slowly across the centuries as a modification of structure and ornament, but in the last fifty years steel and concrete have brought new conquests, which are the index of a greater capacity for construction, and of an architecture in which the old codes have been overturned. If we challenge the past, we shall learn that 'styles' no longer exist for us, that a style belonging to our own period has come about; and there has been a Revolution,"—Le Corbusier, *Towards a New Architecture,* trans. F. Etchells (New York: Frederick Praeger, 1960), p. 13.

3. Arguments that have been made periodically during the past fifty or seventy years have touched on this point. In the early 1930s, Hans Poelzig wrote that the new architecture was as ornamental as the old, implying that modernists had not banished all ornament, merely traditional ornament. More recently, David Pye argued that the various principles guiding modern design were not the means by which design decisions were made—David Pye, *The Nature of Design* (New York: 1964); see also Robert Venturi, *Complexity and Contradiction in Architecture* (New York: The Museum of Modern Art, 1966).

4. Charles Eastlake, *Hints on Household Taste* (1868; reprint, New York: Dover Publications, 1969), p. 40.

5. Walter Gropius, *New Architecture and the Bauhaus,* trans. P. Morton Sand (Cambridge: MIT Press, 1965), p. 20.

6. Pugin said that the structure should be decorated, rather than decoration constructed. Occasionally this structural bias may be camouflaged, by terms such as "appropriate" versus "inappropriate," but these surrogates almost always carry the connotation "linked to structure."

7. Another view—a cousin of the structure-related camp—holds that ornament comprises whatever is uneconomical or unessential. But if this were so, as Sir John Summerson has pointed out, the entasis of a Doric column is ornament, while the rest of the column is not. Here, too, the implicit comparison is between what is essential and unessential—to the structure. See John Summerson, "What Is Ornament and What Is Not," in Stephen Kieran, ed., *Via III: Ornament. Journal of the Graduate School of Fine Arts, University of Pennsylvania* (Philadelphia: The Graduate School of Fine Arts, University of Pennsylvania, 1977), p. 7.

8. John Ruskin, "The Two Paths," in E. T. Cook and A. Wedderburn, eds., *The Works of John Ruskin,* (39 vols., London: George Allen, 1903–12), 16:320.

9. Theo Van Doesburg, "The Will to Style" (1922), in Benton, Benton, and Sharp, eds., *Architecture and Design,* p. 94.

10. Robert Mallet-Stevens, "Architecture and Geometry" (1924) in Benton, Benton, and Sharp, eds., *Architecture and Design,* p. 131.

11. Hans Poelzig, "The Architect" (1931), in Benton, Benton, and Sharp, eds., *Architecture and Design,* p. 57.

12. The "pure form" which evoked eloquent praise from Le Corbusier was the same that had

been written about by Walter Crane in *Line and Form* (London: G. Bell & Sons, 1921), Geoffrey Scott in *Architecture of Humanism* (2nd ed. 1924; reprint, New York: Charles Scribner's Sons, 1969), and Clive Bell in *Art* (1923; reprint, New York: Capricorn Books, 1958).

13. By traditional ornamental styles, I mean those based, however loosely, on natural forms and/or historical precedent.

14. Curiously enough, the uninterrupted planes associated with early modern design are generally traced to designers' fascination with technical forms, although most machines of that era—as well as most bridges, ships, cars, and other modern creations—had complicated surfaces, cluttered with knobs, gears, rivets, tubes, piping, and the like. This is another indication of a conflict between theory and practice, which points up the hostility toward popular taste that had created the need for such theories in the first place.

15. Indeed, it was often said that modern design was not a "style" at all, in the traditional sense of that word, but was the "inevitable" consequence of following "rational" precepts, although those same "rational" precepts had already been used to explain a number of styles that were distinctly different from the "modern" one.

16. See Chapter X for a discussion of borrowing as a traditional means of creating new ornament.

CHAPTER IX

Ornament Returns

"Modernism is dead!" we are told. In some obvious ways that is true. Although the percentage of designers who follow the new faith is small, they are influential, and seem capable of holding the professional media firmly under their spell. The most convincing indication that modernism is at least tilting toward the grave is that it has again become fashionable for designers to be inspired by history, thanks largely to the writings and work of Robert Venturi. [204] Because of this, thanks also to Venturi, traditional ornament has once again become respectable, at least in certain important circles. In his *Complexity and Contradiction in Architecture,* Venturi proposed that the simple, unornamented, universal solutions of modernism should be replaced by ones that offered the opposite: complex, ambiguous, and individualized attention to specific problems. In brief, he said, "Less is a bore." These preferences were buttressed with meticulous documentation of art historical precedents in which such complex and contradictory elements had been juxtaposed to the advantage of the whole.[1]

"Postmodern" architecture, an approach that treats historical precedent as an aid to design rather than an obstacle to creativity, would have been unthinkable without Venturi's ground-breaking works and theoretical writing. Those who followed his bold lead have been freed to dip into the full resources of history, and their openness to ornament is unprecedented in "high-style" design in our times. While modernism was supposed to have freed designers from the corset of the past, it only put them in one of its own making, by introducing an element of negativism that has cast its shadow over every decision of "creative" designers since the first decades of this century: Whatever you do, *don't*

Fig. 204.   The public never embraced modernism. Modernists passed this off as a failure to understand. But the vocabulary of modernism was not rejected because of a simple misunderstanding. And even less, as some postmodernists are heard to claim, because its symbolism was obscure and unfamiliar. An illiterate could tell that modern buildings looked like factories; the symbolic vocabulary fairly screamed out its origins. Modernism was rejected by the majority of people because they did not like the way it looked. Weissenhof Settlement, Stuttgart, 1927.

204

do anything historical! The new approach is more positive (perhaps "less destructive" is a more accurate formulation), even permitting borrowing from the "modern" past, and promises to be far better in the long run than the narrow negativism of the Modern movement.

Breaking with modernism has not been without its risks, all too apparent in the awkwardness—downright ugliness—of much postmodern ornament. Even the most avid and prolific proponent of the new movement acknowledges that "one is not overwhelmed by the sensitivity or discrimination of the final products" of these designers.[2] If designers are ill at ease when handling ornament today, the discomfort is understandable. They are breaking taboos that have gone unquestioned for generations. In addition to the psychological strain accompanying such a schism, these explorers are embarking on the search for ornament with, relatively speaking, a neophyte's knowledge to guide them. There may still be a few old-timers around who actually studied it in school, but the ranks are depleted. The only way to reacquaint ourselves with its many, subtle uses is to try to get a "feel" for ornamenting by studying case histories—the buildings of the past. Not impossible, to be sure, but not the easiest way, either. Like other crafts, ornamenting is probably best learned from a master. It is one thing to study the end result, quite another to be there at the birth; to listen and watch as the experienced voice tells you why, and the knowing hand breathes life into lines and forms, refining each detail until it adds its harmony to the chorus of embellishment that makes the whole more than the sum of the parts.

There seem to be two different approaches to the awkward use of ornament in postmodern architecture. One has been mainly the province of Venturi: the purposeful—one could almost say perversely— clumsy distortion of traditional symbols in an effort to make the building look "almost" all right. [205] In both his writing and his work, Venturi continually reminds us that he favors "conventional element[s] used slightly unconventionally"—the "ugly and ordinary," as he so precisely put it; his aim is to make "commonplace elements . . . uncommon through distortion . . . change in scale . . . and change in context."[3] [206, 207]

Examples of this arch awkwardness are found in all his work. One of his more recent buildings, Wu Hall, at Princeton University, has to be considered an all-too-rare achievement in one respect: a remarkably good, background building (in the best sense of that word). It is unostentatious, fits well with its neighbors and yet is also interesting in its own right. As one approaches it, however, bits of gratuitous clumsiness soon become apparent. [208, 209] Two of the "keystones," anyway rather thickly proportioned, are sliced with calculated haphazardness by expan-

205

Fig. 205.   Robert Venturi uses conventional forms with unconventional twists. In this early house in Chestnut Hill, Pennsylvania, the traditionally important symbolism of the entrance is emphasized by an arc of molding, which is then canceled out by a lintel that seems to have no structural purpose. The roof is almost peaked—the traditional symbol of "home"—but has a gap where the peak should be.

206

207

Figs. 206, 207. The intentional awkwardness of many of Venturi's designs works to advantage in the Brant House, in Bermuda (206). Its oddities, including truncated roofs and an oversized, oculus window, match (in spirit) those of other, local builder–designed houses (207). In short, it becomes "indigenous" in the friendliest sense of the word.

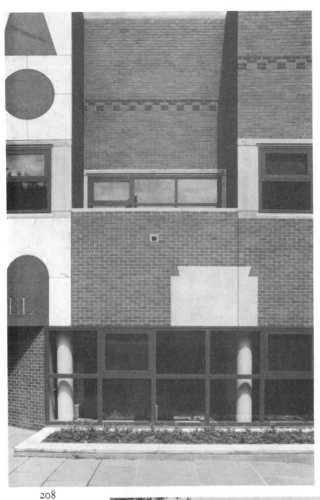

Figs. 208, 209. Wu Hall, at Princeton University, is a complex mixture. It is undeniably friendly to both the general atmosphere of what feels like "university," and to its immediate context. In a broader sense, it is also a condescending, almost hostile, gesture. How else can one interpret it—a superbly skilled designer making a conscious effort to be awkward when the traditional expectation is beauty. Princeton University, 1984, Venturi Rauch & Scott Brown.

208

209

sion joints. A maintenance man characterized the building by saying it was probably designed as a "rush job." Why else, he said, would the architect have cut the decorative "keystones" like that?

Few people would attach much significance to an "uneducated" observer's remark, but under the circumstances, it cannot be dismissed casually. After all, he is allegedly a consumer of "popular culture," and Venturi has written at length about the importance of popular culture in daily life and as the inspiration for his own work.

The curious, plain-Jane appeal of his work is marred by coy condescension—an obviously sophisticated and skilled designer who seems to be trying to make buildings look as though they had been designed in the early fifties by the U.S. Post Office. Such patronizing may be unavoidable in an aesthetic with a pretended link to "popular culture," which conscientiously strives for banality.

It surfaces, among other places in the assumption that the "common man," supposed lover of "popular culture," cannot tell the difference between traditional refinement in detailing and composition, and Venturi's lovingly and cleverly contrived ugliness. His fascination with the symbols of "pop" culture offers other instances. He would have giant signs lighting up all over town, announcing this or that cultural institution, although the speed that demands huge signs on highways is not possible in cities. And who really believes that most people like those signs, or find them either amusing or of cultural interest? If it is any indication, rarely does the value of a house go up when the A&P plants a giant logo next door, and paves over three acres of suburban meadowland. [210]

Venturi has compared the awkwardness of his own work to sixteenth-century Mannerist exaggerations of the Renaissance vocabulary of forms.[4] The comparison overlooks a critical difference. Borromini chose the high art of his time as his model, deforming Renaissance ideals into more emotional and dramatic extensions of their parent forms. Undeniably different from Renaissance architecture, these are beautiful because they grow out of an effort to create beauty. Venturi has no such aim. He fine-tunes his designs to be just a notch or two above the admitted

210

Fig. 210.   Robert Venturi's approach to postmodern architecture has suggested that we can learn about the use of symbols which will be appropriate to our time by studying commercial strip development, the archetypal example being The Strip of Las Vegas. The relevance of such studies to noncommercial, urban or suburban design is debatable. (*Photograph courtesy of Las Vegas Chamber of Commerce*)

ordinariness of almost-all-right (in his terms) Main Street. Here, we come full circle in the evolution of the Kantian artist: the greater talent who demonstrates his "genius" (i.e., originality) by trying to appear the lesser.

Nevertheless, the précieux awkwardness of his work would be infinitely more disturbing in less skillful hands. In spite of a surprisingly original effort to avoid the beautiful, there is a sureness in some of Venturi's contrived clumsiness that comes from its relation to the building's context, and makes it seem less out of place than if the oddness had grown out of a naked urge to be bizarre.

The second kind of postmodern awkwardness is probably best illustrated in the work of Michael Graves, who may well be the Frank Furness of our time. [211] Although the buildings are sometimes bumptiously grotesque, this quality does not seem to arise out of an overt search

Fig. 211. There is a certain awkwardness to much postmodern design. Whether it comes from an unfamiliarity with ornament, a caution about wholeheartedly embracing the past, or some other reason is often hard to tell. Plocek House, Warren, New Jersey; construction view from street. (*Courtesy Michael Graves, Architect. Photograph: Proto Acme Photo*)

for the clumsy, as does Venturi's, but from a more traditionally motivated search for a personalized expression of Beauty. Both cases, however, seem to owe a great deal to the designers' caution in embracing the newly rediscovered history. After all, in the eyes of the great majority of their peers, returning to the past still carries the stigma of copying, and to copy still means violating Kant's first rule of "genius." One need not be on intimate terms with the *Critique* to know that originality remains a highly valued commodity in the world of design.

All of this does not mean that modernism has vanished without a trace from the work of the small group of postmodernist architects. To pick up its trail, we must again look to the founder of the movement, Robert Venturi. [212, 213] Although his erudite writings debunk the

212

213

Figs. 212, 213.   Robert Venturi attacked the fundamental tenets of modernism, pointing out, among other things, that the "honest" expression of the interior on the exterior was the exception rather than the rule—even in modern buildings which have been highly praised. Both the Royal Crescent at Bath, England (212) —whose individual townhouses form a palatial and monolithic facade (by the younger John Wood, 1757–75)—and the High Court Building at Chandigarh, India (213)—with its camouflaging sun breakers (Le Corbusier, 1953-on)—share the "dishonest" quality of disguising what is behind their walls. Yet Venturi's own work is frequently justified in precisely the same terms as that of modernists, and the 19th-century reformers, namely, as the reflection of interior complexities on the exterior.

modernist's naively simplistic expression of function, he explains his own love of complexity in precisely the same terms the modernists used to explain their love of simplicity, namely, as the desire to honestly express function: "the architectural complexities and distortions [of the] inside are reflected on the outside." The wonderfully flexible "principle" of the expression of function is alive and well, and has now been called into service to explain *post*modern architecture.

Other threads also tie the patchwork quilt of postmodernism to the purer cloth of its namesake. The familiar "spirit of the times" approach is retained too, as Venturi argues that "meeting the architectural implications and the critical social issues of our era will require that we drop our involuted, architectural expressionism and our mistaken claim to be building outside a formal language and find formal languages suited to our times."[5]

The fact that Venturi talks about expressing function in form or capturing the "spirit of the time"—like Gropius, and Ruskin, and Pugin before him—is as irrelevant to his work as it was to theirs. These are the same, simple devices being used to rationalize yet another style preference.

Venturi's "gentle manifesto" has other parallels with the more violent, modernist revolution. Perhaps the most obvious—from his work —is the need to shock, and the bias against conventional taste demonstrated by that need. From before the turn of the century, "progressive" designers consciously flouted popular and academic conventions, claiming the imagery of technology must replace that of nature as the standard of beauty. Venturi, too, flouts conventions but they are those of modernism. Designers should seek inspiration in the vernacular of strip development, he says, fixing his aesthetic sights on the epitome of vulgar commercialization, which art reformers have been objecting to for more than a century. The purpose of this foray into the demimonde of architecture is "to *shock our sensibilities* towards a new architecture" (my emphasis).[6] The only difference between this aspect of Venturi's design strategy and the corresponding facet of modernism is that the target has changed; it is no longer *épater le bourgeoisie,* but *épater les modernistes.*

One could argue that the revolt against modernism was instigated because the original revolution had come full circle. Modernism is now the bourgeois style, and Venturi, like his predecessors, must reject those values. This is appealing, but not true. Modernism's success has been limited to the corporate world—that anonymous part of our lives which can be satisfactorily divorced from personal values. The fact of the matter is that the middle class is no longer the focus of artists' attacks because the design elite has finally freed itself from the constraints of the mass market. [214] Beyond the occasional bit of rhetoric—architecture as a political gesture—there is little pretext about being involved with problems that concern the larger social issues of our time, which the Modern movement felt it was addressing. Today's designers do not pretend to create inexpensive accouterments for the "masses"—no "utilitarian" kitchen furniture to populate contemporary *Siedlungen.* They devote their talents to satisfying a small clientele of culture-consumers, which is characterized by a blind willingness to accept the "experts' " taste. There are furniture designs, tableware, and the like, by Richard Meier, Michael Graves, and other "names," most with phenomenal price tags. One recent entry into this market, a line of furniture designed by Robert Venturi and manufactured by Knoll International, boasts laminated wood chairs with an average price of around $1,100 (without cushion). [215] They are cartoon gestures to the past, for those who eagerly look to embrace the next "new wave" as the least painful way to demonstrate their sophistication, just as the upwardly mobile, mid-nineteenth-century gentleman and lady coveted lavish ornament as a sign of culture and good taste.

The "postmodernism" label is unfortunate. The potential value of these buildings is not simply that they fill the next slot in the art historical march of styles, nor even that they use ornament. Their great value is in the openness they demonstrate toward a variety of sources of decorative inspiration, an attitude which makes it much easier for buildings to respect their neighbors. If designers can be uninhibited enough to take advantage of this freedom, it may be possible to make new buildings

214

Fig. 214. Long past are the days when workers' housing and grand urban renewal schemes formed the meat of the designer's interest, and the middle class is no longer the butt of instructions to improve taste. High-style practitioners have given up trying to establish "good design" in the mass market—unless you consider the elegant Braun calculator, which performs basic arithmetic functions for a stylish price tag of $80, a mass-market item. (*Photograph by Brent C. Brolin. Courtesy of The Museum of Modern Art Gift Shop, New York*)

Fig. 215. The successful designer of today makes no pretense of confronting the larger marketplace. He or she deals with a limited clientele, which eagerly, and virtually uncritically, awaits each new artistic pronouncement. Chairs designed by Robert Venturi for Knoll International. (*Photograph by Brent C. Brolin. Courtesy of Knoll International, New York*)

215

that are sympathetic to the old, by using ornament in ways that have not been available to designers for almost a century.

The demand for a sympathetic relationship between new and old is an ancient one: "See that your work harmonizes well with the old," admonished an Imperial Roman decree of the sixth century, in describing the duties of the Palace Architect.[7] [216] Throughout history, the careful use of ornament has made an incalculable contribution to this harmony.[8] Just how the craft was passed along to succeeding generations is hard to say. I know of no treatise which speaks of it directly. Perhaps the inertia of tradition made it the only acceptable path. Or it may be that the unquestioned acceptance of ornament and the "borrowing tradition" were enough to ensure this kind of visual unity. It is even possible that it was an acknowledged skill, consciously passed from master to apprentice, but the value of which was so self-evident that no one ever thought to record the techniques by which it was accomplished. However it was done, this knack has atrophied in our century. As ornament returns, this skill, too, may be regained.

The most obvious pitfall along this road is that designers will lapse into doing "ornament for ornament's sake." That would leave us only slightly better off than when they indulged in "no ornament for no ornament's sake." The promise of postmodernism would then fade, to become just another alleged "style of the times," to be followed, at some later date, by the next in line.

Since the middle of the nineteenth century, the "style of the times" has been the Holy Grail of design. It would be more accurate to characterize it as a red herring. By the time designers had declared that there was such a thing as a "style of the times," their notions of "good design" no longer qualified for that label. The first mouthing of that phrase marked the designers' acknowledgment that their taste was no longer acceptable in the marketplace. The search for that elusive commodity was part of a comprehensive strategy aimed at wresting the power to determine fashion from those whose vision of "the times" did not coincide with that of the designer.

216

Fig. 216.　These two Bavarian town halls, one Gothic (1240) the other Renaissance (1572), demonstrate a fact of architectural life in the past. New buildings almost always respected their older neighbors, even when built—as in the case of the building on the right—in a "modern style." Rothenburg on the Tauber, Bavaria.

Figs. 217, 218. The traditional assumption that new buildings should be sympathetic to old has fallen by the wayside in our century for several reasons, not the least of them being the wholesale rejection of middle-class values and the demand for originality in the arts. The result is frequently "designer architecture," offering viewers the dubious convenience of being able identify the designer of a building, regardless of where it is built. (217) Portland Building, Portland, Oregon, by Michael Graves. (*Courtesy Michael Graves, Architect. Photograph: Proto Acme Photo*). Designer clothing by Calvin Klein.

217

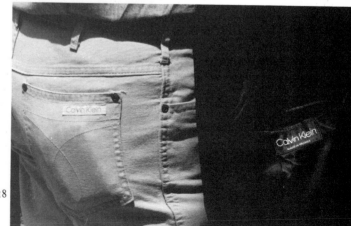

218

219

Fig. 219. Anyone with a casual knowledge of modern architecture will recognize this as one of Le Corbusier's famous brise-soleil, or sunbreakers. But where? In India, France, America? Pursuit of a personal style has led to a world populated by buildings guaranteed to have nothing to do with their visual surroundings. This is Carpenter Center for the Visual Arts, Cambridge, Mass., 1963.

This circle can only be broken if we recognize that it is impossible for us to have any single "style of the times." That would only be possible in a homogeneous culture. There are many versions of "our times," each equally valid as far as those who hold it are concerned.[9] To search one's creative soul for *the* expression of "our times" is at best a thankless task; at worst, a crude form of self-deception.

Another significant obstacle threatens to squelch the potential of the new, ornamented architecture to evolve as a way of relating new to old. "Designer architecture," like "designer jeans," seems to demand that the architect's name be written across a work before it can be of value. [217, 218] As architects have not yet taken to literally signing their buildings, they have resorted to the symbolic "signature," the personal style. The designer building "explores a personal style," regardless of who or what gets in its way. It is easy to tell a Le Corbusier building regardless of where it is in the world. [219] With an occasional exception in the oeuvre of each, the same can be said of Wright, Mies, and so on, down to the present-day "stars"—Meier, Graves, Venturi, et al. Ultimately the seed of what has become an essentially destructive drive for purely personal artistic expression can be traced back to Kant, who laid the burden of originality solely upon the shoulders of the artist.[10]

If there is a hope in the new, ornamented style called postmodernism, it lies in the flexibility which the work of Venturi and a few others seen in these pages shows in its openness to all influences. Not the license to dig into any dish on the smorgasbord of historical ornament, but the knowledge that the real freedom of history comes only from understanding the tradition of borrowing, which has enriched the entire history of art. Truly skillful designers can do this in ways that enhance the surroundings, and also offer the satisfaction that now seems to come only with a "personal artistic statement." [220–225]

Fig. 220.   Burdened by the weight of modernist ideology, and determined to demonstrate "good taste" when dealing with so delicate a matter as the artistic past, many historical preservation groups have guidelines which claim that one of the most important ways to relate new buildings to old is the use of similar materials. In practice, this is seldom the decisive factor. The new glass and steel Chicago Board of Trade Building establishes a definite rapport with the old masonry Board of Trade Building, seen behind. Murphy Jahn, Architects, 1984. (*Photograph: Palmer/Steinkamp*)

220

221

223

222

Figs. 221, 222, and 223.   Capturing the true flavor of a location takes a kind of courage that architects have rarely demonstrated in this century—the confidence that their building need not assault the eye by its inappropriateness in order to be considered "creative" or beautiful. This new building, (221) for downtown La Jolla, California, will look as though it had been there for decades—a feat that will be welcomed by all those who consider architecture an art with a social responsibility rather than some cumbersome vehicle for immortalizing the current definition of "creative." (*Rendering courtesy of Robert A.M. Stern, Architects.*) The same is true of the Regent Hotel and Office Building (222) and Jefferson Court (223), both by the Washington, D. C. office of Skidmore, Owings & Merrill. (*Renderings by Carlos Diniz Associates.*)

224

225

Figs. 224, 225. Establishing a sympathetic relationship between new buildings and old was not just something for the unknown builders whose work borders this Dutch street (224), but also for the likes of Michelangelo, whose New Sacristy (225), in the Church of San Lorenzo, Florence (1521–34), was designed with an eye toward respecting the Old Sacristy of Brunelleschi (1421–28).

NOTES: CHAPTER IX

1. Robert Venturi, *Complexity and Contradiction in Architecture* (New York: The Museum of Modern Art, 1966).
2. Charles Jencks, "Free-Style Classicism: The Wider Tradition," *Free-Style Classicism* (London: Architectural Design, 1982), p. 20.
3. Robert Venturi, Denise Scott Brown, and Steven Izenour, *Learning from Las Vegas, The Forgotten Symbolism of Architectural Form* (1972; rev. ed. Cambridge: MIT Press, 1977), p. 91.
4. *New York Times,* June 7, 1984, sect. 3:10.
5. Venturi, Scott-Brown, and Izenour, *Learning from Las Vegas,* p. 161.
6. Ibid. See Peter Blake, *God's Own Junkyard* (New York: Holt, Rinehart and Winston, 1964), intended as a condemnation of American cities and suburbs, but cited by Venturi as proof that Main Street America is almost all right.
7. Cassiodorus, *The Letters of Cassiodorus, being a condensed translation of the Variae epistolae of Magnus Aurelius Cassiodorus Senator,* trans. Thomas Hodgkin (London: H. Frowde, 1886), bk. 7, formulae 5, p. 323.
8. The difficult problem of designing new buildings to fit with existing contexts is only now being recognized as a substantial task of the profession, although I would not be surprised if the Modern movement's failure to address this problem had, by itself, been responsible for the birth of the entire historic preservation movement.
9. I recommend Herbert Gans, *The Levittowners* (New York: Pantheon, 1967), to all architects and designers. It is an enlightened and enlightening view of the lower middle class—a group that designers have always considered underprivileged in terms of their designed environment. In Levittown, they have found their own, quite satisfactory "style of the times."
10. I do not mean that Kant foresaw that his ideas would lead to minimalist art, any more than Darwin could have foreseen that the doctrine of natural selection (which held that animals evolved in part through adaptation to their surroundings) would play a major role in the American urban renewal policies of the 1950s and 1960s (which tore out the hearts of cities in order to provide a "better" environment and so make "better" citizens). But the ideas of both men undoubtedly influenced these apparently unrelated events.

CHAPTER X

Ornament and the Borrowing Tradition

Until quite recently, if you said a designer "borrowed," it was an accusation. He or she lacked the requisite inner resources to be truly "original" and "creative," and therefore had no choice but to rely on someone else's talents. This taboo still haunts the arts, even after it has once again become acceptable to use the past. While postmodernists acknowledge history, many seem compelled to torture it until an "original" contribution to artistic Progress has been made.

This myopic vision of the "creative act" persists even though it is evident that virtually all societies before our own treated the past as an integral part of the present. The vast majority of designers today still crave the accolade of originality, with little thought about how earlier artists—those whose artifacts make our museums of art possible—gracefully incorporated elements of earlier and contemporaneous cultures into their own artistic constellations.

"Borrowing," as I use the word, should not be confused with "revivalism"—the dogmatic replication of a style, which, however wrongly, is often used to characterize nineteenth-century design. The borrowing about which I speak is the kind that yields traces of Etruscan art in Roman works, Romanesque in Gothic, and early Le Corbusier in Michael Graves and Richard Meier. "Borrowing," in this sense, also encompasses a less conscious process, through which new elements find their way into the arts, a phenomenon perhaps best described as "affinitive seeing."[1] Designers are usually sensitive souls, and are rarely oblivious to the world around them, so bits and pieces of what they see frequently turn up in their work. The romance of space found its way into design in the sixties and seventies in much the same way that the romance of machines did in the twenties, and the magic promised by computers does today. [226, 227]

The notion of borrowing from the past to aid in creating new ornamental designs is probably as old as the second artisan. [228–273] The acceptability of a borrowed element is usually a function of its source. "New and recently-coined words will win acceptance if they are borrowed from Greek sources and drawn upon sparingly," wrote the Roman poet Horace.[2] And Richard Meier's eclecticism has escaped professional criticism because he does his borrowing from early "Corbu." (Had he chosen early James Gamble Rogers as his mentor, whose neo-Gothic colleges grace the campus of Yale University, it is unlikely that he would have received the same warm reception.)

A contemporary of Horace produced the only literary work on art or architecture that has come down to us from antiquity. *The Ten Books on Architecture,* by the Roman engineer-architect Vitruvius, is a two-thousand-year-old state-of-the-art treatise based on earlier writings and his own practical experience. The following observation gives some idea of his matter-of-fact attitude toward borrowing: "What could not happen in the original [style] would have no valid reason for existence in the copy."[3] As we can see, borrowing was a completely unself-conscious act for Vitruvius. More than unself-conscious, it was a natural step in the course of designing, a way to establish an essential connection to a respected and valued tradition. (Perhaps "inventive borrowing" would be a more accurate term, for the Romans freely adapted Greek motifs to their own needs and architectural forms.)

Vitruvius gave no indication that he would have understood what we have learned to think of as the "morality" of such an artistic venture. Borrowing, in our terms, implies *false* principles. The specter of this kind of personal, moral failure was inconceivable to Vitruvius. Our ancient Roman was not in the least offended that the Greeks had created structurally meaningless details by translating the forms of wood construction into stone; his only mention of "false" principles comes in reference to a failure to copy accurately.[4]

One might argue that the Romans borrowed from the Greeks because of proximity, both geographical and chronological. The same might be said of early Christian art, which was inspired by classical culture. Although it may be surprising, the Europeans of the Middle Ages also had a strong sense of the continuity with classical culture, no feeling of being *here* in time, separated from *there*. As one of his many titles, Charlemagne chose "Roman Emperor" when he was crowned in A.D. 800, for he thought of himself as continuing the line of emperors that had begun with Julius Caesar. And the art and architecture of that time shows its own direct relationship to Imperial Rome.

For a number of reasons, among them the many classical ruins, and a strong sense of nationalism, the poets and artists of the Italian Renaissance skipped over the recent, Gothic example, and also borrowed from the classical past. For Plutarch (1304–1374) and later humanists, the northern barbarian (the "Goth" of Gothic) had irreparably severed the continuous thread of history, creating the sense of isolation from the past that is an essential quality of the modern world. Yet the lack of self-consciousness with which Renaissance craftsmen relied on the artistic past for their inspiration was in no way impaired by the loss of this sense of continuity.

Largely because travel was difficult, borrowing from truly exotic cultures was relatively limited in the past.[5] In addition to transportation difficulties, the inertia of tradition severely limited the degree to which outside influences were incorporated into traditional styles. By the early eighteenth century, however, new ingredients were affecting the evolution of styles. The colonization of the world, which was in full swing by that time, was bringing the exotica of four continents into the marketplaces of Europe. And the class whose energies were responsible for this exponential expansion was presenting its own demands for novelty and variety in the trappings of life.

The eighteenth century also saw the growth of an interest in archeology, which, in the most obvious way, expanded the decorative artist's palette. More importantly, however, the discovery of these ancient sites raised the decorative expectations of the public. The excavations of Pompeii and Herculaneum showed the new middle class that a richness of embellishment associated only with the aristocracy in modern times had once been the standard even in middle-class homes.[6]

Borrowing only became tainted during the nineteenth century. After the gods of genius and originality had been enshrined in the artistic pantheon, there was a painful conflict between the new demand for originality and the traditional approach of borrowing. Nineteenth- and twentieth-century theoreticians handled this conflict differently. The former decided that the safest use of history was as a giver of abstractions —the principles of past decorative art were to be emulated, rather than its forms. As borrowing fell from favor, other explanations had to be found for the origins of historical ornament. Viollet-le-Duc voiced a popular view when he wrote that primitive ornament took the forms it did because of the nature of the materials: "Higher" civilizations, he declared, learned to combine this principle with functional and climatic demands to determine the form of their decoration.[7] Structure and function were also named as generating forces in earlier, decorative styles. No one seemed to consider the possibility that borrowing, itself, might have been a prime principle in the creation and evolution of ornamental styles.

While twentieth-century modernists tried to give the appearance of having abandoned that ancient tradition, they did not in fact do so. The revolutionary shapes of modernism did not come about because borrowing had stopped, but because they borrowed from new sources. Where their predecessors had taken from nature and other styles, modernists, in their effort to turn away from conventions, looked only to the imagery of industry and technology.

226

Figs. 226. Postmodern architects have tended to favor classical ornament. Few buildings in recent years have recalled Romanesque architecture, for example (226). (*Office Building, Connecticut Ave., Washington, D.C., David M. Schwarz. Photo: Courtesy David M. Schwarz.*)

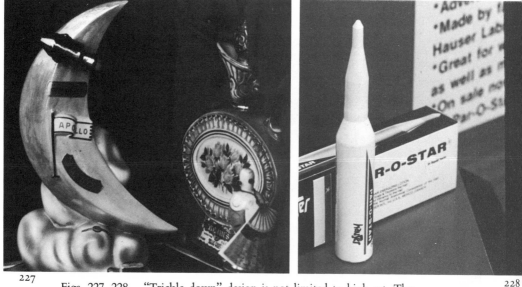

227

228

Figs. 227, 228. "Trickle down" design is not limited to high art. The paraphernalia of space travel became the focus of attention in the 1960s and early 1970s, as we shot men into space and landed them on the moon. The result: radios that looked like space helmets, whiskey decanters recounting astronautical adventures in fashions befitting the Crystal Palace Exhibition, and shampoo containers and bottles that changed their silhouettes overnight to take on the forms of the rockets and space capsules. (227) Whiskey decanter, 1960s; (228) cosmetics container, late 1960s.

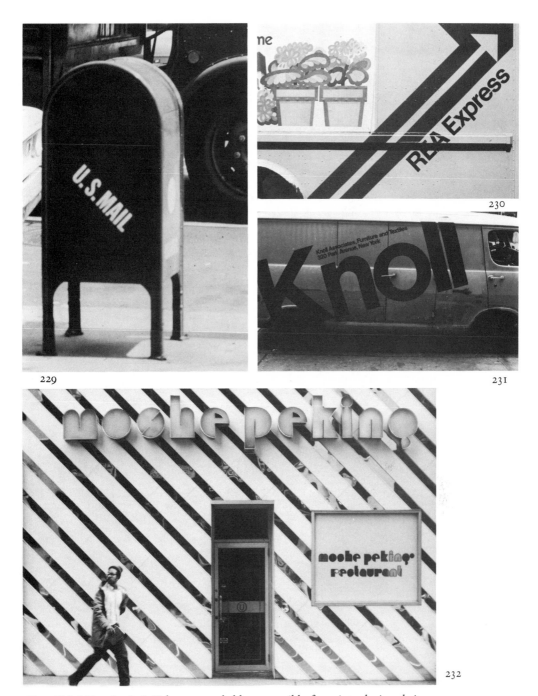

Figs. 229–232.   Louis I. Kahn was probably responsible for reintroducing designers
to the diagonal in the 1960s. Shortly thereafter, it became fashionable as a
decorative motif for a variety of uses. (229) Mailbox, U.S. Post Office, ca. 1970;
(230) Railway Express truck, ca. 1970; (231) Knoll International Truck, early 1970s;
(232) restaurant, New York City, ca. 1968.

233

Fig. 233. This 7th-century B.C. silver bowl was found in Praeneste, Italy. Part of its ornament illustrates a crucial facet of the borrowing tradition: it is a visual, not an intellectual phenomenon. The artist who engraved the two concentric rings of hieroglyphs was enchanted by their decorative quality, not their meaning. They translate into gibberish. (*From Donald B. Harden,* The Phoenicians, *1963. Courtesy Thames & Hudson, Ltd.*)

Figs. 234–246. Many decorative elements appear in a variety of different styles. Changes in the form of the acanthus leaf over the centuries may have been the result of different levels of skill, or of interpretations based in new views of the world. These illustrations begin with the real acanthus plant—photographed in the Roman Forum—and follow some of its decorative incarnations over the past two thousand years. (234) Actual acanthus; (235) Forum, 1st century B.C.; (236) Mausoleum of Galla Placidia, Ravenna, 420; (237) San Vitale, Ravenna, 526–47; (238) Worms Cathedral, 1110–81; (239) Romsey Abbey, England, ca. 1130; (240) Wells Cathedral, 1180–1425; (241) Duomo, Florence, 1296–1462; (242) Pazzi Chapel, Florence, 1429–46; (243) St. Paul's, London, 1675–1710; (244) porch, St. Bartholomew's, New York, 1902; (245) Music School, Yale University, 1930s; (246) Rockefeller Center, New York, 1931–40.

234

235

236

237

238

239

240

241

242

243

244

245

246

248

247

Figs. 247–251. The anthemion, an ancient
decoration perhaps derived from the honeysuckle
blossom, has been a decorative element in Western
art for the past 2,500 years. (247) End tile from the
Parthenon, mid-5th century B.C.; (248) anthemion
and acanthus, Roman Forum; (249) stair railing,
apartment house by Otto Wagner, Vienna; (250)
library, Springfield, Mass., ca. 19th century; (251)
Rockefeller Center, New York, 1930s.

249

250

251

252

253

254

255

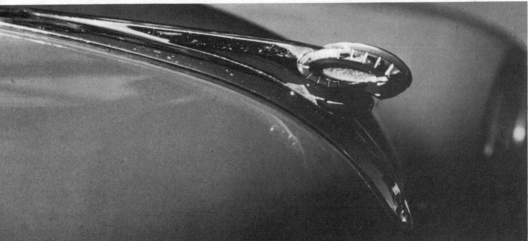

256

Figs. 252–256.   Animals, in decorative form, have symbolized the power and
strength of the elite throughout the history of art. The lion entered English
heraldry early; here it appears, rampant, in 13th-century encaustic tiles in
Winchester Cathedral (252). It has come down through the ages, styles, and social
classes, to grace not only the Art Deco British Empire Building in Rockefeller
Center (253) but also a Ford tail light (254).

   The ram, symbol of stubbornness and power, has had an equally far-ranging
ornamental life. The detail shows a grouping of rams' heads surrounding a gold
clasp from ancient Iran (255). The more familiar head (256) is attached to the hood
of a Dodge, vintage 1950s.

257

258

259

Figs. 257, 258, and 259. The organic, almost treelike nature of Gothic structure has been rendered in more and less sophisticated interpretations over the past one thousand years. (257) St. Stephen's, Vienna; (258) St. Saviour's Parish Church, Tetbury, England; (259) farmhouse porch, upper New York State.

260

262

261

263

s. 260–263.   Without a readily apparent meaning, scrolls
ve been used, over the centuries, to soften the meeting of
perpendiculars. (260) Santo Spirito, Florence; (261) Santa
Maria Novella, Florence; (262) Rome, 16th century; (263)
house entrance, Nüremberg, ca. 18th century.

264

26

265

268

266

269

270

271

272

Figs. 264–272. An antique form taken over by the early Christians, the shell lost first its pagan, then its Christian connotations, and has been incorporated into a variety of different styles. (264) Rome, 4th century; (265) early Christian bas-relief, 4th century (Photograph: Brent C. Brolin. Courtesy of the Vatican Museum); (266) Tempietto, Rome, by Bramante, 1502; (267) Rome, 16th century; (268) house entrance, Nuremberg, 18th century; (269) house entrance, Tetbury, England, 18th century; (270) Vienna, 18th century; (271) Vienna, ca. 1880; (272) Vienna, ca. 1880.

Fig. 273. The mechanistic, decorative style called Art Deco continued another kind of borrowing. For centuries, religious reliquaries had been made in the form of buildings: this bookcase and desk takes the form of an Art Deco skyscraper. Paul T. Frankl, designer, ca. 1928. (*Collection of John Axelrod. Photograph: Yale University Art Gallery*)

It is difficult to imagine a designer of today gaining a major reputation without in some way being "different." Robert Venturi, the original "bad boy" of postmodernism, and perhaps the most talented of the well-known architects who embrace history, is also the clearest illustration of the persistent and demanding nature of Kant's notion that the genius must defy conventions. The scenario is appropriately complex. The conventional style against which he rebelled was modernism; but, as there was nowhere else to go, the required unconventionality led back to earlier conventions, which could not be used in the traditional way because that would not satisfy the old demand for an original artistic statement.

A tangible burden of guilt still weighs on those who would deal with the past unself-consciously, without coyness or irony. To regain fluency in the traditional language of design—and to make the product of such a collaboration with past centuries accessible to a broad cross-section of society—designers and critics must shed the sense of guilt and feelings of creative inadequacy that have arisen from both nineteenth- and twentieth-century attitudes toward borrowing. To do this effectively

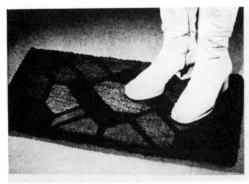

MAGNIFICENT MONDRIAN MAT! What an eye catcher front door . . . exotic mu muted red, gold, and green, with bold black lines to form ing design, a la the famou Mondrian. A real dirt catch The practically indestructibl fiber gives shoes the brush-i shrugs off moisture . . . stays and useful for years! 16"; sharp front door accent . . some gift!
H7049 Mondrian Door Mat

274

Fig. 274. Early modernists often spoke of the need to design for the masses. When bits and pieces of that movement finally trickled down into everyday life, it was seldom in a form which modernists would endorse. Doormat à la Mondrian, 1970s.

requires a redefinition of the very heart of artistic creativity, which was put forth nearly two hundred years ago in an esoteric philosophical treatise that has had an extraordinary influence well beyond its readership.

NOTES: CHAPTER X

1. I first heard this term from the ceramist Eva Zeisel. She pointed out that, in the multitude of shapes available in nature, different historical periods have had affinities for specific decorative lines, so much so that the silhouettes of certain flowers look as though they belong to specific historical periods.
2. Horace, "On the Art of Poetry," in *Classical Literary Criticism,* trans. T. S. Dorsch (Baltimore: Penguin Books, 1965), lines 29–56, p. 80.
3. Vitruvius, *The Ten Books on Architecture,* trans. Morris Micky Morgan (New York: Dover Publications, 1960), 4.3.109.
4. Ibid.
5. In 1845, a reviewer of the Munich Exhibition of Art observed that "the easier means of transportation and the constantly increasing interest in travel, had led to a previously unknown interest in paintings of distant regions and peoples"—Ernst Förster, "The Munich Art Exhibition of 1845," in Elizabeth Holt, *The Triumph of Art for the Public* (Garden City, N.Y.: Doubleday Anchor Books, 1979), pp. 446–7.
6. Herculaneum was known about as early as 1719, and serious excavations began in 1738 (*Encyclopaedia Britannica,* 11th ed., s.v. "Herculaneum"). Systematic excavations of Pompeii began in 1763 (*Encyclopaedia Britannica,* 11th ed., s.v. "Pompeii").
7. Eugène Emmanuel Viollet-le-Duc, *Lectures on Architecture,* trans. Benjamin Buckwall (1889; New York, 1959), p. 173.

APPENDIX

Some Origins of the Modern Notion of "Genius"

The present-day definition of "genius" closely parallels that of Kant in *Critique of Judgment*. Its origins are found in the Renaissance ideas of inborn talent (*inventione* and *ingenium*) and, after the sixteenth century, in the idea of "grace" or *"je ne sais quoi."*[1] Just who was privileged to receive this accolade in the Renaissance is not entirely clear. As late as the fifteenth century, there was no consensus among the learned as to which groups had been granted this innate gift. The art historian Martin Kemp does say, however, that "generally it is characteristic of the humanists that they find it easier to attribute *ingenium* to the safely-deceased artists of Antiquity than to those contemporary painters and sculptors who represented a socially-ambitious group within their own society."[2]

References to ideas we now associate with "artistic genius" exist in the literature of the Renaissance, but with an important difference in connotation. "Originality," for example, was frequently mentioned in warnings against imitating other artists. While this sounds like our demand, that the artist be "true" to his or her individual creative spirit, the worry at that time was not that the copiers would appear "unoriginal" because they imitated others. The concern was rather that these artists were restricting themselves unnecessarily, nature being a much richer source to draw upon than the works of other painters.[3]

Renaissance theoreticians also implied that artists had no need of rules, which sounds at first like Kant's description of genius ("for which no definite rule can be given"); but they seem to have had something different in mind. According to Erwin Panofsky, at that time it was felt that artists *intuitively* transformed nature into an Idea, in the Platonic sense. "But—and this is the important point—*the Renaissance proper no more arrived at this explicit, almost polemical emphasis on artistic genius than it did at an express formulation of the concept of 'the ideal.' It knew no more of a conflict between genius and the rule than of a conflict between genius and nature*" (my emphasis).[4] A very different approach from that of Kant.

One of the more surprising facts we learn in scanning the evolution of the concept of genius from the Renaissance on is that this quality was attributed to writers far more frequently than to those in the arts of design, and that writings on the subject discussed "almost exclusively poetry and poets."[5] If most of the more sensitive Renaissance artists assumed that *ingenium* was necessary to their trade, few of the intellectual elite of that time, the literary humanists, cared to admit that painters, sculptors, or architects could possess inborn genius.[6] In fact, most humanists remained remarkably insensitive to the new ideals expressed by their painter-contemporaries,[7] presumably because of the inferior social status which still attached to those who practiced the manual arts. The Platonic Academy, established at the Medici villa by the philosopher Marsilio Ficino, discussed the most compelling intellectual matters of the day, but barely touched upon art or art theory.[8]

In the seventeenth century, Roget de Piles, a leading French art historian and theorist of his day, wrote of the relationship between genius and other necessary attributes of the artist. "Genius is the first Thing we must suppose in a Painter," he said, " 'tis a part of him that cannot be acquir'd by Study or Labour."[9] But de Piles did not emphasize originality as an ingredient of genius, rather, "a person that has a Genius may invest a subject in general, but will be embarrast [sic] in the Execution of his Work, unless he has recourse to the Works of another."[10] Far from depending on originality, genius enabled painters to store and make use of images taken from nature, as well as those borrowed "without scruple" from other painters, enabling them to keep a veritable resource library of inspiration subject matter at their fingertips: "Thus Genius makes use of the Memory, as a Vessel wherein it keeps all the Ideas that present themselves to it."[11] Nor did de Piles loose genius from the rein of reason and other moderating forces; the possessor of that quality should be subject to the lessons of the past, and, above all, it was to be tempered with Reason, and corrected by "Rules, Reflections and Industry."[12]

For at least one well-known commentator of that period, "genius" hardly seemed to matter. In noting the talents required of an artist, Charles Alphonse du Fresnoy said only that "the Qualities requisite to form an excellent Painter are, a true discerning Judgment, a Mind which is docible [sic], a noble Heart, a sublime Sense of things, and Fervour of Soul; after which follow Health of Body, a convenient Share of Fortune, the Flower of Youth, Diligence, an Affection for the Art, and to be bred under the Discipline of a knowing Master."[13]

The earl of Shaftesbury, writing in the early eighteenth century, did consider genius and inventiveness (originality) important: "The mere face-painter . . . has little in common with the poet; but like the mere historian, copies what he sees and minutely traces every feature and odd mark. 'Tis otherwise with the men of invention and design."[14] Yet he too seemed to require that, however artistic judgments were made, they be subordinated to reason: " 'Tis evident however from Reason it-self, as well as from History and Experience, that nothing is more fatal, either to Painting, Architecture, or the other Arts, than this *false Relish* which is govern'd rather by what immediately strikes the Sense, than by what consequently and by reflection pleases the Mind, and satisfies the Thought and Reason."[15]

Dr. Johnson also urged novelty in the sense of originality, saying:

No man ever became great by imitation. Whatever hopes for the veneration of mankind must have *invention* in the design or the execution; either the effect must itself be new, or the means by which it is produced. Either truths hitherto unknown must be discovered, or those which are already known enforced by stronger evidence, facilitated by clearer method, or elucidated by brighter illustrations.

Yet at the same time he cautioned against too great a reliance on this intuitive faculty: "The mental disease of the present generations, is impatience of study, contempt of the great masters of wisdom, and a disposition to rely wholly upon unassisted genius and natural sagacity."[16]

Alexander Gerard was equally firm about the need for constraints. While genius might choose and dispose in artistic matters, it could not complete a work of art without reason "to guide and moderate its exertions."[17]

Even Sir Joshua Reynolds spoke of the limitations of genius in these same terms. In an address to the students of the Royal Academy given just a few years before the publication of *Critique of Judgment,* he admonished the would-be artists:

> You may have no dependence on your own genius. If you have great talents, industry will improve them: if you have but moderate abilities, industry will supply their deficiency. Not to enter into metaphysical discussions on the nature or essence of genius, I will venture to assert, that assiduity unabated by difficulty, and a disposition eagerly directed to the object of its pursuit, will produce effects similar to those which some call the result of natural powers.[18]

Conventional rules did not fetter genius, in Reynolds's eyes, leaving some intellectual distance to travel before arriving at the modern conception of a unique power whose productions lie beyond anything that could come from mere "industry."

With the acceptance of Kant's definition of genius—emphasizing originality above all—the confounding of artistic conventions eventually became, if not conclusive proof that one was a serious artist, at least evidence that you were making your own rules rather than pandering to fashion. This expectation gave rise to a mythical image of art lore, which remains potent to this day: that of the artist who chooses poverty and privation rather than prostitute his art by yielding to the pressures of the marketplace. In reviewing the work of Horace Vernet, a successful French painter of battle scenes, a critic of the Salon of 1822 pleaded that the painter's "life should not be so easy. Horace Vernet should be tormented. Let his torment be the ideal of perfection, may this ideal pursue him unceasingly. He is worthy of aspiring to this. Everything calls him to it; his genius, his age and his country, which worships a free, enlightened and generous talent."[19]

The vision of the artist-genius unhampered by society's conventions remains an undeniable euphoric even today, and it has frequently encouraged the kind of hyperbole found in the following advertisement, written by William Blake for a show of his own paintings that had been refused by the Royal Academy:

> If Italy is enriched and made great by Raphael, if Michael Angelo is its supreme glory, if Art is the glory of a Nation, if Genius and Inspiration are the great Origin and Bond of society, the distinction my works have obtained from those who best understand such things, calls for my Exhibition as the greatest of Duties to my country.[20]

A curious thing happened to the reputations of great artists of earlier eras when remeasured by the new yardstick of originality: their stature came to be determined more by quirk of birth than by the artistic fame or worldly riches that accrued to them in their lifetime. Phidias, Shakespeare, and Michelangelo all excelled because they lived in pivotal ages, times of intense aesthetic innovation: "What placed these men beyond all comparison were the era and circumstances under which they lived," wrote a French critic in 1827. Unfortunates like Praxiteles and Raphael, on the other hand, lived in periods of artistic refinement and so were "too late to find, to discover, to invent," and, therefore, they were denied a chance to demonstrate that special quality of originality which marked the Artist.[21] Even Michelangelo could not escape the recalculation of his worth in the new coinage of originality. Benjamin Haydon declared him overrated because this Renaissance giant had not expressed his artistic individuality by choosing his subjects himself.[22]

NOTES: APPENDIX

1. *Dictionary of the History of Ideas,* s.v. "Genius: Individualism in Art and Artist."
2. Martin Kemp, "From Mimesis to Fantasia: The Quattrocento Vocabulary of Creation, Inspiration and Genius in the Visual Arts," *Viator,* 8 (1977):358ff., 386, 391, and 392–3.
3. Erwin Panofsky, *Idea: A Concept in Art Theory,* trans. Joseph J. S. Peake (Columbia, S.C.: University of South Carolina Press, 1968), p. 67.
4. Ibid.
5. *Dictionary of the History of Ideas,* s.v. "Genius." The prejudice favoring the arts of literature should come as no surprise, given the lowly origins of the design arts, and it continued well into the nineteenth century. Yet even the literary man, in England, was hard-pressed to make it in society: "As, for instance, my friend the Rev. James Asterisk, who has an undeniable pedigree, a paternal estate, and a living to boot, once dined in Warwickshire, in company with several squires and parsons of that enlightened county. Asterisk, as usual, made himself extraordinarily agreeable at dinner, and delighted all present with his learning and wit. 'Who is that monstrous pleasant fellow?' said one of the squires. 'Don't you know' replied another. 'It's Asterisk, the author of so-and-so, and a famous contributor to such and such a magazine.' 'Good heavens!' said the squire, quite horrified! 'a literary man! I thought he had been a gentleman'"—William Makepeace Thackeray, "On the French School of Painting," *The Paris Sketch Book* . . . (Boston: Lee & Shepard, 1888), p. 44.
6. *Dictionary of the History of Ideas,* s.v. "Genius." See also Kemp, "From Mimesis to Fantasia."
7. Kemp, "From Mimesis to Fantasia," pp. 359, 392.
8. Rudolf Wittkower and Margot Wittkower, *Born Under Saturn, The Character and Conduct of Artists: A Documented History from Antiquity to the French Revolution* (New York: W. W. Norton, 1963), p. 232; see André Chastel, *Marsile Ficin et l'art* (Geneva-Lille: 1954), pp. 7ff.
9. Roger de Piles, *The art of painting, and the lives of the painters, containing a compleat treatise of painting, designing, and the use of prints* (London: Printed for J. Nutt, 1706), p. 1.
10. Ibid., p. 12.
11. Ibid., p. 11.
12. Ibid., p. 10.
13. Charles Alphonse du Fresnoy, *The Art of Painting,* trans. John Dryden (2nd ed. London, 1716), in Elizabeth Holt, *A Documentary History of Art* (2 vols., New York: Doubleday Anchor Books, 1958), 2:174.
14. Shaftesbury, "Freedom of Wit and Humour," in Albert Hofstadter and Richard Kuhns, eds.,

Philosophies of Art & Beauty, various trans. (Chicago: University of Chicago Press, 1976), p. 243.

15. Shaftesbury, "An Essay on Painting, being a Notion of the Historical Draught or Tablature of the Judgment of Hercules" (London, 1713), in Holt, *Documentary History of Art,* 2:259.

16. Samuel Johnson, *The Rambler,* 3, no. 154 (Sept. 7, 1751):273, 277.

17. Alexander Gerard, *An Essay on Taste* (3rd ed. 1780; reprint, Gainesville, Fla.: Scholars' Facsimiles & Reprints, 1963), pp. 163, 166.

18. Sir Joshua Reynolds, *A Discourse Delivered to the Students of the Royal Academy, on the Distribution of the Prizes* (London: Thomas Davies, 1769), p. 19.

19. Thiers, "Salon of 1822," in Elizabeth Holt, *The Triumph of Art for the Public* (Garden City, N.Y.: Doubleday Anchor Books, 1979), p. 237.

20. William Blake, advertisement for an exhibition of his own work, 1809, reprinted in Holt, *The Triumph of Art,* p. 137. The myth of the demands of artistic creativity for complete freedom and the reality of the creative process do not necessarily agree: "A number of studies have indicated that creators are communicating with an audience, real or imagined, even in high culture, and that the stereotypes of the lonely high culture artists who creates [*sic*] only for himself or herself, and of the popular culture creators who suppress their own values and cater only to an audience, are both false. . . . Moreover, the freedom of the popular culture creator to ignore user perspectives is not as limited, and that of the high culture creator not as limitless as is often thought. In fact, a recent study of Hollywood studio musicians suggested that the men who perform the background music for the movies found their work more creative and their working conditions freer than when they played for symphony orchestras" —Herbert Gans, *Popular Culture and High Culture* (New York: Basic Books, 1974), pp. 23, 26.

21. Étienne Delécluze, "On the 1827 Salon," in Holt, *The Triumph of Art,* p. 289.

22. Benjamin Robert Haydon, *Lectures on Painting and Design* (2 vols., London, 1844–6), 1:302–3.

Bibliography

Ackerman, J. "Concluding Remarks: Science and Art in the Work of Leonardo." In *Leonardo's Legacy*. Berkeley: University of California Press, 1969, pp. 205–25.

Alberti, Leon Battista. *On Painting*. 2nd rev. ed. Translated by John R. Spencer. New Haven: Yale University Press, 1966.

————. *Ten Books on Architecture* (1485). Translated by James Leoni, 1755. Edited by Joseph Rykwert. Reprint with addition of the "Life" from the 1739 ed. London: A. Tiranti, 1955.

"An Art Nouveau Edifice in Paris." *Architectural Record,* 12 (May 1902): 52–66.

Antal, Frederick. *Florentine Painting and Its Social Background: 14th and Early 15th Centuries. The Bourgeois Republic Before Cosimo de'Medici's Advent to Power, XIV and Early XV Centuries.* New York: Harper & Row, 1948.

Aquinas, Thomas. *An Aquinas Reader.* Edited by Mary T. Clark. Garden City, N.Y.: Doubleday, 1972.

————. *Summa Theologiae.* Edited and translated by Thomas Gilby. Garden City, N.Y.: Doubleday, 1969.

"Architectural Expression in a New Material." *Architectural Record,* 23 (April 1908): 249–68.

Aristotle. *The Ethics of Aristotle: The Nicomachean Ethics.* 2nd rev. ed. Edited by Betty Radice, translated by J. A. K. Thomson. Baltimore: Penguin Books, 1976.

————. *Metaphysics.* Translated by Richard Hope. Ann Arbor: University of Michigan Press, 1960.

————. *Poetics.* Translated with an introduction by Gerald F. Else. Ann Arbor: University of Michigan Press, 1970.

————. *The Politics.* Edited by Betty Radice, translated by T. A. Sinclair, Baltimore: Penguin Books, 1962.

Arnold, Matthew. *Culture and Anarchy.* London: Smith & Elder, 1869.

"Art for the People." *Harper's Weekly,* 37 (1893):394–5.

The Art-Journal Illustrated Catalogue: The Industry of All Nations, 1851. London: George Virtue, 1851. Reprint ed. New York: Dover Publications, 1970.

Arts and Crafts Essays. By members of the Arts and Crafts Exhibition Society. Preface by William Morris. London: Rivington, Perceval & Co., 1893.

Augustine. *City of God.* Translated by Henry Bettenson. Baltimore: Penguin Books, 1972.

———. *Confessions.* Edited by Betty Radice and Robert Baldick, translated by R. S. Pine-Coffin. Baltimore: Penguin Books, 1961.

Barnard, Julian. *The Decorative Tradition.* Princeton: The Pyne Press, 1973.

Baron, Hans. *The Crisis of the Early Italian Renaissance.* Rev. ed. Princeton: Princeton University Press, 1966.

Barzun, Jacques. *The Use and Abuse of Art.* Bollingen Series XXXV·22. Princeton: Princeton University Press, 1974.

Bate, Walter Jackson. *From Classic to Romantic: Premises of Taste in 18th Century England.* Cambridge: Harvard University Press, 1961.

Batteux, Abbé Charles. *Les Beaux Arts réduits à une même principe.* Paris: Durand, 1747.

Beardsley, Monroe C. *Aesthetics from Classical Greece to the Present.* University, Ala.: University of Alabama Press, 1966.

Bell, Clive. *Art* (1923). New York: Capricorn Books, 1958.

Bell, Quentin. *The Schools of Design.* London: Routledge & Kegan Paul, 1963.

Benton, Tim, Charlotte Benton, and Dennis Sharp, eds. *Architecture and Design: 1890–1939.* New York: Whitney Library of Design, 1975.

Beule, M. "M. Beule on Greek Polychromy." *American Architect,* 1 (1877): 271–2; 278–80.

Billings, Robert William. *An Attempt to Define the Geometric Proportions of Gothic Architecture: as Illustrated by the Cathedrals of Carlisle and Worcester.* London, 1840.

"Birmingham and Wolverhampton—Effects of the Great Exhibition—Schools of Design." *Journal of Design and Manufactures,* 6, no. 31 (1852):149–52.

Blake, Peter. *God's Own Junkyard: The Planned Deterioration of America's Landscape.* New York: Holt, Rinehart and Winston, 1964.

Bolgar, R. R. *The Classical Heritage and Its Beneficiaries.* Cambridge: Cambridge University Press, 1954.

Bowditch, John, and Clement Ramsland. *Voices of the Industrial Revolution:*

Selected Readings from the Liberal Economists and Their Critics. Ann Arbor: University of Michigan Press, 1961.

Brandt, William J. *The Shape of Medieval History: Studies in Modes of Perception.* New York: Schocken Books, 1973.

Braudel, Fernand. *Capitalism and Material Life: 1400–1800.* Translated by Miriam Kochan. New York: Harper & Row, 1973.

————. *The Structures of Everyday Life.* Translated by Siân Reynolds. New York: Harper & Row, 1981.

————. *The Wheels of Commerce.* Translated by Siân Reynolds. New York: Harper & Row, 1981.

Briggs, Martin Shaw. *The Architect in History* (1927). Reprint ed. New York: Da Capo Press, 1974.

Bronowski, Jacob, and Bruce Maylish. *The Western Intellectual Tradition.* New York: Harper & Row, 1962.

Bulwer-Lytton, Edward. *England and the English* (1833). Reprint ed. Chicago: University of Chicago Press, 1970.

Burchett, Richard. "The Central Training School for Art." *Introductory Addresses on the Science and Art Department and the South Kensington Museum,* no. 4, delivered Dec. 7, 1857. London, 1858.

Burford, Alison. "The Builders of the Parthenon." *Parthenos and Parthenon, Supplement to Greece and Rome,* 10 (1963):23–43.

Burke, Edmund. *A Philosophical Enquiry into the Origin of Our Ideas of the Sublime and Beautiful.* Edited with an introduction and notes by J. T. Boulton, New York: 1958.

Cassiodorus. *The Letters of Cassiodorus, being a condensed translation of the Variae epistolae of Magnus Aurelius Cassiodorus Senator.* Translated by Thomas Hodgkin. London: H. Frowde, 1886.

Chamberlayn, Edward. *Angliae Notitia: or the Present State of England.* London: printed and sold by S. Smith and B. Walford, 1707.

Chambers, Frank P. "The Aesthetic of the Ancients." *RIBA Journal,* 32 (Feb. 21, 1925):241–52.

————. *Cycles of Taste: An Unacknowledged Problem in Ancient Art and Criticism.* Cambridge: Harvard University Press, 1928.

Cicero. *De Officiis/On Duties.* Translated by Harry G. Edinger, Indianapolis: Bobbs-Merrill, 1974.

Cole, Henry. "The Functions of the Science and Art Department." *Introductory*

Addresses on the Science and Art Department and the South Kensington Museum, no. 1, delivered Nov. 16, 1857. London, 1857.

Coleridge, S. T. *Coleridge: Select Poetry, Prose, Letters.* Edited by Stephen Potter. London: The Nonesuch Press, 1971.

Condivi, Ascanio. *The Life of Michelangelo.* Edited by Hellmut Wohl. Translated by Alice Sedgwick Wohl. Baton Rouge, La.: Louisiana State University Press, 1976.

Crane, Walter. *The Bases of Design.* London: G. Bell & Sons, 1904.

————. *The Claims of Decorative Art.* Boston: Houghton Mifflin, 1892.

————. *Line and Form.* London: G. Bell & Sons, 1921.

————. *William Morris to Whistler: Papers and Addresses on art and craft and the commonweal.* London: G. Bell & Sons, 1911.

Crawford, Donald W. *Kant's Aesthetic Theory.* Madison, Wis.: University of Wisconsin Press, 1974.

Cuffin, Charles H. "Leaders of the New Salon." *Harper's Magazine,* 118 (December 1908):99–108.

Day, Lewis Foreman. *Every-Day Art.* London: B. T. Batsford, 1882.

"Decadence in Modern Art." *Forum & Century,* 15 (1894):428–38.

Dervaux, A. *L'Architecture Étrangère: A l'exposition international des arts décoratifs et industriels moderns.* Paris: Charles Moreau, 1925.

Dickens, Charles. *American Notes.* New York: American News Co., 1842.

Dictionary of the History of Ideas: Studies of Selected Pivotal Ideas. Edited by Philip P. Wiener. 4 vols. New York: Charles Scribner's Sons, 1973.

Diocletian. *An Edict of Diocletian Fixing a Maximum of Prices through the Roman Empire.* Edited by Leake. London, 1826.

"Domestic Architecture at the Arts and Crafts Exhibit." *International Studio,* 19 (June 1903):249–60.

Dresser, Christopher. *Principles of Decorative Design.* 4th ed. London: Cassell, Petter, Galpin & Co., 1883.

Dunlop, Ian. *The Shock of the New.* New York: McGraw-Hill, American Heritage Press, 1972.

Durant, Stuart. "Ornament: In an Industrialized Civilization." *Architectural Review* (September 1976):139–43.

Dvorak, Max. *Idealism and Naturalism in Gothic Art* (1927). Translated by Randolph J. Klawiter. Notre Dame, Ind.: University of Notre Dame Press, 1967.

Dyce, William. "Education of Artists and Designers." *Journal of Design and Manufactures,* 6 (1852):131–5, 165–7.

———. "Lecture on Ornament Delivered to the Students of the London School of Design." *Journal of Design and Manufactures,* 1 (1849):26ff.

———. *The National Gallery, Its Formation and Management.* London, 1853.

———. "Theory of the Fine Arts: An Introductory Lecture." London: James Burns, 1844.

———. "Universal Infidelity in Principles of Design." *Journal of Design and Manufactures,* 6, no. 31 (1852):1–6.

———. "Which direction is ornamental art likely to take in this country, toward elaboration or simplicity?" *Journal of Design and Manufactures,* 6, no. 31 (1852):135–37.

———, and Charles H. Wilson. "Letter to Lord Meadowbank, and the Committee of the Honourable board of trustees for the encouragement of the arts and manufactures of Scotland in point of taste." Edinburgh: T. Constable, 1837.

Eastlake, Charles. *Hints on Household Taste* (1868). Reprint ed. New York: Dover Publications, 1969.

——— [Jack Easel, pseud.]. *Our Square and Circle, or the Annals of a Little London House.* New York, 1895.

Edgerton, Samuel Y., Jr. "The Art of Renaissance Picture-Making and the Great Western Age of Discovery." In *Essays Presented to Myron P. Gilmore.* Florence: La Nuova Italia, 1978.

———. "Icons of Justice." *Past and Present,* no. 89 (November 1980), 23–38.

———. "Linear Perspective and the Western Mind." *Cultures,* no. 3 (1976): 77.

———. *The Renaissance Rediscovery of Linear Perspective.* New York: Harper & Row, 1976.

Edwards, Edward. *The Administrative Economy of the Fine Arts in England.* London: Saunders & Otley, 1840.

Elton, G. R., ed. *Renaissance and Reformation: 1300–1648.* New York: The Macmillan Company, 1963.

Fergusson, James. "On a National Collection of Architectural Art." *Introductory Addresses on the Science and Art Department and the South Kensington Museum,* no. 6. London, 1857.

Ferree, Barr. "Utility in Architecture." *Popular Science,* 37 (1890):202–11.

———. "Architecture and the Environment." *Popular Science,* 38 (1890): 194–204.

Fitch, Cleo Rickman. "The Lamps of Cosa." *Scientific American,* 247 (1982): 148–60.

Freart, Roland. *A Parallel of the Ancient Architecture with the Modern.* Translated by John Evelyn. London, 1707.

Fred, W. "The Work of Professor J. M. Olbrich at the Darmstadt Artists' Colony." *International Studio,* 15 (December 1901):91–100.

Frothingham, A. L. "Greek Architects, Contractors and Building Operations." *The Architectural Record,* nos. 23, 24 (1908):81–96, 321–38.

Fry, Roger. *Vision and Design* (1924). Reprint ed. New York: P. Smith, 1947.

Fuller, Edward. "Art for Art's Sake." *Bookman,* 1 (1895):241–3.

Furst, Lilian R. "Zola's Art Criticism." In *French Nineteenth Century Painting and Literature.* Edited by Ulrich Finke. New York: Harper & Row, 1972.

Gans, Herbert. *Popular Culture and High Culture.* New York: Basic Books, 1974.

Garland, Hamlin. "Successful Efforts to Teach Art to the Masses." *Forum & Century,* 19 (1895):606–17.

Gerard, Alexander. *An Essay on Taste* (3rd ed. 1780). Reprint ed. Introduction by Walter J. Hipple, Jr. Gainesville, Fla.: Scholars' Facsimiles & Reprints, 1963.

Giedion, Seigfried. *Space, Time and Architecture: The Growth of a New Tradition.* 3rd ed. Cambridge: Harvard University Press, 1959.

Gies, Joseph, and Frances Gies. *Life in a Medieval City.* 2nd ed. New York: Thomas Y. Crowell, 1973.

Gimpel, Jean. *The Medieval Machine: The Industrial Revolution of the Middle Ages.* Baltimore: Penguin Books, 1977.

Gombrich, E. H. *Art and Illusion.* 2nd rev. ed. Princeton: Princeton University Press, 1969.

———. *The Heritage of Apelles: Studies in the Art of the Renaissance.* Ithaca, N.Y.: Cornell University Press, 1976.

———. *Meditations on a Hobby Horse: And Other Essays on the Theory of Art.* 3rd ed. New York: Phaidon Press, 1978.

———. *The Sense of Order.* Ithaca, N.Y.: Cornell University Press, 1979.

Gottesman, Rita Susswein. *The Arts and Crafts in New York, 1777–1799: Advertisements and News Items from New York City Newspapers.* New York: The New-York Historical Society, 1954.

Grant, Edward. *Physical Science in the Middle Ages.* Cambridge History of Science Series, edited by George Basalla and William Coleman. Cambridge: Cambridge University Press, 1977.

Gropius, Walter. *New Architecture and the Bauhaus.* Translated by P. Morton Sand. Cambridge: MIT Press, 1965.

Gutherie, William. *A New Geographical, Historical, and Commercial Grammar; and Present State of the Several Kingdoms of the World.* London, 1771.

Gwynn, John. *London and Westminster Improved* (1776). Facsimile ed. Westmead, U.K.: Gregg International, 1969.

Harrison, Frederic. "Influence of Historic Homes on English Character." *Forum & Century,* 15 (1894):232–41.

Hartt, C. F. "Evolution in Ornament." *Popular Science Monthly,* 6 (January 1875):266–75.

Hastings, Thomas. "The Relation of Life to Style in Architecture." *Harper's Monthly,* 88 (May 1894):957–62.

Hauser, Arnold. *The Social History of Art.* 2 vols. Translated by Stanley Godman. New York: Alfred A. Knopf, 1951.

Haydon, Benjamin Robert. *Lectures on Painting and Design.* 2 vols. London, 1846.

Herlihy, David, ed. *Medieval Culture and Society.* New York: Harper & Row, 1968.

Herodotus. *The Histories.* 2nd rev. ed. Edited by E. V. Rieu, translated by Aubrey de Selincourt. Baltimore: Penguin Books, 1972.

Hofstadter, Albert, and Richard Kuhns, eds. *Philosophies of Art & Beauty: Selected Readings in Aesthetics from Plato to Heidegger.* Various translators. Chicago: University of Chicago Press, 1976.

Hogarth, William. *The Analysis of Beauty: Written with a view of fixing the fluctuating ideas of taste.* London: printed by J. Reeves 1753.

Hollanda, Francisco de. *Four Dialogues on Painting.* Translated by Aubrey F. G. Bell. London: Oxford University Press, 1928.

Holmes, George. *The Florentine Enlightenment: 1400–1450.* New York: Pegasus Books, 1969.

Holt, Elizabeth Gilmore, *The Art of All Nations: 1850–1873: The Emerging Role of Exhibitions and Critics.* Garden City, N.Y.: Doubleday Anchor Books, 1979.

——— comp. and ed. *Documentary History of Art.* 2 vols. Garden City, N.Y.: Doubleday Anchor Books, 1958.

———. *From the Classicists to the Impressionists.* Garden City, N.Y.: Doubleday Anchor Books, 1966.

———. *The Triumph of Art for the Public: The Emerging Role of Exhibitions and Critics.* Garden City, N.Y.: Doubleday Anchor Books, 1979.

Hulme, F. E. *Suggestions in Floral Design.* London: Cassell, Petter & Galpin, ca. 1880.

Hume, David. *Of the Standard of Taste and Other Essays* (1826). Reprint ed. Indianapolis: Bobbs-Merrill, 1965.

Hyman, Isabelle, ed. *Brunelleschi in Perspective.* Englewood Cliffs, N.J.: Prentice-Hall, 1974.

The Idler. Edited by Samuel Johnson. Nos. 36 and 85 (Dec. 23, 1758; Dec. 1, 1759).

International Studio. "Some Recent Work by M. C. F. A. Voysey." 22 (April 1904):127–34.

Itten, Johannes. *Design and Form.* Rev. ed. New York: Van Nostrand Reinhold, 1975.

Ivins, William M. *On the Rationalization of Sight.* Metropolitan Museum of Art Papers, no. 8. New York, 1938.

Jarves, J. Jackson. "Ethics of Taste: The Duty of Being Beautiful." *Art-Journal,* (1875):315ff.

Jeanneret, Charles-Édouard [Le Corbusier]. *Étude sur le mouvement d'art décorativ en Allemagne* (1912). Reprint ed. New York: Da Capo Press, 1968.

Jones, Owen. *Grammar of Ornament* (1856). Reprint ed. New York: Van Nostrand Reinhold, 1972.

Journal of Design and Manufactures. Edited by Henry Cole. London: Chapman & Hall, 6 vols, 1849–52.

Kant, Immanuel. *Critique of Judgment* (1790). Translated by J. H. Bernard. New York: Hafner Publishing Company, 1951.

Kemp, Martin. "From Mimesis to Fantasia: The Quattrocento Vocabulary of Creation, Inspiration and Genius in the Visual Arts." *Viator,* 8 (1977):347–98.

———. "Science, Non-Science and Nonsense: The Interpretation of Brunelleschi's Perspective." *Art History,* 1, no. 2 (1978):134–61.

Kinross, Albert. "The Secession Movement in German Art." *The Century Magazine,* 70 (1905):323–39.

Koestler, Arthur. "The Aesthetics of Snobbery." *Horizon* (Winter 1965):50–53.

Kristeller, Paul Oskar. *Eight Philosophers of the Italian Renaissance.* Stanford: Stanford University Press, 1964.

———. "The Modern System of the Arts." *Journal of the History of Ideas,* 12, 13 (1951, 1952):496ff, 17ff.

Landucci, Luca. *A Florentine Diary: from 1450–1516.* Translated by Alice de Rosen Jervis, 1927. Reprint ed. Freeport, N.Y.: Books for Libraries Press, 1971.

Langley, B., and T. Langley. *Gothic Architecture Improved by Rules and Proportions.* London, 1742.

Lee, Rensselaer W. *Ut Pictura Poesis: The Humanistic Theory of Painting.* New York: W. W. Norton, 1966.

Leonardo da Vinci. *Paragone.* Translated by I. A. Richter. London: Oxford University Press, 1949.

Lessing, Gotthold Ephraim. *Laocoön.* Translated by Ellen Frothingham. New York: The Noonday Press, 1968.

Letheve, Jacques. *Daily Life of French Artists in the Nineteenth Century.* Translated by Hilary E. Paddon. New York: Frederick Praeger, 1972.

Lowenthal, Leo, and Marjorie Fiske. "The Debate Over Art and Popular Culture in Eighteenth Century England." In Mirra Komarovsky, ed., *Common Frontiers of the Social Sciences.* Glencoe, Ill.: The Free Press, 1957, pp. 33–96.

Lucretius. *On the Nature of the Universe.* Edited by Betty Radice, translated by Ronald Latham. Baltimore: Penguin Books, 1951.

————. *On the Nature of Things.* Translated by Palmer Bovie. New York: New American Library, 1974.

Lux, J. A. "Workman's Home in Vienna." *International Studio,* 21 (December 1903):150–53.

Malek, James S. *The Arts Compared: An Aspect of Eighteenth-Century British Aesthetics.* Detroit: Wayne State University Press, 1974.

Manetti, Antonio di Tuccio. *The Life of Brunelleschi.* Translated by Catherine Enggass. University Park, Pa.: Pennsylvania State University Press, 1970.

Marshall, Henry Rutgers. "Expression in Architecture." *Architectural Record,* 9 (January 1900):254–67.

Martin, W. "The Life of a Dutch Artist, Part 6: How the Painter Sold His Work." *Burlington Magazine,* 11, no. 54 (September 1907):357–69.

Martines, Lauro. *Power and Imagination: City-States in Renaissance Italy.* New York: Alfred A. Knopf, 1979.

Matthews, Eva. "The Study of Ancient History in the Middle Ages." *Journal of the History of Ideas,* 5 (1944):221ff.

Meyer, Franz Sales. *Handbook of Ornament.* 8th ed. Montreal, 1894.

Milizia, Francesco. *The Lives of Celebrated Architects Ancient and Modern.* 2 vols. Translated by Mrs. Edward Cresy. London, 1826.

Mill, John Stuart. *Autobiography.* London, 1873.

Mooney, Michael, ed. *Renaissance Thought and Its Sources.* New York: Columbia University Press, 1979.

Moore, Julian. "Principles of Beauty in Architecture." *Fortnightly Review,* 72 (December 1899):936–43.

Morazé, Charles. *The Triumph of the Middle Classes.* Translated by Weidenfeld & Nicolson. London: Weidenfeld & Nicolson, 1966.

Morris, Colin. *The Discovery of the Individual: 1050–1200.* New York: Harper & Row, 1973.

Morris, William. *Aims of Art.* London: Strangeways & Sons, 1887.

————. *Arts and Its Producers, and The Arts and Crafts of To-day: Two Addresses Delivered before the National Association for the Advancement of Art.* London: Longmans & Co., 1901.

————. *The Decorative Arts and Their Relation to Modern Life and Progress.* Boston: Roberts Bros., 1878.

————. *Hopes and Fears for Art.* 5th ed. New York: Longman, Green, & Co., 1898.

Nicolson, Benedict. *The Treasures of the Foundling Hospital.* Oxford: The Clarendon Press, 1972.

Nochlin, Linda. *Realism.* Baltimore: Penguin Books, 1971.

Osborne, Harold. *Aesthetics and Art Theory: An Historical Introduction.* New York: E. P. Dutton, 1970.

Panofsky, Erwin. *Idea: A Concept in Art Theory.* Translated by Joseph J. S. Peake. Columbia, S.C.: University of South Carolina Press, 1968.

————. *Renaissance and Renascences in Western Art.* New York: Harper & Row, 1972.

Pausanias. *Guide to Greece.* 2 vols. 2nd rev. ed. Edited by Betty Radice, translated by Peter Livi. Baltimore: Penguin Books, 1979.

Piles, Roger de. *The Art of Painting, and the Lives of the Painters, containing a compleat treatise of painting, designing, and the use of prints.* London: Printed for J. Nutt, 1706.

Piozzi, Hester Lynch. *Observations and Reflections Made in the Course of a Journey Through France, Italy and Germany.* Edited by Herbert Barrows (1798). Reprint ed. Ann Arbor: University of Michigan Press, 1967.

Pirenne, Henri. *Medieval Cities.* Garden City, N.Y.: Doubleday Anchor Books, 1956.

Plato. *Gorgias.* 2nd rev. ed. Edited by Betty Radice, translated by Walter Hamilton. Baltimore: Penguin Books, 1971.

————. *The Last Days of Socrates: Euthyphro, The Apology, Crito.* Edited by Betty Radice and C. A. Jones, translated by Hugh Tredennick. Baltimore: Penguin Books, 1954.

————. *The Laws.* Translated by Thomas L. Pangle. New York: Basic Books, 1980.

————. *Phaedo.* 3rd rev. ed. Edited by Betty Radice and C. A. Jones, translated by Hugh Tredennick. Baltimore: Penguin Books, 1959.

————. *Phaedrus & Letters VII and VIII.* Edited by Betty Radice, translated by T. S. Dorsch. Baltimore: Penguin Books, 1965.

————. *Protagoras and Meno.* Edited by Betty Radice, translated by W. K. C. Guthrie. Baltimore: Penguin Books, 1956.

————. *The Republic.* Edited by Betty Radice and Robert Baldick, translated by H. D. P. Lee. Baltimore: Penguin Books, 1955.

————. *The Symposium.* Edited by Betty Radice, translated by Walter Hamilton. Baltimore: Penguin Books, 1951.

Pliny the Elder. *Natural History.* Translated by H. Rackham. 10 vols. Cambridge: Harvard University Press, 1938–63.

Pliny the Younger. *The Letters of the Younger Pliny.* Edited by Betty Radice and Robert Baldick, translated by Betty Radice. Baltimore: Penguin Books, 1963.

Plutarch. *The Age of Alexander: Nine Greek Lives by Plutarch.* Edited by Betty Radice, translated by Ian Scott-Kilvert. Baltimore: Penguin Books, 1973.

————. *Fall of the Roman Republic: Six Lives by Plutarch.* 2nd rev. ed. Edited by Betty Radice, translated by Rex Warner. Baltimore: Penguin Books, 1972.

————. *Makers of Rome: Nine Greek Lives by Plutarch.* Edited by Betty Radice, translated by Ian Scott-Kilvert. Baltimore: Penguin Books, 1965.

————. *The Rise and Fall of Athens: Nine Greek Lives by Plutarch.* Edited by Betty Radice, translated by Ian Scott-Kilvert. Baltimore: Penguin Books, 1960.

Polanyi, Michael. *The Tacit Dimension.* Garden City, N.Y.: Doubleday, 1966.

Pugin, Augustus Welby Northmore. *Contrasts: or A Parallel Between the Noble Edifices of the Middle Ages and Corresponding Buildings of the Present Day, Shewing the Present Decay of Taste.* 2nd ed. London: Charles Dolman, 1841.

————. *The True Principles of Pointed or Christian Architecture.* London: J. Weale, 1841.

Pye, David. *The Nature of Design.* New York: Reinhold Publishing Corporation, 1964.

Redgrave, Richard. *Manual of Design.* Compiled by Gilbert R. Redgrave. New York: Scribner, Welford and Armstrong, 1876.

―――――. "On the Necessities of Principles in Teaching Design, Being an address given at the opening session of the Department of Science and Art, Oct. 1853." London: Chapman & Hall, 1853.

―――――. "Supplementary Report on Design." In *Great Exhibition of the Works of Industry of All Nations, 1851, Reports by the Juries.* 2 vols. London: Spicer Bros., 1852. 2:1588–682.

Redivius, Palladio [pseud.]. "Prospects of Iron and Glass Edifices, and of novel forms of architecture arising from the use of these materials." *Journal of Design and Manufactures,* 6 (1851–2):16.

Repository of Arts, Literature, Fashions etc. Edited by Rudolph Ackerman (London, 1809–10).

Reynolds, Sir Joshua. *A Discourse Delivered to the Students of the Royal Academy, on the Distribution of the Prizes, December 11,* 1769. London: Thomas Davies, 1769.

―――――. *Discourses on Art.* Reprint ed. Edited by R. T. Wark. San Marino, Calif.: Huntington Library, 1959.

Roebuck, Carl, ed. *The Muses at Work: Arts, Crafts, and Professions in Ancient Greece and Rome.* Cambridge: MIT Press, 1969.

Rosenberg, Jakob. *On Quality in Art.* Princeton: Princeton University Press, 1967.

Ruskin, John. *The Seven Lamps of Architecture.* London, 1848. Reprint ed. New York: The Noonday Press, 1961.

―――――. *The Stones of Venice.* 3 vols. New York: John Wiley, 1851.

―――――. "The Two Paths." In *The Works of John Ruskin.* 39 vols. Edited by E. T. Cook and A. Wedderburn. London: G. Allen, 1903–12, 15:344, 16: 259–411.

Schiller, Friedrich. *On the Aesthetic Education of Man, in a Series of Letters* (1795). Translated by Reginald Snell. New York: Frederick Ungar, 1965.

Scott, Geoffrey. *The Architecture of Humanism.* 2nd ed. New York: Charles Scribner's Sons, 1969.

Scranton, Robert. "Greek Building." In *The Muses at Work: Arts, Crafts, and Professions in Ancient Greece and Rome.* Edited by Carl Roebuck. Cambridge: MIT Press, 1969.

Sedgewick, Theodore. "First Annual Report." *Association for Exhibition of Industry of All Nations.* New York, 1853.

Seneca. *Epistles.* 3 vols. Translated by Richard M. Gummere. London: W. Heinemann, Loeb Classical Library, 1917–25.

Southern, R. W. "Medieval Humanism." In *Medieval Humanism and Other Studies*. London: Oxford University Press, 1970, pp. 29–60.

Sparkes, John. *The Schools of Art: Their Origin, History, Work, and Influence*. London, 1884.

Stanton, Phoebe. "The Sources of Pugin's Contrasts." In *Concerning Architecture: Essays on Architectural Writers and Writing Presented to Nikolaus Pevsner*. Edited by John Summerson. London: Allen Lane, 1968, pp. 120–39.

Stevenson, R. L. "A Plea for Gaslamps." In *A Book of English Essays*. Baltimore: Penguin Books, 1963, pp. 204–8.

"The Struggle of Architecture Against Ugliness." *Review of Reviews*, 34 (July 1906):93–5.

Summerson, Sir John. "What Is Ornament and What Is Not." In *Via III: Ornament. Journal of the Graduate School of Fine Arts, University of Pennsylvania*. Edited by Stephen Kieran. Philadelphia: The Graduate School of Fine Arts, University of Pennsylvania (1977):5–9.

Tacitus. *The Annals*. Translated by D. R. Dudley. New York: New American Library, 1966.

Thackeray, William Makepeace. *The Paris Sketch Book of Mr. M. A. Titmarsh and Easter Sketches, A Journey from Cornhill to Cairo, The Irish Sketch Book, Character Sketches*. Boston: Lee & Shepard, 1888.

Thucydides. *History of the Peloponnesian War*. 2nd rev. ed. Edited by Betty Radice, translated by M. I. Finley. Baltimore: Penguin Books, 1952.

Tocqueville, Alexis de. *Democracy in America*. Translated by John Stuart Mill. 2 vols. New York: Schocken Books, 1961.

Vasari. *Lives of the Artists*. 2nd ed. Translated by George Bull. Baltimore: Penguin Books, 1965.

———. "The Bicentennial Commemoration—1976." *Architectural Forum* (October 1969):66ff.

Venturi, Robert. *Complexity and Contradiction in Architecture*. New York: The Museum of Modern Art, 1966.

———. "Ugly Is Beautiful," *Atlantic Monthly* (May 1973):33–43.

———, Denise Scott Brown, and Steven Izenour. *Learning from Las Vegas: The Forgotten Symbolism of Architectural Form*. Rev. ed. Cambridge: M.I.T. Press, 1977.

———, and Denise Scott-Brown. "A Significance for A&P Parking Lots or Learning from Las Vegas." *Architectural Forum* (March 1968):36–43.

———, and Denise Scott-Brown. "Ugly & Ordinary Architecture or The Decorated Shed." *Architectural Forum* (November 1971):64–7.

Vergo, Peter. *Art in Vienna, 1898–1918.* London: The Phaidon Press, 1975.

Viollet-le-Duc, Eugène Emmanuel. *Lectures on Architecture.* Translated by Benjamin Bucknall, 1889. Reprint of first American ed. New York 1956.

Vitruvius. *The Ten Books on Architecture.* Translated by Morris Hicky Morgan, 1914. Reprint ed. New York: Dover Publications, 1960.

Voltaire. *Letters Concerning the English Nation* (1733). Translated by John Lockman. London: P. Davies, 1926.

Wackernagel, Martin. *The World of the Florentine Renaissance Artist.* Translated by Alison Luchs. Princeton: Princeton University Press, 1981.

Ward, James. *Elementary Principles of Ornament.* London, 1890.

Watkin, David, *Morality and Architecture.* Oxford: The Clarendon Press, 1977.

Wheeler, Sir Mortimer. *Roman Art and Architecture.* New York: Frederick Praeger, 1964.

White, John. "Developments in Renaissance Perspective—I." *Journal of Warburg and Courtauld Institute,* 12 (1949):58–79.

Wightwick, George. *Hints to Young Architects.* Introduction by A. J. Downing. New York: John Wiley, 1851.

Wilde, Oscar. *The Soul of Man Under Socialism.* Portland, Me.: Thomas B. Mosher, 1909.

Williams, Raymond. *Culture and Society: 1780–1950.* Harmondsworth: Penguin Books, 1958.

Wittkower, Rudolf. "Brunelleschi and 'Proportion in Perspective.' " *Journal of Warburg and Courtauld Institute,* 16 (1953):75–291.

————, and B. A. R. Carter. "The Perspective of Piero della Francesca's 'Flagellation.' " *Journal of Warburg and Courtauld Institute,* 16 (1953):292–302.

————, and Margot Wittkower. *Born Under Saturn: The Character and Conduct of Artists. A Documented History from Antiquity to the French Revolution.* New York: W. W. Norton, 1963.

Wolfe, Tom. *The Painted Word.* New York: Farrar, Straus and Giroux, 1975.

Wornum, Ralph Nicholson. *Analysis of Ornament: The Characteristics of Styles.* 9th ed. London, 1884.

————. "The Exhibition as a lesson in taste: An essay on ornamental art as displaced in the Industrial exhibition in Hyde Park, in which different styles are compared with a view to the improvement of taste in home manufactures." *The Art-Journal Illustrated Catalogue: The Industry of All Nations, 1851.* London, 1851. Reprint ed. New York: Dover Publications, 1970.

————. "The Government Schools of Design." The *Art Union Journal,* 4 (1852):16, 39.

Index

Illustrations and information mentioned in captions are indicated in italics.

About the Author

Brent C. Brolin has a bachelor's degree in art history and a master's degree in architecture from Yale University, and practiced architecture for eight years in the United States and the West Indies. His books include *The Failure of Modern Architecture* (1976, translated into Greek and German), *Architecture in Context: Fitting New Buildings with Old* (1980), and *Sourcebook of Architectural Ornament* (1982, translated into Spanish and Serbo-Croatian). He is at work on a book about New York City's St. Bartholomew's controversy. His many articles have appeared in magazines from *Penthouse* to *The Harvard Architecture Review,* and he has lectured at universities and to community and business organizations around the country. Brolin is a consultant to planning departments, design review boards, and community groups on guidelines for the design of new buildings. He lives in Greenwich Village with his wife, actress Jean Richards, and daughter, Tally.